God's Wisdom Is Available to **You**

Jack and Judy Hartman

Lamplight Ministries, Inc.
PO Box 1307
Dunedin, Florida 34697-2921
Phone: 1-800-540-1597
Fax: 1-727-784-2980
email: gospel@tampabay.rr.com
Website: www.lamplight.net

ISBN 0-915445-08-5

Dedication

We dedicate this book to our cherished friend, Terry Lemerond. Terry has been a constant encouragement to us as a friend, a mentor and a member of our Board of Directors. We thank you, Terry, for your friendship, wisdom and support for many years. You are a blessing in our lives. We love you. We thank you for the wisdom of God that has come through you to us.

Foreword

I wrote the first two drafts of this book by myself. When I gave the third draft to my wife for editing, I found that I received a lot more than her normal editing. Judy gave me numerous suggestions to rewrite portions of this book. As I studied Judy's recommendations I believed that they had merit. I incorporated many of Judy's suggested changes into the next draft.

I gave the fourth draft to Judy asking her specifically to *only* edit for grammar and punctuation. I received much more than I expected. When Judy gave me her proposed revision she once again included a substantial amount of rewriting. Each time Judy did any rewriting she included the words, "I humbly submit."

My initial reaction to all of Judy's changes was one of frustration. *Why* did Judy continue to rewrite at this late stage? However, I humbly read Judy's recommended changes. I repeatedly concluded that her changes were correct. I knew that I needed to make these significant changes no matter how many drafts of the book had been completed.

Judy continued to give me constructive criticism throughout Draft #9 and Draft #10. She has contributed a significant amount to the writing of this book. Judy's repeated suggestions have caused me to make extensive changes. Because of what Judy has done, I have concluded that she should legitimately be listed as the co-author of this book because that it is exactly what Judy is.

I have not removed several first person references that I used in writing my portion of the book, but I want to emphasize that Judy definitely is the co-author of this book. I am indebted to Judy for hearing God and for all of the constructive rewriting she has done. Thank you, my dear wife. I believe the readers of this book also will thank you as they read the following pages.

Jack Hartman

All Scripture quotations, unless otherwise indicated, are taken from *The Amplified Bible, Old Testament, copy*right 1965, 1987 by the Zondervan Corporation or *The Amplified Bible, New Testament,* copyright 1954, 1958, 1987 by the Lockman Corporation. Used by permission.

I first started using this version of the Bible when I bought a paperback version of *The Amplified New Testament* many years ago because of the inscription on the cover. This inscription said, "...the best study Testament on the market. It is a *magnificent* translation. I use it constantly." (Dr. Billy Graham).

As I read about the history of this version of the Bible, I found that a group of qualified Hebrew and Greek scholars had spent a total of more than 20,000 hours amplifying the Bible. They believed that traditional word-by-word translations often failed to reveal the shades of meaning that are part of the Hebrew and Greek words.

After almost twenty-seven years of extensive Bible study I have found that *The Amplified Bible* reveals many spiritual truths that I cannot find in other versions of the Bible. Because of this amplification I now use this version of the Bible exclusively in all of our books and Scripture Meditation Cards.

Please be patient with the brackets and parentheses if you aren't familiar with this translation of the Bible. They are used to indicate what has been added in the amplification. I don't want to bury you under a mass of parentheses and brackets, but I have found that *The Amplified Bible* is filled with specific and practical information that I believe will help *you* to receive the wisdom our Father has made available to each of His beloved children.

TABLE OF CONTENTS

Introduction

The Book of Proverbs contains a significant amount of information pertaining to the wisdom of God. *Strong's Exhaustive Concordance* indicates that the words "wisdom," "wise," "wisely" and "wiser" are used more than five hundred times in the Book of Proverbs alone. In this book we will carefully study many of these Scripture references from the Book of Proverbs. We also will study many other Scripture references throughout the Bible to learn everything we can about the wisdom of God.

Access to God's wisdom is available to every person who has received Jesus Christ as his or her Savior. If you have not come to this knowledge, you will find information pertaining to eternal salvation in Chapter #3 and also in the Appendix at the end of this book.

We each should learn from the holy Scriptures exactly what our Father wants us to do to receive manifestation of the wisdom He has offered to us. Unbelievers cannot receive the wisdom of God. I believe that only a small percentage of all believers have learned how to receive God's wisdom. All people who have received Jesus Christ as their Savior should take full advantage of the wonderful privilege we have been given of being able to receive wisdom directly from heaven.

God's wisdom is available to each of us to use throughout every day of our lives. Our Father has given us His wisdom to show us how to find and carry out His will for our lives, to improve our marriages, to raise our children effectively, to do an excellent job in our vocations and to receive His answers to the problems we face.

In addition to studying the Word of God to learn about the wisdom of God, we also will study the holy Scriptures to learn what they say about the knowledge, understanding and guidance our loving Father has provided for us. We will see from God's Word exactly how God's wisdom, knowledge, understanding and guidance are meant to work together in our lives.

This book is solidly anchored upon 501 Scripture references that tell us how to receive wisdom, knowledge, understanding and guidance from God. These instructions and promises from God are meant to be studied, not just to be read. Our Father wants His promises and instructions to fill our eyes, our ears, our minds, our hearts and our mouths. We must *know* and *obey* the *instructions* our Father has given to us if we sincerely desire to receive His wisdom. We must *know* God's *promises* and *act* in *faith* upon these promises if we sincerely desire to receive our Father's wisdom.

Receiving God's wisdom isn't simply a matter of our saying, "God, I want Your wisdom" and God saying, "Okay. Here it is." Our heavenly Father loves us much more than any parent here on earth has ever loved his or her children. Our Father wants very much to pour out His wisdom and many other blessings upon His beloved children.

God's wisdom isn't something we labor for. Our loving Father will reveal His wisdom to us if we continually seek a close and intimate personal relationship with Him. Our Father will reveal His wisdom to us if we learn how to spend a great deal of time in His presence.

Unfortunately, some of God's children actually block their loving Father from giving them the wisdom He so very much wants to give to them. Some of us block Him because we haven't taken the time to obey His instructions to study and meditate on His Word daily. As a result, some of us simply do not know what our Father instructs us to do in order to receive His wisdom and the many other blessings He wants to give to us.

Some of us know what our Father promises He will do for us in regard to giving us His wisdom and many other blessings, but we block Him from giving us these blessings because of doubt and unbelief. We must obey our Father's instructions that tell us exactly what He wants us to do so that our faith in Him will be strong, absolute and unwavering.

In the following forty-three chapters we will give you a detailed scriptural explanation of exactly what our loving Father wants His children to do to receive His wisdom and the many other blessings He wants to give us. We pray that these instructions from God's Word will enable you to receive full manifestation of the wisdom and the other blessings your loving Father has made available to you.

Chapter 1

Remarkable Facts about the Wisdom of God

In this first chapter we will look into the Bible to see many remarkable facts that the holy Scriptures tell us about the wisdom of God. We will begin by defining God's wisdom. The best definition of God's wisdom that I have found comes from *The Amplified Bible.* The following amplification in parentheses explains what I believe to be God's wisdom. "...wisdom (comprehensive insight into the ways and purposes of God)..." (Colossians 1:28).

Our goal in each chapter of this book will be to help each person reading the book to receive more "comprehensive insight into the ways and purposes of God." On many occasions we will study exactly what the Bible says about receiving wisdom from God. At other times we will study passages of Scripture that, although not referring specifically to the wisdom of God, always will be able to pass the test of giving us more comprehensive insight into the ways and purposes of God.

Our Father knows exactly what we should do to receive His wisdom. Only God can tell us how to receive His wisdom. "God understands the way [to Wisdom] and He knows the place of it [Wisdom is with God alone]" (Job 28:23).

We will begin this book by carefully studying the theme passage of Scripture of this book that is shown on the front cover. This wonderful promise from God says, "If any of you is deficient in wisdom, let him ask of the giving God [Who gives] to everyone liberally and ungrudgingly, without reproaching or faultfinding, and it will be given him" (James 1:5).

Let's examine this passage of Scripture carefully. The all-inclusive words "any of you" apply to every person who believes in Jesus Christ as his or her Savior. Please personalize this passage of Scripture. Know that this promise from God applies to *you* because you definitely are included in the words "any of you."

We are told that God will give us His wisdom "liberally and ungrudgingly, without reproaching or faultfinding." Our loving Father doesn't withhold His wisdom because of our faults and shortcomings. He doesn't accuse us, blame us or find fault with us. Our Father knows that we are imperfect. By God's grace we are able to receive His wisdom because we have placed our faith in His Son, Jesus Christ, as our Savior.

We have just seen in James 1:5 that our Father promises to give us His wisdom "liberally and ungrudgingly." Another passage of Scripture expands on this statement by telling us that God actually has "lavished" His wisdom upon us. "In Him we have redemption (deliverance and salvation) through His blood, the remission (forgiveness) of our offenses (shortcomings and trespasses), in accordance with the riches and the generosity of His gracious favor, which He lavished upon us in every kind of wisdom and understanding (practical insight and prudence), making known to us the mystery (secret) of His will (of His plan, of His purpose)..." (Ephesians 1:7-9).

The word "lavish" in Ephesians 1:8 means "extremely generous, extravagant or abundant." Our Father is very generous. We did not earn and we do not deserve His wisdom. We should be very thankful for all of the wisdom and understanding our Father has made available to us. Because of His grace we have been given the opportunity to put His wisdom to practical use throughout every day of our lives.

We must not underestimate the magnitude of the wisdom of God that has been given to us. "Oh, the depth of the riches and wisdom and knowledge of God! How unfathomable (inscrutable, unsearchable) are His judgments (His decisions)! And how untraceable (mysterious, undiscoverable) are His ways (His methods, His paths)!" (Romans 11:33).

The depth of God's wisdom and knowledge is immeasurable by any human standard of measurement. We are told that God's ways are "unfathomable." This word is based upon the word "fathom" which is a six foot unit of measurement that is used to measure the depth of water. If the depth of water is fathomable, the number of fathoms can be measured. When something is unfathomable, it is so deep that it cannot be measured.

We also are told that the wisdom and knowledge of God are "inscrutable." When something is inscrutable, it is mysterious and unable to be understood. We cannot even begin to grasp the magnitude of our Father's wisdom with the limitations of our finite minds. We can only begin to understand His wisdom as a result of continual study and meditation on His Word and revelation we receive from the Holy Spirit.

We can receive a glimpse of the magnitude of God's wisdom by considering the great variety of creatures He has created. All of the streams, rivers, lakes and oceans on earth also were created through the wisdom of God. "O Lord, how many and varied are Your works! In wisdom have You made them all; the earth is full of Your riches and Your creatures. Yonder is the sea, great and wide, in which are swarms of innumerable creeping things, creatures both small and great" (Psalm 104:24-25).

Please pause for a moment to meditate on the significance of the statements in this passage of Scripture. Know that the same Almighty God who created the earth, the sea and everything and everyone on the earth and in the sea has made His magnificent wisdom available to *you*.

God created so many billions of stars that astronomers cannot begin to measure their number with the most precise instruments that are available to them. God's wisdom is so great that He knows the exact number of stars He created. God also knows the names of every one of these billions of stars. "He determines and counts the number of the stars; He calls them all by their names. Great is our Lord and of great power; His understanding is inexhaustible and boundless" (Psalm 147:4-5).

God's wisdom set specific times for daylight and night in each area of the world. God also has established the four different seasons of spring, summer, winter and fall throughout the earth. "...Blessed be the name of God forever and ever! For wisdom and might are His! He changes the times and the seasons; He removes kings and sets up kings. He gives wisdom to the wise and knowledge to those who have understanding! He reveals the deep and secret things..." (Daniel 2:20-22).

God is so wise and powerful that He is able to remove the leaders of countries. He can instantly put new leaders into positions of authority. As we reach out in faith to continually seek the wisdom of God, we can be certain that He will give His wisdom to us. Our Father very much wants to "reveal the deep and secret things" to each of His beloved children.

As we read these passages of Scripture we are able to obtain increasing insight into the awesome might and power of God and the unlimited scope of God's wisdom, knowledge, understanding and guidance. Our Father knows everything about every person on earth. The psalmist David said, "O Lord, You have searched me [thoroughly] and have known me. You know my downsitting and my uprising; You understand my thought afar off. You sift and search out my path and my lying down, and You are acquainted with all my ways. For there is not a word in my tongue [still unuttered], but, behold, O Lord, You know it altogether" (Psalm 139:1-4).

Our Father knows when we sit down, when we lie down and when we stand up. He knows every thought that goes through our minds. He knows what we are going to say before we say it. He knows what we are going to do before we do it. "...not a creature exists that is concealed from His sight, but all things are open and exposed, naked and defenseless to the eyes of Him with Whom we have to do" (Hebrews 4:13).

Our Father is omniscient. This word means "all knowing." The word "omniscient" comes from the word "omniscience." The last part of this word is the word "science" which means "facts or knowledge." The prefix "omni" means "all." God has all facts. God's knowledge is infinite.

God also is omnipotent. This word means "all power." God also is omnipresent. He is able to be in all places at the same time. *Why* would we ever attempt to rely upon our limited human wisdom when we have the magnificent wisdom of the omnipotent, omnipresent and omniscient God available to us?

No person on earth can even begin to be compared to God. Our beloved Father is glorious in His holiness and awesome in His splendor. There is no limit to the wonders He is able to perform. "Who is like You, O Lord, among the gods? Who is like You, glorious in holiness, awesome in splendor, doing wonders?" (Exodus 15:11).

This chapter is filled with many important facts about the power, the might, the wisdom, the knowledge, the understanding and the guidance that are available to us from Almighty God. We pray that this chapter has helped to birth within you a deep and sincere desire to learn how to receive the magnificent supernatural wisdom your loving Father has made available to you. We now are ready to proceed together in an in-depth study of the holy Scriptures to learn many additional facts about the wisdom of God and to learn how we can obtain our Father's wisdom for practical use in our lives here on earth.

Chapter 2

We Can Receive the Blessings of God's Wisdom

The Bible is filled with many promises from God telling us about the numerous blessings our loving Father will give to us if we learn how to receive and utilize His wisdom in our lives. "...by me [Wisdom from God] your days shall be multiplied, and the years of your life shall be increased" (Proverbs 9:11).

This passage of Scripture explains that our lives will be long and fulfilling if we learn to receive the wisdom that is available to us from God. Our Father loves us so much that He promises to bring us safely through our entire lives if we will trust Him completely. "Even to your old age I am He, and even to hair white with age will I carry you. I have made, and I will bear; yes, I will carry and will save you" (Isaiah 46:4).

Our lives will flow like a fountain if we learn how to appropriate God's wisdom. We can avoid the penalty of premature death by learning how to receive and utilize God's wisdom. "The teaching of the wise is a fountain of life, that one may avoid the snares of death" (Proverbs 13:14).

Our Father doesn't want us to die prematurely. He wants each of His beloved children to live a long and full life in good health so that we each can carry out His will for our lives. "Skillful and godly Wisdom is more precious than rubies; and nothing you can wish for is to be compared to her. Length of days is in her right hand, and in her left hand are riches and honor. Her ways are highways of pleasantness, and all her paths are peace. She is a tree of life to those who lay hold on her; and happy (blessed, fortunate, to be envied) is everyone who holds her fast" (Proverbs 3:15-18).

This passage of Scripture is filled with many wonderful blessings that our Father promises to us if we learn how to be guided by His wisdom. We are told that God's wisdom is "more precious than rubies" (or any other rare gem). Nothing on earth can even remotely compare to the blessings that are available to us through the wisdom of God.

We are told that God's wisdom will give us "length of days" – a long and a full life. God's wisdom will give us "riches and honor." We can live a much more pleasant and peaceful life with God's wisdom than we ever could experience operating within the limitations of our human wisdom. We are told that everyone who holds fast to God's wisdom will be blessed by God.

Our Father places great emphasis on the power of His wisdom which is far superior to anything in the world that is powerful and mighty. "...wisdom is better than might..." (Ecclesiastes 9:16). God also tells us that His wisdom is more powerful than any of the worldly weapons human beings use when they are engaged in warfare. "Wisdom is better than weapons of war…" (Ecclesiastes 9:18).

The Word of God tells us that we will be strong in the Lord when we are wise in the Lord. We can increase our strength through our knowledge of God. "A wise man is strong and is better than a strong man, and a man of knowledge increases and strengthens his power…" (Proverbs 24:5).

Rulers and generals received great honor when the Old Testament was written. We are told that the wisdom of God is able to give us more strength than ten rulers or generals combined. "[True] wisdom is a strength to the wise man more than ten rulers or valiant generals who are in the city" (Ecclesiastes 7:19).

We will be able to solve problems that seem to be unsolvable when we learn how to receive wisdom from God. The Bible says that we can bring down our enemies through God's wisdom and power. "A wise man scales the city walls of the mighty and brings down the stronghold in which they trust" (Proverbs 21:22).

People who are operating in the limitations of human wisdom often believe they have to force the issue when they are faced with difficult and seemingly insurmountable problems. The wisdom of God will enable us to be successful when we cannot possibly solve difficult problems with our limited human wisdom and strength. "If the ax is dull and the man does not whet the edge, he must put forth more strength; but wisdom helps him to succeed" (Ecclesiastes 10:10).

Our Father wants to bless each of us just as loving parents here on earth want to bless each of their children. Unfortunately, some children on earth fail to receive the blessings their parents want to give them because they make unwise decisions instead of receiving wisdom from their parents. We will receive wonderful blessings and favor from our Father if we are able to receive His wisdom. "...whoever finds me [Wisdom] finds life and draws forth and obtains favor from the Lord" (Proverbs 8:35).

Our Father loves us so much that He wants to pour out a virtual stream of His wisdom upon us. God's wisdom is fresh and sparkling like a gushing stream of water. Our Father's wisdom is so pure that it gives us life. "...the fountain of skillful and godly Wisdom is like a gushing stream [sparkling, fresh, pure, and life-giving]" (Proverbs 18:4).

We have seen that our Father has promised to make His wisdom available to every one of His children. The Bible says that God's wisdom actually cries out to us. We will not be simple people who are open to the evil influence of Satan if we know how to receive wisdom from God. "Wisdom cries aloud in the street, she raises her voice in the markets; she cries at the head of the noisy intersections [in the chief gathering places]; at the entrance of the city gates she speaks: How long, O simple ones [open to evil], will you love being simple?..." (Proverbs 1:20-22).

Our Father hasn't saved His wisdom for us to use when we get to heaven. He has made His wisdom fully available to us while we are here on earth. I pray that you will be able to see the enormity of the precious gift of wisdom our Father has made available to us.

Our Father has given us the tremendous gift of His wisdom by His love and by His grace. We should be very grateful for the precious gift of God's wisdom. We should take full advantage of this wonderful gift our Father has made available to us.

In the first chapter of this book we studied several Scripture references that explained the magnificence and the awesome depth of the wisdom of God. In this chapter we have looked into the Word of God to see the many blessings that are available to God's children who will learn how to walk in His wisdom. Now that we have laid this scriptural foundation pertaining to the wisdom of God, we are ready to carefully and thoroughly study in the next forty-one chapters exactly what the holy Scriptures tell us to do if we deeply yearn to live our lives guided by the wisdom of Almighty God.

Chapter 3

Jesus Christ Enables Us to Receive God's Wisdom

Most of the Scripture references in the first two chapters of this book are from the Old Testament. We now are ready to learn how the price that Jesus Christ paid for us at Calvary has given us the ability to bring these Old Testament promises and much more into manifestation in our lives.

Some people who are reading this book have not yet asked Jesus Christ to be their personal Savior. Let's look into the Word of God to see what it says about eternal life through Jesus Christ. We will learn how asking Jesus Christ to be our Savior enables us to receive wisdom from God.

Any person who has not asked Jesus Christ to be his or her Savior has been blinded by Satan regarding God's plan of salvation. Jesus said, "He has blinded their eyes and hardened and benumbed their [callous, degenerated] hearts [He has made their minds dull], to keep them from seeing with their eyes and understanding with their hearts and minds and repenting and turning to Me to heal them" (John 12:40).

Satan does everything he can to blind unbelievers from understanding their need for repentance. Satan wants people to have dull minds and hard hearts in regard to their need for eternal salvation through Jesus Christ. The last thing Satan wants is for any of us to repent of our sins and to turn to Jesus Christ with absolute faith that our sins are forgiven.

I would like to give you an example of how Satan blinded me for many years. I had a sincere desire to learn the truth before I was saved. I purchased several hundred secular "self-help, success" books over a period of several years because I yearned to find answers to the problems in my life. I read these books constantly. I took copious notes from them. I then compiled many large three ring binders that were filled with the detailed information I learned from these books.

I spent *nine years* studying these books. At the end of this time my large three ring binders contained 1,392 different items on faith, 246 items on fear, 343 items on worry, 1,090 items on overcoming adversity, 933 items on prosperity, 34 items on patience and 134 items on perseverance. These notebooks also contained additional information filed under many additional categories.

After nine years of intense study I had compiled almost one hundred of these large three-ring binders that were filled with a massive amount of material. These notebooks contained hundreds of Scripture references I had read in some of the "success" books. I had a genuine desire to learn from the Bible before I was saved, but all of the Scripture references in these notebooks were like a foreign language to me until I asked Jesus Christ to be my Savior.

All unsaved people, whether they have a sincere desire to learn the things of God or not, are under the influence of Satan. The apostle Paul told the Ephesians, "...You were following the course and fashion of this world [were under the sway of the tendency of this present age], following the prince of the power of the air. [You were obedient to and under the control of] the [demon] spirit that still constantly works in the sons of disobedience [the careless, the rebellious, and the unbelieving, who go against the purposes of God]" (Ephesians 2:2).

People who have not received Jesus Christ as their Savior follow the customs and traditions of the world. Although they may not realize it, they are followers of Satan who is referred to here as "the prince of the power of the air." They are knowingly or unknowingly following the directions of a demonic spirit that influences people who do not have a sincere desire to learn and obey God's instructions.

Satan was able to deceive me even though I had a sincere desire to learn the things of God. I tried hard, but Satan was able to prevent me from understanding God's truths. "...the god of this world has blinded the unbelievers' minds [that they should not discern the truth], preventing them from seeing the illuminating light of the Gospel of the glory of Christ (the Messiah), Who is the Image and Likeness of God" (II Corinthians 4:4).

When this passage of Scripture speaks of "the god of this world," it refers to Satan. He is able to blind unbelievers so they do not understand that the Word of God is the Truth and that God sent His beloved Son, Jesus Christ, to be their Savior. "...the mind of the flesh [with its carnal thoughts and purposes] is hostile to God, for it does not submit itself to God's law; indeed it cannot" (Romans 8:7).

Unbelievers who are influenced by the ways of the world actually are "hostile to God." They don't obey God's instructions because they are incapable of understanding and obeying the holy Scriptures unless they are saved. Jesus said, "Whoever is of God listens to God. [Those who belong to God hear the words of God.] This is the reason that you do not listen [to those words, to Me]: because you do not belong to God and are not of God or in harmony with Him" (John 8:47).

Jesus spoke these words to a group of Jews on the Mount of Olives. The apostle Paul spoke similar words in his letter to the Ephesians. Paul said, "...you must no longer live as the heathen (the Gentiles) do in their perverseness [in the folly, vanity, and emptiness of their souls and the futility] of their minds. Their moral understanding is darkened and their reasoning is beclouded. [They are] alienated (estranged, self-banished) from the life of God [with no share in it; this is] because of the ignorance (the want of knowledge and perception, the willful blindness) that is deep-seated in them, due to their hardness of heart [to the insensitiveness of their moral nature]" (Ephesians 4:17-18).

Paul told the Ephesians that they shouldn't have vain and empty minds. He explained that their thinking was cloudy. They were alienated from God because of their spiritual ignorance that was caused by their hard hearts.

Some unbelievers are very intelligent in regard to the wisdom of the world. Some of these intelligent people are very philosophical. The word "philosopher" means "to love wisdom." The philosophy of the world is empty and theoretical because it is not solidly anchored upon God. "...the world with all its earthly wisdom failed to perceive and recognize and know God by means of its own philosophy..." (I Corinthians 1:21).

Many highly educated people know absolutely nothing about God. Human logic enables us to deal with the facts of this world. God's ways supercede human logic. The instructions in the Word of God are contrary to the ways of the world. God's ways are much higher and very different from the world's ways (see Isaiah 55:8-9).

The teaching of the Bible makes no sense to intellectual people who are slaves to the world's way of thinking. Many people who are extremely intelligent from the world's perspective cannot begin to understand how ignorant they actually are. Their intellectual awareness actually blocks them from understanding God's ways and knowing Him personally.

People cannot escape from this sad state of affairs unless they ask Jesus Christ to be their Savior. They cannot come to Jesus unless *God Himself actually draws them to Him and gives them the desire to come to Christ.* Jesus said, "No one is able to come to Me unless the Father Who sent Me attracts and draws him and gives him the desire to come to Me..." (John 6:44).

I thank God that, at a time in my life when I was on the verge of business failure, bankruptcy and a nervous breakdown, a friend of mine told me about eternal salvation through Jesus Christ. My life was falling apart. I had a tremendous desire to learn the things of God. However, I was unable to learn these great spiritual truths until Almighty God drew me to Himself on the day my friend was used by God to lead me to Jesus Christ.

God wants everyone on earth to be saved. He wants everyone to have a hunger for His Word. He wants each of us to grow and mature continually. The Bible speaks of "...God our Savior, Who wishes all men to be saved and [increasingly] to perceive and recognize and discern and know precisely and correctly the [divine] Truth" (I Timothy 2:3-4).

There is no question that God wants everyone to be saved and to understand His Word. However, He has given each of us freedom of choice. He never violates our right to choose. We can only come to God if He draws us to Himself and if we freely and willingly make the choice to ask Jesus Christ to be our Savior.

Jesus Christ explained this spiritual principle to a Jewish leader named Nicodemus. Jesus told Nicodemus that no one can experience the magnificence of the kingdom of God unless that person is "born again." Jesus said, "...I assure you, most solemnly I tell you, that unless a person is born again (anew, from above), he cannot ever see (know, be acquainted with, and experience) the kingdom of God" (John 3:3).

On another occasion Jesus explained the absolute necessity of repenting of our sins. We must understand that we will suffer eternally if we don't repent of our sins and change our ways. Jesus said, "...unless you repent (change your mind for the better and heartily amend your ways, with abhorrence of your past sins), you will all likewise perish and be lost eternally" (Luke 13:5).

What exactly does it mean to be born again? What must we do to repent of our sins? The Bible answers these questions. "...if you acknowledge and confess with your lips that Jesus is Lord and in your heart believe (adhere to, trust in, and rely on the truth) that God raised Him from the dead, you will be saved" (Romans 10:9).

We can only be born again if we know in our hearts that we are sinners and if we believe that God sent His beloved Son, Jesus Christ, to earth to die on a cross at Calvary to pay for our sins. We must believe in our hearts that God raised Jesus Christ from the dead. We will be saved if we believe these spiritual truths in our hearts and if we open our mouths to confess that Jesus Christ is our Savior.

Unfortunately, many "religious" people do not believe they are sinners. They think they are living a good life. They think their "good life" will get them to heaven. People who think they are not sinners make a big mistake. They cannot be saved. They cannot learn eternal truths from the Word of God. "If we say we have no sin [refusing to admit that we are sinners], we delude and lead ourselves astray, and the Truth [which the Gospel presents] is not in us [does not dwell in our hearts]" (I John 1:8).

All people who admit their sins, repent of these sins and believe that Jesus Christ died on a cross at Calvary for their sins and rose from the dead are saved. God sets us free from the dominion of Satan when this most important of all decisions is made. We then become members of the family of God. "[The Father] has delivered and drawn us to Himself out of the control and the dominion of darkness and has transferred us into the kingdom of the Son of His love..." (Colossians 1:13).

The spiritual veil that prevented us from understanding the things of God is removed when we repent of our sins and ask Jesus Christ to be our Savior. We then are given the ability to understand the Word of God. We are able to see, learn and comprehend the ways of Almighty God. "...whenever a person turns [in repentance] to the Lord, the veil is stripped off and taken away" (II Corinthians 3:16).

I still marvel at the transformation that took place in my life when I was saved. On the day that I asked Jesus Christ to be my Savior, I suddenly was able to understand the Scripture references that were in my notebooks. The meaning of the holy Scriptures wasn't hidden to me any more. "...even if our

Gospel (the glad tidings) also be hidden (obscured and covered up with a veil that hinders the knowledge of God), it is hidden [only] to those who are perishing and obscured [only] to those who are spiritually dying and veiled [only] to those who are lost" (II Corinthians 4:3).

Everything changes when we are saved. Vast new spiritual horizons open up to us. Everything is fresh and new and wonderful. Praise the Lord! "...if any person is [ingrafted] in Christ (the Messiah) he is a new creation (a new creature altogether); the old [previous moral and spiritual condition] has passed away. Behold, the fresh and new has come!" (II Corinthians 5:17).

When we are saved, we are transformed in an instant from spiritual death to spiritual life. We still look the same on the outside, but we have changed completely on the inside.

Because Jesus Christ was raised from the dead, everything changes in a wonderful way for each person who trusts Him for eternal salvation. We are raised from spiritual death. We are able to live in the wonder of our new life in Christ. "...just as Christ was raised from the dead by the glorious [power] of the Father, so we too might [habitually] live and behave in newness of life" (Romans 6:4).

After I was saved I was amazed that I had a hunger and thirst for the Word of God that could not be quenched. I had a tremendous desire to learn everything I could about the ways of God. "...I endorse and delight in the Law of God in my inmost self [with my new nature]" (Romans 7:22).

Before we are saved we have to "limp along" within the limitations of our human wisdom. After we are saved we never again will have to depend upon human wisdom. God's wisdom is made available to us when we are saved. We must understand that we miss the glorious operation of God's wisdom when we live our lives within the limitations of our human wisdom.

In this chapter we have seen that we cannot receive the wisdom of God or any other blessings from the kingdom of God without being saved. You could give this book to a friend of yours who has not been saved. Your friend could read this book and it wouldn't make any sense whatsoever to him or her.

Even though this book is written in English it might as well be written in a foreign language for any person who has not asked Jesus Christ to be his or her Savior. Our spirits become alive in Christ Jesus the moment Jesus Christ becomes our Savior. We are given the opportunity to receive many blessings from our loving Father, including His wisdom.

If you have received Jesus Christ as your personal Savior after reading this chapter, please write to us (Jack and Judy Hartman, PO Box 1307, Dunedin, FL 34697-2921), call us at 1-800-540-1597, send us a fax message at 1-727-784-2980 or email us at gospel@tampabay.rr.com and tell us of your decision. We would like to rejoice with you. We also will send you some material free of charge that will help you in your new life as a member of the family of God.

Chapter 4

The Hidden Wisdom of God Has Been Revealed to Us

We have just learned many spiritual truths about eternal salvation through Jesus Christ. After we are saved we have access to secrets from God that were previously hidden from us. Jesus said, "...To you it has been given to know the secrets and mysteries of the kingdom of heaven, but to them it has not been given" (Matthew 13:11).

One of the secret mysteries of the kingdom of heaven is the wisdom of God. God hides His wisdom from unbelievers. He has stored up His wisdom for the righteous. We become righteous before God when Jesus Christ becomes our Savior (see Philippians 1:11). At that time we receive access to the wisdom of God. "He hides away sound and godly Wisdom and stores it for the righteous (those who are upright and in right standing with Him)..." (Proverbs 2:7).

We have just read in the Old Testament that God's wisdom was hidden and stored up for the righteous. The New Testament confirms that God's wisdom that once was hidden now is available to us. "...what we are setting forth is a wisdom of God once hidden [from the human understanding] and now revealed to us by God - [that wisdom] which God devised and decreed before the ages for our glorification [to lift us into the glory of His presence]" (I Corinthians 2:7).

God's wisdom is no longer hidden from human understanding. This wisdom that has been revealed to us because of the sacrifice of Jesus Christ is *so powerful that it actually is able to lift us into the glory of the presence of God.*

Our Father wants us to take full advantage of the opportunity we have been given to partake of the treasures of His wisdom. "...that mystic secret of God, [which is] Christ (the anointed One). In Him all the treasures of [divine] wisdom (comprehensive insight into the ways and purposes of God) and [all the riches of spiritual] knowledge and enlightenment are stored up and lie hidden" (Colossians 2:2-3).

We must not allow the sacrifice of Jesus Christ to go in vain. Jesus died on a cross at Calvary so that we could live eternally with Him in heaven. He also died so that we can receive God's wisdom. Jesus Christ *is* the Wisdom of God. "...Christ [is] the Power of God and the Wisdom of God" (I Corinthians 1:24).

In addition to being the wisdom of God, Jesus Christ also is the Word of God. "In the beginning [before all time] was the Word (Christ), and the Word was with God, and the Word was God Himself" (John 1:1). Jesus Christ has been given the title of The Word of God. "...the title by which He is called is The Word of God" (Revelation 19:13).

The Word of God is the living Christ. The Word of God is alive. We don't study the Bible just to learn about Jesus Christ. We study the Bible to know Jesus Christ personally. We will meet Jesus Christ if we continually study and meditate on the holy Scriptures. Jesus said, "...these [very Scriptures] testify about Me!" (John 5:39).

The Word of God enables us to receive revelation of the wisdom of God and many other blessings from God. Unfortunately, some Christians fail to receive manifestation of the power of the Word of God in their lives. Jesus said, "...for the sake of your tradition (the rules handed down by your forefathers), you have set aside the Word of God [depriving it of force and authority and making it of no effect]" (Matthew 15:6).

This passage of Scripture tells us that *we actually can make the mighty power of the Word of God ineffective in our lives.* How can we do this? We can deprive the Word of God of its immense power through the religious tradition that has been handed down from generation to generation. We must be totally open and receptive when we study and meditate on the Word of God. We must not allow religious tradition to stop us from being able to receive the secrets and mysteries of the kingdom of heaven.

When Jesus Christ becomes our Savior, we are given the ability to be set free from the religious tradition that has blinded so many people from one generation to another. "You must know (recognize) that you were redeemed (ransomed) from the useless (fruitless) way of living inherited by tradition from [your] forefathers ..." (I Peter 1:18).

Some Christians who are extremely intellectual in the ways of the world are unable to learn the great spiritual truths that are contained in the Word of God. Their intellectual knowledge complicates the truth of the Word of God that is able to make simple people wise. "...the testimony of the Lord is sure, making wise the simple" (Psalm 19:7).

We need to be "simple" enough to turn away from religious tradition and worldly, intellectual understanding to obey God's specific instructions to constantly study and meditate on His Word. Our Father promises to flood our minds and our hearts with light if we will fill our minds and our hearts with His living Word. As the Word of God unfolds in our minds and our hearts, we will receive "understanding, discernment and comprehension" from God. "The entrance and unfolding of Your words give light; their unfolding gives understanding (discernment and comprehension) to the simple" (Psalm 119:130).

Little children have open minds. They are simple, humble and teachable. They are not bound up by the intellectual complications of many years of traditional thinking. Our Father wants us to be like little children as we seek the revelation of wisdom, knowledge, guidance and understanding He has made available to us through Jesus Christ.

We cannot become Christians unless we enter the kingdom of heaven with simple childlike trust. Jesus said, "...Truly I say to you, unless you repent (change, turn about) and become like little children [trusting, lowly, loving, forgiving], you can never enter the kingdom of heaven [at all]" (Matthew 18:3).

Jesus thanked His Father for hiding the secrets and mysteries of the kingdom of heaven from worldly religious leaders. Jesus said that our Father will reveal great spiritual truths to His children who do not succumb to the influence of worldly wisdom. Jesus said, "...I thank You, Father, Lord of heaven and earth [and I acknowledge openly and joyfully to Your honor], that You have hidden these things from the wise and clever and learned, and revealed them to babies [to the childish, untaught, and unskilled]" (Matthew 11:25).

Some of the disciples of Jesus Christ were fishermen who came to Jesus directly from their fishing boats. These simple, unlearned men ultimately were filled with the power of God. They were used in a mighty way by God. We also must be simple if we want to be used by God today. We must turn away from traditional intellectual thinking and test everything in our lives against the Word of God.

We can only grow spiritually after we are saved if we are able to acknowledge that our preconceived opinions in many areas must be changed. We must approach God's Word each day with a humble, teachable attitude. We must be willing to change our long established opinions if we see that the Word of God says something that is different from what we previously believed.

We block our Father from teaching us and from revealing His wisdom to us if we have a "know-it-all-attitude." The Bible refers to people like this as "scoffers." These people cannot receive wisdom from God. Our Father will only reveal His magnificent wisdom and knowledge to His children who are humble and teachable. "A scoffer seeks Wisdom in vain [for his very attitude blinds and deafens him to it], but knowledge is easy to him who [being teachable] understands" (Proverbs 14:6).

Our Father looks for His children who are in awe of the power of His Word. He wants us to tremble as we approach His Word each day with humble reverence. "...this is the man to whom I will look and have regard: he who is humble and of a broken or wounded spirit, and who trembles at My word and reveres My commands" (Isaiah 66:2).

Pride blocks us from learning from the Word of God. Our Father wants us to turn away from all preconceived opinions that are contrary to His Word to humbly receive the wonderful instructions He has given us. "...in a humble (gentle, modest) spirit receive and welcome the Word..." (James 1:21).

Jesus Christ is our example in every area of life. He was humble and teachable throughout His earthly ministry. We first see an example of His eager desire to learn when He was twelve years old. At that time His parents took Him to Jerusalem for the annual Passover Feast. Jesus became separated from His parents in the large crowds of people. They looked feverishly for Him.

The following passage of Scripture tells us that they found Him. It also shows us the humble and respectful attitude of Jesus Christ. "After three days they found Him [came upon Him] in the [court of the] temple, sitting among the teachers, listening to them and asking them questions. And all who heard Him were astonished and overwhelmed with bewildered wonder at His intelligence and understanding and His replies" (Luke 2:46-47).

Joseph and Mary found Jesus in a synagogue. Everyone in the synagogue was astonished by His wisdom and understanding. Nevertheless, Jesus was humble and respectful. We are told that Jesus listened carefully to the teachers in the synagogue. He asked many questions. We should follow His example. We should always be humble and teachable.

In the first two chapters of this book we learned about the magnitude of God's wisdom and the blessings that are available to us from God's wisdom. In the last two chapters we have learned that the wonderful secrets and mysteries of the kingdom of heaven are available to us through Jesus Christ. With this foundation we now are ready to study many specific instructions from the Word of God that tell us exactly *how* to receive manifestation of God's wisdom in our lives.

Chapter 5

The Fear of the Lord Is the Beginning of Wisdom

In this chapter we will learn from several passages of Scripture that *the fear of the Lord* should be our first priority if we sincerely desire to receive wisdom from God. We should define the topic of this chapter before we study these Scripture references. What is the fear of the Lord?

I believe the two words that best describe the fear of the Lord are "awe" and "reverence." We should always be in absolute awe of the majesty and greatness of the Lord. We should always have an attitude of absolute reverence toward Him. Our attitude should be one of deference and profound respect. We should adore the Lord. Our thoughts, words and actions should always indicate that we honor Him and love Him.

As we grow and mature in the Lord, we will understand more and more how weak and inadequate we actually are. As we continually draw closer to the Lord, we will comprehend how great, awesome, powerful and mighty He is. We will become increasingly aware of our absolute inadequacy and of His magnificent splendor. Every aspect of our lives will revolve around His indwelling presence.

Our awe will increase as we learn more and more about our Father's wonderful love for each of His children. We will look at our Father with wonder as we begin to comprehend that He loves each of us with an unconditional love. As we grow closer to God, we will be in constant awe of our Father's incomparable love, His magnificent holiness, His limitless power and His infinite wisdom.

Our thoughts, words and actions should exhibit a constant attitude of gratitude toward the Lord. We should thank Him continually. We should praise Him throughout the day and night. We should be so grateful to Him that we couldn't begin to express our heartfelt gratitude if we praised Him and thanked Him continually throughout every hour of every day during the remainder of our lives. We should praise Him continually here on earth just as we will praise Him continually when we are in heaven (see Revelation 19:1-6).

Some Christians do not fear the Lord. Some of us treat the Lord lightly. Only Christians who have not experienced the magnificence of God's presence treat Him lightly. As we come to know the Lord personally, we will revere Him, honor Him and hold Him in absolute awe.

God is the Creator of heaven and earth. He is the Creator of every person who has ever walked the face of this earth. How can we possibly center our lives around anything or anyone except the Lord? How can we live one day of our lives without being in continual reverent awe of His magnificence, His splendor and His glory?

The following passage of Scripture gives us a definition of the fear of the Lord. "...what does the Lord your God require of you but [reverently] to fear the Lord your God, [that is] to walk in all His ways, and to love Him, and to serve the Lord your God with all your [mind and] heart and with your entire being, to keep the commandments of the Lord and His statues which I command you today for your good?" (Deuteronomy 10:12-13).

If we reverently fear the Lord, we will be eager to learn and obey all of His instructions. Our hearts will be filled with love for Him. We will yearn to serve Him. Our lives will be committed to serving Him and to obeying His instructions. We will have the attitude of the prophet Jeremiah who said, "Who would not fear You, O King of the nations? For it is fitting to You and Your due! For among all the wise [men or gods] of the nations and in all their kingdoms, there is none like You" (Jeremiah 10:7).

Who wouldn't fear the Lord if he or she truly understood Who He is? No one on earth can even remotely compare to the splendor and magnificence of the Lord. He reigns over the entire universe. "The Lord reigns, let the peoples tremble [with reverential fear]!" Psalm 99:1).

Our Father wants every person on earth to fear Him, to revere Him and to worship Him just as everyone in heaven does. Please understand that the Lord is speaking to *you* when you read the word "all" that is used twice in the following passage of Scripture. "Let all the earth fear the Lord [revere and worship Him]; let all the inhabitants of the world stand in awe of Him" (Psalm 33:8).

We shouldn't fear the Lord occasionally. We shouldn't fear the Lord most of the time. We should fear the Lord continually throughout every minute of every hour of every day of our lives. "...continue in the reverent and worshipful fear of the Lord all the day long" (Proverbs 23:17).

Now that we have learned what the fear of the Lord is and why we should fear the Lord, we are ready to learn from the Word of God how the fear of the Lord applies to receiving manifestation of His wisdom. "The reverent fear and worship of the Lord is the beginning of Wisdom and skill [the preceding and the first essential, the prerequisite and the alphabet]..." (Psalm 111:10).

This passage of Scripture explains that the fear of the Lord is the beginning of His wisdom. God often uses repetition in the Bible for the purpose of emphasis. He makes a similar statement in the Book of Proverbs. "The reverent and worshipful fear of the Lord is the beginning (the chief and choice part) of Wisdom..." (Proverbs 9:10).

This passage of Scripture tells us that the fear of the Lord is "the chief and choice part" of God's wisdom. There is no question that we must fear the Lord if we truly want to receive manifestation of His wisdom. "The reverent and worshipful fear of the Lord brings instruction in Wisdom..." (Proverbs 15:33).

If we want to receive wisdom and understanding from the Lord, we must understand where wisdom can be found. God's wisdom does *not* come from the world. "...where shall Wisdom be found? And where is the place of understanding? Man knows not the price of it; neither is it found in the land of the living" (Job 28:12-13).

Where can we find God's wisdom? It is hidden from the eyes of all living people who do not know Jesus Christ as their Savior. We will learn in subsequent chapters that God's wisdom comes to us from the inside out, not from the outside in.

"From where then does Wisdom come? And where is the place of understanding? It is hidden from the eyes of all living..." (Job 28:20-21).

Jesus Christ is our example in every area of our lives. Jesus was heard by God because He feared God and revered Him. "...He was heard because of His reverence toward God [His godly fear, His piety, in that He shrank from the horrors of separation from the bright presence of the Father]" (Hebrews 5:7).

Jesus was in such awe of His Father that He was horrified at the thought of being separated from His presence. Jesus knew that, when He took the sins of the entire world upon Himself, the appropriation of this sin would separate Him from God. Just before He died on the cross Jesus said, "My God, My God, why have You forsaken Me [deserting Me and leaving Me helpless and abandoned]?" (Mark 15:34).

We also should revere God so much that we have a deep and sincere desire to remain in His presence continually, never to be separated from Him. In subsequent chapters we will learn from the holy Scriptures how to enter into the presence of God and remain there. The fear of God is vital if we truly want to live in God's presence and to receive manifestation of His wisdom.

Now that we have seen the importance of fearing the Lord, we are ready to look into God's Word for more scriptural instruction pertaining to the relationship between the fear of the Lord and receiving His wisdom. "...if you cry out for insight and raise your voice for understanding, if you seek [Wisdom] as for silver and search for skillful and godly Wisdom as for hidden treasures, then you will understand the reverent and worshipful fear of the Lord and find the knowledge of [our omniscient] God" (Proverbs 2:3-5).

Our Father wants us to yearn so much to receive insight and understanding from Him that we cry out to Him. He wants us to continually search for His wisdom because we understand what a magnificent treasure His wisdom is. We will understand the reverent fear of the Lord when we yearn to receive His wisdom. Then we will find the knowledge of God.

We must understand that the fear of the Lord is positive, not negative. The fear of the Lord is not a fear that makes us want to run away from Him. Instead, the fear of the Lord makes us want to run *to Him.* If we truly fear and revere the Lord, we will have a deep and fervent desire to draw as close to Him as we possibly can throughout every day of our lives here on earth.

God actually created us for the purpose of fearing, revering and worshipping Him. "...Fear God [revere and worship Him, knowing that He is] and keep His commandments, for this is the whole of man [the full, original purpose of his creation, the object of God's providence, the root of character, the foundation of all happiness, the adjustment to all inharmonious circumstances and conditions under the sun] and the whole [duty] for every man" (Ecclesiastes 12:13).

We will grow and mature if we obey God's instructions to fear Him and to do what His Word tells us to do. Our character will develop and mature if we obey these instructions from God. We will live happy, fulfilled and harmonious lives if we live the way our Father instructs us to live.

As we study the Word of God in more detail, we will see the relationship between fearing the Lord, studying His Word continually and obeying His instructions. "...he shall keep it with him, and he shall read in it all the days of his life, that he may learn [reverently] to fear the Lord his God, by keeping all the words of this law and these statues and doing them…" (Deuteronomy 17:19).

We are instructed to keep our Bibles with us and to study them constantly. If we obey our Father's instructions, we will fear Him and we will live our lives in obedience to the instructions in His Word. A definite relationship exists between fearing the Lord and understanding the Word of God. "Establish Your word and confirm Your promise to Your servant, which is for those who reverently fear and devotedly worship You" (Psalm 119:38).

If we truly fear the Lord, our lives will be solidly anchored upon the Word of God. We'll be certain that every promise from God is absolutely true and completely reliable. We'll step out in faith on these promises with absolute assurance that our loving Father will always do exactly what He promises to do.

Our hearts will rejoice if we fear the Lord. We'll hunger and thirst to learn more from the holy Scriptures. "The precepts of the Lord are right, rejoicing the heart; the commandment of the Lord is pure and bright, enlightening the eyes. The [reverent] fear of the Lord is clean, enduring forever; the ordinances of the Lord are true and righteous altogether. More to be desired are they than gold, even than much fine gold; they are sweeter also than honey and drippings from the honeycomb" (Psalm 19:8-10).

The Word of God is pure. Our hearts will sing with joy if we continually fill our minds and our hearts with the holy Scriptures. We will be enlightened continually if we obey our Father's instructions to study and meditate on His Word daily. The Word of God is much more desirable than gold or any other earthly treasure. "…I love Your commandments more than [resplendent] gold, yes, more than [perfectly] refined gold" (Psalm 119:127).

Some people despise the Bible. These people are blinded by Satan. They will ultimately pay a severe price if they don't change their ways. Our Father will reward us if we fear and respect His Word just as we fear and respect Him. "Whoever despises the word and counsel [of God] brings destruction upon himself, but he who [reverently)] fears and respects the commandment [of God] is rewarded" (Proverbs 13:13).

In subsequent chapters we will study many Scripture references pertaining to the relationship between the Word of God and the Holy Spirit. For now, let's look at one passage of Scripture that tells us about the relationship between the fear of the Lord and the Spirit of the Lord. "...the Spirit of the Lord shall rest upon Him – the Spirit of wisdom and understanding, the Spirit of counsel and might, the Spirit of knowledge and of the reverential and obedient fear of the Lord – and shall make Him of quick understanding, and His delight shall be in the reverential and obedient fear of the Lord. And He shall not judge by the sight of His eyes, neither decide by the hearing of His ears..." (Isaiah 11:2-3).

This passage of Scripture is a prophetic passage referring to Jesus Christ. It accurately prophesied that the Holy Spirit would rest on Jesus Christ throughout His earthly ministry. We can see that we can receive wisdom, understanding and knowledge from the Holy Spirit because He is referred to as "the Spirit of wisdom and understanding" and as "the Spirit of knowledge." We are not limited to what we can see with our eyes and hear with our ears.

Jesus Christ received wisdom, understanding, knowledge and guidance from the Holy Spirit throughout His earthly ministry. This same wonderful wisdom, understanding, knowledge and guidance are available to all Christians today from the same Holy Spirit Who lives in our hearts.

If we truly want to receive these blessings from God, we must learn how to hear the voice of the Holy Spirit just as Jesus heard His voice throughout His earthly ministry. If we learn to obey the instructions of the Holy Spirit, we will turn away from the limitations of knowledge received from our senses. We won't make decisions based only on what we see with our eyes and what we hear with our ears.

In subsequent chapters we will study Scripture references explaining that the Lord is our teacher. The following passage of Scripture shows us the relationship between fearing the Lord and being taught by the Lord as He tells us what choices He wants us to make. "Who is the man who reverently fears and worships the Lord? Him shall He teach in the way that he should choose" (Psalm 25:12).

We are able to come into the Lord's presence when we truly fear Him and revere Him. "The secret [of the sweet, satisfying companionship] of the Lord have they who fear (revere and worship) Him, and He will show them His covenant and reveal to them its [deep, inner] meaning" (Psalm 25:14).

This passage of Scripture is absolutely awesome. It actually tells us *the secret of enjoying sweet and satisfying companionship with the Lord.* We will be able to enjoy this wonderful companionship when we fear the Lord, revere the Lord and worship the Lord. Worship isn't a mental decision. Worship is our whole self loving God. Our worship will increase as we revere God and experience His presence.

This passage of Scripture goes on to say that the Lord will show us His covenant if we fear Him. A covenant is an agreement between two people. As we continually draw closer to the Lord, He will reveal to us the "deep inner meaning" of a continual close relationship with Him.

We won't be proud and arrogant if we truly fear the Lord. Satan fell because of pride. Satan wants us to fall because of pride. Our Father wants us to be humble at all times. If we truly fear the Lord, we will hate evil, pride, arrogance and every other influence that Satan's demons attempt to put into our minds. "The reverent fear and worshipful awe of the Lord [includes] the hatred of evil; pride, arrogance, the evil way…" (Proverbs 8:13).

If we truly fear the Lord, we will experience the satisfaction, meaning and fulfillment that all people yearn for. Satan's evil influence will not be able to get a foothold in our lives. "The reverent, worshipful fear of the Lord leads to life, and he who has it rests satisfied; he cannot be visited with [actual] evil" (Proverbs 19:23).

We should have no greater desire than to fear the Lord at all times. Our Father looks constantly for His children who truly "fear Him, revere Him and worship Him with awe." "…the Lord's eye is upon those who fear Him [who revere and worship Him with awe]…" (Psalm 33:18).

How do we fear the Lord? We choose to spend time alone with Him daily. We study His Word and talk to Him. We worship Him and praise Him constantly. We learn to be quiet enough to hear Him. We listen to Him talk to us. Nothing in life is more valuable than the time we spend communicating with our wonderful Lord for no other purpose than to love Him.

This chapter is filled with several Scripture references explaining the relationship between the fear of the Lord and receiving manifestation of God's wisdom, guidance, knowledge and understanding. We have learned that fearing the Lord is the secret to a close and satisfying relationship with the Lord. We are now ready to build upon this foundation to learn many additional scriptural truths pertaining to the wisdom of God. In the next chapter we'll learn how to place the same priority on the wisdom of God that our Father puts on His wisdom.

Chapter 6

God Places a High Priority on His Wisdom

We should set our priorities in life to be the same as God's priorities. Our priorities are wrong if our Father tells us to put something first in our lives and we fail to comply with His instructions. Let's look at the Word of God to see what our Father says about the priority His wisdom should have in our lives. "The beginning of Wisdom is: get Wisdom (skillful and godly Wisdom)! [For skillful and godly Wisdom is the principal thing.] And with all you have gotten, get understanding (discernment, comprehension, and interpretation)" (Proverbs 4:7).

Our Father begins this passage of Scripture by telling us to "get" His wisdom. We then are told that God's wisdom is "the principal thing." *Webster's New World Dictionary* says that "principal" means "first in rank, authority, importance, degree." Our Father tells us to place our desire to receive His wisdom in first place ahead of our other desires.

There are other places in the Bible where we also are told to put things first in our lives. I'm not in any way saying that our desire for God's wisdom should come ahead of God's instructions in both the Old Testament and the New Testament to love Him with all of our hearts. "...you shall love the Lord Your God with all your [mind and] heart and with your entire being and with all your might. And these words which I am commanding you this day shall be [first] in your [own] minds and hearts..." (Deuteronomy 6:5-6).

Jesus Christ emphasized this Old Testament instruction to put our love for God in first place in our lives. Jesus said, "...You shall love the Lord your God with all your heart and with all your soul and with all your mind (intellect). This is the great (most important, principal) and first commandment" (Matthew 22:37-38).

Jesus gave us one additional instruction about what we should put first in our lives. He said, "...seek (aim at and strive after) first of all His kingdom and His righteousness (His way of doing and being right), and then all these things taken together will be given you besides" (Matthew 6:33).

I believe we are talking about the same thing as we compare the "firsts" in the Bible. Let's go back to the amplification from *The Amplified Bible* that we are using as our definition of wisdom in this book. This amplification defines wisdom as "comprehensive insight into the ways and purposes of God." We will receive comprehensive insight into the ways and purposes of God if we love Him with all of our hearts and all of our souls and all of our minds and if we always seek His kingdom and His righteousness.

I believe that our primary goal in life should be to draw closer to the Lord. We should have a deep and continuing desire to live more and more in the presence of the Lord throughout every day of our lives. When we have this continual close relationship with the Lord, we will receive His wisdom as well as the other blessings He gives to His children who walk closely with Him.

Proverbs 4:7 also tells us that, as we receive God's wisdom, we will "get understanding." We'll be able to discern great spiritual truths as our Father gives us His understanding. We'll be able to see things more and more from God's perspective.

If we go back a little before Proverbs 4:7, which I put first because it is the key passage of Scripture in this chapter, we will learn more about wisdom and understanding. Let's look now at the two verses immediately preceding Proverbs 4:7. "Get skillful and godly Wisdom, get understanding (discernment, comprehension, and interpretation); do not forget and do not turn back from the words of my mouth. Forsake not [Wisdom], and she will keep, defend, and protect you; love her, and she will guard you" (Proverbs 4:5-6).

The word "get" is used twice in Proverbs 4:5 just as it is used twice in Proverbs 4:7. We have seen that God often uses repetition in the Bible for emphasis. There is no question that our Father has emphatically instructed us to "get" His wisdom and His understanding. He doesn't want us to forget about our desire to receive His wisdom. He doesn't want us to forsake His wisdom. Our Father wants us to love His wisdom because His wisdom is so powerful that it will keep us, defend us, protect us and guard us.

God gives us additional information pertaining to His wisdom immediately after Proverbs 4:7. "Prize Wisdom highly and exalt her, and she will exalt and promote you; she will bring you to honor when you embrace her. She shall give to your head a wreath of gracefulness; a crown of beauty and glory will she deliver to you" (Proverbs 4:8-9)

Our Father wants us to prize His wisdom highly. When we prize something, we give it a very high priority. God tells us to exalt His wisdom. When we exalt something, we lift it up. Our Father promises that we will receive promotions and honor if we embrace His wisdom. We will receive "gracefulness, beauty and glory." We also will receive many blessings from our Father if we learn how to receive manifestation of His wisdom.

Our Father has given us the example of King Solomon to emphasize the priority He wants us to place on receiving comprehensive insight into His ways and His purposes. One night when King Solomon was sleeping, God appeared to him in a dream. He said, "...Ask what I shall give you" (I Kings 3:5). Solomon had his priorities right. He said, "...give Your servant an understanding mind and a hearing heart to judge Your people, that I may discern between good and bad..." (I Kings 3:9).

God was pleased with Solomon's response. "It pleased the Lord that Solomon had asked this. God said to him, Because you have asked this and have not asked for long life or for riches, nor for the lives of your enemies, but have asked for yourself understanding to recognize what is just and right, Behold, I have done as you asked. I have given you a wise, discerning mind, so that no one before you was your equal, nor shall any arise after you equal to you. I have also given you what you have not asked, both riches and honor, so that there shall not be any among the kings equal to you all your days" (I Kings 3:10-13).

King Solomon didn't ask to live a long life, to be rich or that his enemies would be killed. Instead, he asked God for understanding to recognize what is good and right (comprehensive insight into the ways and purposes of God). Solomon had a deep desire to see things from God's perspective. He asked for an understanding heart.

God answered Solomon's prayer. He gave him a brilliant mind that surpassed the wisdom of anyone before him or after him. God also gave King Solomon the riches and honor he didn't ask for. (You might want to read II Chronicles 1:7-12 for a similar version of this story).

Solomon didn't reply the way many of us would reply when God asked him that he wanted above all else. He didn't ask for material benefits. What would you have replied if God had appeared to you and asked you the same question He asked King Solomon? Are your priorities the same as Solomon's? Do you have a deep and sincere desire to receive manifestation of God's wisdom in your life? Do you truly crave more comprehensive insight into the ways and purposes of God?

Let's look again at the first chapter of Kings for additional information pertaining to the wisdom that God gave to King Solomon. "...God gave Solomon exceptionally much wisdom and understanding, and breadth of mind like the sand of the seashore. Solomon's wisdom excelled the wisdom of all the people of the East and all the wisdom of Egypt. For he was wiser than all other men..." (I Kings 4:29-31).

God gave Solomon exceptional wisdom and understanding. Solomon's wide range of wisdom and understanding is compared to sand on the seashore. Think about the hundreds of millions of grains of sand on the shore of the sea and you will begin to comprehend the magnitude of the wisdom and understanding God gave to King Solomon.

We will live in God's presence both now and in heaven if we learn how to receive wisdom from Him. "So shall you know skillful and godly Wisdom to be thus to your life; if you find it, then shall there be a future and a reward, and your hope and expectation shall not be cut off" (Proverbs 24:14).

Most of us would put the well-being of the members of our family at or near the top of any list of priorities. "Through skillful and godly Wisdom is a house (a life, a home, a family) built, and by understanding it is established [on a sound and good foundation], and by knowledge shall its chambers [of every area] be filled with all precious and pleasant riches" (Proverbs 24:3-4).

This passage of Scripture applies to you and your family. Know that your family will be established on a solid foundation if you learn how to receive wisdom and understanding from God. If you receive God's wisdom and share His wisdom with the members of your family, they will receive manifestation of the precious treasures our Father wants to give to all of His children who live the way He wants us to live.

What are your goals in life? Would you like to receive God's wisdom to help you successfully find and carry out God's will for your life? Would you like to receive God's wisdom to be a better husband, wife or parent? Would you like to utilize God's wisdom to be more successful at your vocation and therefore be able to provide more abundantly for your family and to give money liberally into the kingdom of God?

Our Father has provided His wisdom to help us in every area of our lives. God's wisdom is very practical. Our Father wants His children to abound with blessings just as those of us who are parents want our children here on earth to be blessed abundantly. Because of the price that Jesus Christ paid for us, the manifestation of God's wisdom is vital so that we can receive all of the blessings our Father has made available to each of His beloved children.

In this chapter we have seen the priority that God places on our desire to receive His wisdom. Now we are ready to look into the holy Scriptures to learn what the Word of God has to say about the relationship between receiving God's wisdom and turning away from the ways of the world.

Chapter 7

Receive God's Wisdom by Turning Away from the World

Jesus Christ came to earth from heaven. He was far above every person who was living on earth. The people who lived on earth could only understand things from their limited worldly perspective. "He Who comes from above (heaven) is [far] above all [others]; he who comes from the earth belongs to the earth, and talks the language of earth [his words are from an earthly standpoint]. He Who comes from heaven is [far] above all others [far superior to all others in prominence and in excellence]" (John 3:31).

Christians do not need to look at things from a worldly perspective. All people who receive Jesus Christ as their Savior do not belong to the world any longer. Jesus said, "...you are not of the world [no longer one with it], but I have chosen (selected) you out of the world..." (John 15:19).

When Jesus died on a cross at Calvary to pay the price for our sins, He also made it possible for us to be set free from the influence the world has upon us. "...our Lord Jesus Christ (the Messiah), Who gave (yielded) Himself up [to atone] for our sins [and to save and sanctify us], in order to rescue and deliver us from this present wicked age and world order, in accordance with the will and purpose and plan of our God and our Father..." (Galatians 1:3-4).

Even though all Christians live on earth in their physical bodies, we must understand that, in the spiritual realm, Jesus has lifted us above this world so that we actually can sit with Him in heaven while we are still on earth. We may look like we are of the world, but our home actually is in heaven. "And He raised us up together with Him and made us sit down together [giving us joint seating with Him] in the heavenly sphere [by virtue of our being] in Christ Jesus (the Messiah, the Anointed One)" (Ephesians 2:6).

We have risen to a new life with Jesus Christ. Jesus went from earth to heaven when He was resurrected from the dead. All Christians share in His resurrection. Because of our salvation, we should be heavenly-minded, not earthly-minded. "If then you have been raised with Christ [to a new life, thus sharing His resurrection from the dead], aim at and seek the [rich, eternal treasures] that are above, where Christ is, seated at the right hand of God. And set your minds and keep them set on what is above (the higher things), not on the things that are on the earth" (Colossians 3:1-2).

Before Jesus ascended into heaven He prayed to God asking His Father to purify us and to separate us from the world so that we will be made holy. We will become holy if we continually immerse ourselves in the Word of God and allow its power to transform our lives. Jesus said, "They are not of the world (worldly, belonging to the world), [just] as I am not of the world. Sanctify them [purify, consecrate, separate them for Yourself, make them holy] by the Truth; Your Word is Truth" (John 17:16-17).

We will see things more and more from a heavenly perspective if we obey our Father's instructions to continually fill our minds and our hearts with His Word. As we grow and mature as Christians we will know that this earth is not our home. We may be listed as citizens of a specific town or city and a specific state for voting purposes here on earth, but the Bible teaches us that we actually are citizens of heaven. "...we are citizens of the state (commonwealth, homeland) which is in heaven..." (Philippians 3:20).

We are only visitors here on earth. Because our real home is in heaven and because we are citizens of heaven, we should continually pay the price of daily Bible study and meditation to learn and obey the laws of heaven while we live temporarily on earth. We are "...aliens and strangers and exiles [in this world]..." (I Peter 2:11).

As we study and meditate on these passages of Scripture, we can clearly see that God doesn't want us to identify with the world. Our Father wants us to turn completely away from the things of this world to live our lives according to His instructions. "...Turn away from the irreverent babble and godless chatter, with the vain and empty and worldly phrases, and the subtleties and the contradictions in what is falsely called knowledge and spiritual illumination. [For] by making such profession some have erred (missed the mark) as regards the faith..." (I Timothy 6:20).

The world is filled with "irreverent babble and godless chatter." Many people in the world waste their God-given right to speak constructive words by continually speaking meaningless words about things of the world that have absolutely no eternal significance. We live on earth and we can enjoy godly activities while we are here, but we must not be consumed by them.

We have seen that Christians actually are aliens on earth. We have been given the ability to think different thoughts and to speak a different language than unbelievers. Our hearts should be filled with joy because we know that we are merely passing through this world. Our hearts should rejoice because we are absolutely certain that we have a permanent residence awaiting us in the incomprehensible glory, beauty, magnificence and splendor of heaven. You might want to read our book, *What Will Heaven Be Like?*, if you would like more information on this subject.

Unfortunately, some Christians fail to understand the importance of continually turning away from the ways of the world. We must not be preoccupied with the things of this world because "...the whole world [around us] is under the power of the evil one" (I John 5:19). Satan won control of the world when Adam fell. Jesus Christ once referred to Satan as "...the ruler (evil genius, prince) of this world..." (John 12:31).

Satan has great power over the world. He wants Christians to conform to the ways of the world because Satan and his demons then have a better opportunity to influence our thoughts, our beliefs, our words and our actions. Satan wants our values to be based upon the value system of the world. He has no power over Christians who live in the power of the risen Lord, the power of the Holy Spirit and the power of the living Word of God.

Jesus Christ wants us to constantly walk in the magnificent victory He won for us (see Matthew 28:18). He wants us to turn away from the influence of Satan. Jesus wants us to live our lives in God's presence where we are safe and victorious.

He wants us to believe our Father's promises with absolute and unwavering faith in the reliability of God.

Our Father wants us to look at the ways of the world from His perspective. The things in this world that unsaved people think highly of actually are repugnant to God. Jesus said, "...what is exalted and highly thought of among men is detestable and abhorrent (an abomination) in the sight of God" (Luke 16:15).

All Christians are members of the family of God. We have access to the wisdom of our Father. We should seek this wisdom for every area of life. We should be the best doctors, lawyers, teachers, scientists, mechanics, chefs, housewives or whatever else we do while we are on earth. We should operate in excellence because we are connected to the wisdom of God.

Our Father holds the wisdom of the world in contempt. He has shown us how foolish the world's wisdom is. "Where is the wise man (the philosopher)? Where is the scribe (the scholar)? Where is the investigator (the logician, the debater) of this present time and age? Has not God shown up the nonsense and the folly of this world's wisdom?" (I Corinthians 1:20).

We are deceived if we pursue the wisdom of the world. Our Father wants us to turn completely away from the discernment of the world because we realize how foolish it is. We cannot receive the wisdom of God unless we turn completely away from the wisdom of the world. "Let no person deceive himself. If anyone among you supposes that he is wise in this age, let him become a fool [let him discard his worldly discernment and recognize himself as dull, stupid, and foolish, without true learning and scholarship], that he may become [really] wise" (I Corinthians 3:18).

The Bible tells us that the wisdom of the world is foolish and absurd. God knows that all human wisdom is absolutely useless. "…this world's wisdom is foolishness (absurdity and stupidity) with God, for it is written, He lays hold of the wise in their [own] craftiness; and again, The Lord knows the thoughts and reasonings of the [humanly] wise and recognizes how futile they are" (I Corinthians 3:19-20).

Our Father wants us to learn His ways through continual study and meditation on the precious Book of Instructions He has made available to us because of His love for us. We can easily fall into the trap the apostle Paul warned the Colossians about if we fail to obey God's instructions. Paul said, "See to it that no one carries you off as spoil or makes you yourselves captive by his so-called philosophy and intellectualism and vain deceit (idle fancies and plain nonsense), following human tradition (men's ideas of the material rather than the spiritual world), just crude notions following the rudimentary and elemental teachings of the universe and disregarding [the teachings of] Christ (the Messiah)" (Colossians 2:8).

We must be very careful that we are not taken into captivity by subtle worldly ideas that are deceitful. Our Father wants us to turn away from worldly philosophy that cannot stand the test of scriptural accuracy. We must not make the mistake of disregarding the teachings of Jesus Christ to pursue the wisdom of the world.

God's wisdom is infinitely superior to the wisdom of the world. Some Christians make the mistake of pursing the wisdom of the world because they do not understand the facts about the wisdom of God compared to the wisdom of the world. They waste tremendous amounts of time and energy pursuing the wisdom of the world when they should continually seek the wisdom of God.

When God created us, He knew that the wisdom of the world would be inadequate as we try to solve many of the complex problems we face in our lives. Human wisdom is ineffective. "...in much [human] wisdom is much vexation, and he who increases knowledge increases sorrow" Ecclesiastes 1:18).

The word "vexation" means "to be disturbed, annoyed or irritated." We will experience constant frustration if we attempt to find the answers to complex problems with the wisdom of the world. We ultimately will experience a great deal of sorrow if we continue to pursue worldly knowledge. We should always be aware that the ways of the world can creep into our lives so slowly that we don't notice the change. We should constantly fill our minds and our hearts with the Word of God to protect ourselves against the influence of the world.

The Bible compares Christians who love the ways of the world with wives who are unfaithful to their husbands. We are *unfaithful to God* if we pursue the ways and the wisdom of the world. If we are friends of the ways of the world, we must understand that we actually are *enemies* of God. "You [are like] unfaithful wives [having illicit love affairs with the world and breaking your marriage vow to God]! Do you not know that being the world's friend is being God's enemy? So whoever chooses to be a friend of the world takes his stand as an enemy of God" (James 4:4).

Our Father doesn't want us to live lives that are controlled by our flesh. We cannot please God if we constantly give in to our carnal desires. "...those who are living the life of the flesh [catering to the appetites and impulses of their carnal nature] cannot please or satisfy God, or be acceptable to Him" (Romans 8:8).

Our Father doesn't want us to make the mistake of placing too much emphasis on the pleasures of the world. Some Christians miss God entirely because they are so caught up with worldly hobbies and the pursuit of pleasure. We must understand that all of the ways of the world are merely temporary. The Bible speaks of "...those who deal with this world [overusing the enjoyments of this life] as though they were not absorbed by it and as if they had no dealings with it. For the outward form of this world (the present world order) is passing away" (I Corinthians 7:31).

We should die to a worldly perspective when we become Christians. Jesus Christ has set us free from the crude, external teachings of the world. We must not make the mistake of living our lives the way that unbelievers live. "If then you have died with Christ to material ways of looking at things and have escaped from the world's crude and elemental notions and teachings of externalism, why do you live as if you still belong to the world?..." (Colossians 2:20).

We should prayerfully examine our lives for evidence of the world's ways. Our Father doesn't want us to be contaminated by any influence the world has on us. We are instructed to "...keep oneself unspotted and uncontaminated from the world" (James 1:27).

We can expect to be criticized by others if we make the commitment to continually turn away from the things of this world to pursue a closer relationship with the Lord. People who have not accepted Jesus Christ as their Savior have no frame of reference about what we believe. They think that our Christian beliefs are absurd. "...the story and message of the cross is sheer absurdity and folly to those who are perishing and on their way to perdition..." (I Corinthians 1:18).

I have been called a "Jesus freak" many times. Some members of my family and some people I thought were my friends have turned away from me because of my total commitment to the Lord Jesus Christ. Jesus warned us that some people actually will hate us because we refuse to conform to the ways of the world. He said, "...the world has hated them, because they are not of the world [do not belong to the world]..." (John 17:14).

Are we here on earth to please other people or are we here to please God? During His earthly ministry Jesus found that several "religious" people emphatically disagreed with many of His statements and many of the choices He made. Even members of His own family turned against Him. These people disagreed with Jesus because He was teaching God's ways that are vastly different from the ways of the world. Nothing has changed in this respect during the past two thousand years.

Our Father doesn't want us to focus primarily on things we can see with our eyes. He wants us to focus on things that we cannot contact through our senses. The things we can see with our human eyesight are temporary. The invisible truths of the spiritual realm are eternal. "...consider and look not to the things that are seen but to the things that are unseen; for the things that are visible are temporal (brief and fleeting), but the things that are invisible are deathless and everlasting" (II Corinthians 4:18).

There are two separate realms – the spiritual realm and the natural realm. We are preoccupied with the natural realm if we are preoccupied with the things of the world. Our Father wants us to learn how to live victoriously in the spiritual realm according to the specific scriptural instructions that we will study in detail throughout this book. We must understand that everything we can see with our human eyesight was originally created by God from things that were invisible. "...what we see was not made out of things which are visible" (Hebrews 11:3).

Many unbelievers are searching for the supernatural realm. We have seen increased interest in recent years in the occult, in spiritism, in astrology, fortune telling, palm reading and the many other substitutes Satan has for the kingdom of God. If we fail to grow and mature as Christians, we can easily be trapped through lack of discernment by spiritual events that come from Satan even though they seem to come from God.

A new kingdom was established on earth when Jesus Christ rose from the dead. Our lives should not revolve around the limitations of our senses. The teaching of the Word of God should permeate every aspect of our lives. All of our thoughts, words and actions should be yielded to the Holy Spirit Who lives in our hearts.

We should learn everything we possibly can about the spiritual laws of God's kingdom so that we can successfully carry out God's purpose for our lives. Although we live in a world that is controlled by Satan, higher laws predominate for the believer. Jesus Christ has given us absolute authority and power over Satan (see Luke 10:19). If we learn the higher laws of the kingdom of God, we will be able to receive manifestation of God's wisdom throughout our lives here on earth.

Chapter 8

We Should Pursue God's Wisdom Ahead of Wealth

Several Scripture references compare wisdom with wealth. The Word of God repeatedly instructs us to value God's wisdom more than any worldly treasure. God's wisdom is more desirable than any amount of precious gems or the gold that is prized so highly in the world. "…the possession of Wisdom is even above rubies or pearls. The topaz of Ethiopia cannot compare with it, nor can it be valued in pure gold" (Job 28:18-19).

The value of instruction from the Word of God is much greater than the value of gold. Godly knowledge is better than gold. God's wisdom is far superior to rubies or pearls. King Solomon told his son, "Receive my instruction in preference to [striving for] silver, and knowledge rather than choice gold, for skillful and godly Wisdom is better than rubies or pearls, and all the things that may be desired are not to be compared to it" (Proverbs 8:10-11).

God's priorities are obvious. Are our priorities the same? Do we understand the wonderful blessings we will receive if we know how to operate in God's wisdom? "Wisdom is as good as an inheritance, yes, more excellent it is for those [the living] who see the sun. For wisdom is a defense even as money is a defense, but the excellency of knowledge is that wisdom shields and preserves the life of him who has it" (Ecclesiastes 7:11-12).

Most people would be overjoyed if they received a large inheritance from a wealthy relative that enabled them to be set for life financially. God's wisdom is better than any inheritance. Many people strive to accumulate wealth because they believe this earthly wealth will give them security. These people trust in their wealth to protect them. God's wisdom will lead us to make decisions that will provide all of the security we will ever need. God's wisdom will protect us.

Some Christians devote a disproportionate amount of their time and energy to the pursuit of worldly wealth in spite of God's instructions telling us to put our desire for His wisdom first. Jesus Christ said, "No servant is able to serve two masters; for either he will hate the one and love the other, or he will stand by and be devoted to the one and despise the other. You cannot serve God and mammon (riches, or anything in which you trust and on which you rely)" (Luke 16:13).

If the accumulation of wealth is our top priority, we are told that we will love money and that we will hate the things of God. We cannot serve God if our primary desire is to pursue wealth and to place our reliance upon this wealth. Greed for the wealth of the world will cause us to despise the Lord. "...the one greedy for gain curses and spurns, yes, renounces and despises the Lord" (Psalm 10:3).

Our Father wants us to cease from the human wisdom that causes some people to have a greater desire for worldly wealth than they have for a close, intimate relationship with Him. "Weary not yourself to be rich; cease from your own [human] wisdom" (Proverbs 23:4).

If we are caught up with the pursuit of wealth and the things money can buy, we will miss precious spiritual treasure from the Lord that cannot be purchased with the wealth of this world. "Wait and listen, everyone who is thirsty! Come to the waters; and he who has no money, come, buy and eat! Yes, come, buy [priceless, spiritual] wine and milk without money and without price [simply for the self-surrender that accepts the blessing]. Why do you spend your money for that which is not bread, and your earnings for what does not satisfy? Hearken diligently to Me, and eat what is good, and let your soul delight itself in fatness [the profuseness of spiritual joy]. Incline your ear [submit and consent to the divine will] and come to Me; hear, and your soul will revive..." (Isaiah 55:1-3).

Our Father wants us to thirst for Him. We can come to Him to receive "priceless spiritual wine and milk" even if we don't have any money. Our Father wants us to put our desire for Him above all else. We should obey God and "hearken diligently" to Him instead of pursuing worldly wealth and the things that money can buy. The word "hearken" means to pay close attention.

Our Father wants us to eat the good spiritual food that He will provide for us when we draw close to Him. We will experience tremendous joy if we obey these instructions from God. We will hear our Father's voice speaking to us if we submit and consent to His will for our lives. Our souls will be revived if we continually draw close to Him.

True happiness and fulfillment cannot be found through the accumulation of earthly wealth. True happiness and fulfillment can only be attained by seeking God with all of our hearts. I want to emphasize that I am *not* saying that our Father doesn't want His children to prosper. What loving father here on earth doesn't want his children to prosper? Our heavenly Father wants very much for us to be prosperous (see III John 2), but He wants us to prosper His way, not the world's way.

Our Father wants us to prosper financially for His glory. We will experience severe problems if we trust financial prosperity instead of trusting God. "...those who crave to be rich fall into temptation and a snare and into many foolish (useless, godless) and hurtful desires that plunge men into ruin and destruction and miserable perishing. For the love of money is a root of all evils; it is through this craving that some have been led astray and have wandered from the faith and pierced themselves through with many acute [mental] pangs" (I Timothy 6:9-10).

Money is a wonderful servant, but it is a horrible master. We give Satan and his demons a significant opportunity to deceive us if we crave the wealth of the world. We ultimately will be trapped by our desire for excess worldly wealth. We will pursue many foolish desires that will hurt us if we pursue worldly wealth ahead of God. This desire eventually will destroy us.

This passage of Scripture says that "the love of money is a root of all evil." Sometimes we hear people say that "money is the root of all evil." They fail to state all of the words in this passage of Scripture. Our Father says that the *love* of money will lead us to evil - to the influence of Satan and his demons. We should love God and we should love other people. We should never love money or the things money can buy.

We are told that we will be diverted from having faith in God if we crave the wealth of the world. We will "pierce ourselves with many acute mental pangs" if we make this mistake. On the other hand, we will be truly rich if we obey God's instructions. We will not experience the sorrow that people ultimately experience when they put their craving for worldly wealth and the things that money can buy ahead of the Lord.

If we want to be truly rich from the Lord's perspective, we should prosper according to the specific instructions we have been given in the Word of God. We will receive wonderful blessings from the Lord when we prosper in obedience to His instructions. We won't experience sorrow. We are told that toiling (human efforts) will not increase the true riches the Lord will give us. "The blessing of the Lord – it makes [truly] rich, and He adds no sorrow with it [neither does toiling increase it]" (Proverbs 10:22).

This chapter is filled with biblical instructions pertaining to the pursuit of wealth compared to the pursuit of God. In the next chapter we will look carefully into the Word of God for additional instructions pertaining to financial wisdom.

Chapter 9

We Can Receive Financial Wisdom from God

We saw in the last chapter that, when someone obtains wealth without the wisdom of God, this wealth inevitably will lead that person into bondage. We need our Father's wisdom to understand what He wants us to do with worldly riches. We can see many examples of this principle with professional athletes, movie stars and other people who become very wealthy only to end up being extremely frustrated because they have no comprehension of God's instructions for handling wealth. These people ultimately will find that the wealth they thought was a blessing actually will turn into a curse.

People who attain worldly wealth without the wisdom of God do not understand the reason our Father has made financial abundance possible. Many people are so preoccupied with accumulating earthly wealth that they miss God entirely. They think constantly about accumulating more wealth instead of focusing continually on what God wants them to do with their lives.

In a subsequent chapter we will thoroughly examine the relationship between pride and the wisdom of God. For now, I just want to say that the Bible tells us that God resists the proud (see James 4:6 and I Peter 5:5). Many wealthy people who are conceited because of their wealth mistakenly trust in their human wisdom. "The rich man is wise in his own eyes and conceit..." (Proverbs 28:11).

Instead of being proud of our financial prosperity, we should be humble. We should glorify God instead of glorifying ourselves because of the wealth we have accumulated. "...beware lest you say in your [mind and] heart, My power and the might of my hand have gotten me this wealth. But you shall [earnestly] remember the Lord your God, for it is He Who gives you power to get wealth..." (Deuteronomy 8:17-18).

The first sentence in this passage of Scripture contains the words "my" and "me" three times – "*My* power and the might of *my* hand have gotten *me* this wealth." We should never put ourselves in first place ahead of God. We should always be conscious that God has given us the ability to obtain wealth.

Many Christians need to be educated in regard to what God says about finances. If you would like to learn hundreds of facts from the Word of God pertaining to finances, you might want to study our book, *Trust God for Your Finances*, and our Scripture Meditation Cards and the accompanying 85 minute cassette tape that both have the title, *Financial Instructions from God.*

Our Father has given the following specific instructions to every person who has been blessed financially. "As for the rich in this world, charge them not to be proud and arrogant and contemptuous of others, nor to set their hopes on uncertain riches, but on God, Who richly and ceaselessly provides us with everything for [our] enjoyment. [Charge them] to do good, to be rich in good works, to be liberal and generous of heart, ready to share [with others], in this way laying up for themselves [the riches that endure forever as] a good foundation for the future, so that they may grasp that which is life indeed" (I Timothy 6:17-19).

This passage of Scripture is filled with important advice for wealthy people. Some of these people elevate themselves in their own eyes. They look down at other people with contempt. Wealthy people shouldn't be haughty, self-centered and rude.

This passage of Scripture goes on to say that we shouldn't place our hopes for the future on the uncertainty of worldly riches. Some wealthy people make the mistake of allowing their wealth to become their god. Our Father doesn't want us to ever put anything or anyone ahead of Him (see Exodus 20:3).

We are instructed to set our hopes on God instead of setting our hopes on any wealth we have accumulated. Our Father promises to provide us with everything we need for our enjoyment. If we want to avoid the extreme frustration that many wealthy people inevitably experience, we should focus continually on God instead of being preoccupied with the accumulation of wealth.

This passage of Scripture tells wealthy people what God wants them to do with their wealth. If we have been blessed financially, our Father wants us to be generous with the wealth He has enabled us to obtain. He wants us to share this wealth freely with others.

Our Father never intended for us to accumulate wealth that is far over and above what we actually need. When we have accumulated wealth that is above and beyond the reasonable needs of ourselves and our families, we should invest this money in the kingdom of God.

When we give freely to others, we actually are able to use our earthly wealth in such a way that we will "lay up riches that endure forever." We will be able to grasp the true meaning of life if we are able to appropriate the wisdom of God to guide us financially. We are here on earth to serve God and to help other people.

When a rich man came to Jesus and asked for advice Jesus said, "...One thing you still lack. Sell everything that you have and divide [the money] among the poor, and you will have [rich] treasure in heaven..." (Luke 18:22).

Many wealthy people are unable to understand this eternal financial principle. They are consumed with a desire to accumulate wealth on earth instead of giving freely into the kingdom of God. They do not understand that being liberal and generous with their wealth on earth will give them eternal treasure in heaven.

We cannot possibly understand God's financial principles through human wisdom. God did not place us here on earth to accumulate earthly riches. When you arrive in heaven do you think God will say to you, "Congratulations on the net worth of $4,000,000 you accumulated on earth"? God won't make this statement to anyone. Instead, our Father hopefully will say, "Well done, good and faithful servant" because we have devoted our lives on earth to serving Him and helping others.

Many people mistakenly attempt to find joy and happiness by pursuing selfish desires. They are takers, not givers. The Word of God says, "...It is more blessed (makes one happier and more to be envied) to give than to receive" (Acts 20:35).

Immature little children want to receive, but supposedly mature adults shouldn't focus continually on their desire to receive. As we grow and mature in the Lord, we will understand God's principle that we always are more blessed when we give than we are when we receive.

Our Father wants us to utilize His wisdom to use the money He has blessed us with to plant seeds to serve Him. Wealthy people often consume their seeds. They have no concept whatsoever of the godly principle of planting financial seeds into the kingdom of God as part of what is required of them to carry out God's plan for their lives.

I believe we should pray for financial blessings so that we can be used as an instrument for God. I believe we should have a sincere desire for financial abundance so that we can plant this money into the kingdom of God. Everything we do should be done to serve God. Our Father wants us to be available at all times to be used to spread the gospel in any way He leads us.

Our Father instructs us to tithe ten percent of our income (see Malachi 3:8-11). Our Father can make ninety percent of our income do much more than we can do with one hundred percent of our income. I believe the tithe should be paid to the local church where we are fed spiritually.

In addition, our Father wants us to invest money into evangelistic ministries that share the gospel of eternal salvation with many people. We should use our earthly wealth to help as many people as possible to live eternally in heaven instead of suffering throughout eternity in "...the furnace of fire; there will be weeping and wailing and grinding of teeth" (Matthew 13:42).

What better use can we make of money that God blesses us with than to use this money to sow liberally into ministries that have a proven record of helping large numbers of people to accept Jesus Christ as their Savior? We also should invest in ministries that help Christians to learn God's ways so that they will able to be a blessing to others. Money should be like water in our hands. It should flow through us to others to help them in any way possible.

Our Father wants us to focus our attention on other people who are less fortunate than ourselves. If we are mature in the Lord, we will look continually for ways to help unfortunate people. When we give to the poor, we actually are lending this money to the Lord. We can be absolutely certain that the Lord will repay this money so that we can continue to give freely to poor people. "He who has pity on the poor lends to the Lord, and that which he has given He will repay to him" (Proverbs 19:17).

Our Father wants us to continually sow seeds into His kingdom. He wants us to get our attention off ourselves. He wants us to focus continually on Him and on other people. He wants us to have a deep and sincere desire to be used by Him to be a blessing to others.

In these last days before Jesus Christ returns, our Father wants to bless many of His children financially so that we can be used to fund the Great Commission. Jesus Christ said, "Go then and make disciples of all the nations, baptizing them into the name of the Father and of the Son and of the Holy Spirit, teaching them to observe everything that I have commanded you..." (Matthew 28:19-20).

If we don't go to the nations ourselves, we should financially support those who do go. I believe that some Christians are called into the ministry of distributing wealth. Pray and ask God if He wants to pour large amounts of money through you to fulfill the Great Commission in these last days before the return of our Lord Jesus Christ.

Chapter 10

Receive Wisdom from Heaven through the Word of God

We will increase our ability to receive God's wisdom if we continually fill our minds and our hearts with the living Word of God. We are able to receive God's wisdom from the Word of God because every passage of Scripture in the Bible has been given to us by the inspiration of God. "Every Scripture is God-breathed (given by His inspiration) and profitable for instruction, for reproof and conviction of sin, for correction of error and discipline in obedience, [and] for training in righteousness (in holy living, in conformity to God's will in thought, purpose, and action), so that the man of God may be complete and proficient, well fitted and thoroughly equipped for every good work" (II Timothy 3:16-17).

The inspired Word of God contains numerous instructions from our Father that tell us exactly how He wants us to live our lives. The holy Scriptures show us the mistakes that many people will make if they fail to obey God's instructions. We have been given a standard of measurement for every area of our lives so that we can see where we err. We can learn to make the necessary corrections based upon specific instructions from God.

The Bible is God's training course for a righteous life. It shows us how to live each day in the righteousness that has been provided for us by the shed blood of our Lord Jesus Christ. Our Father shows us in His Word how to live a holy life in conformity to the individual plan He has for each of our lives.

The Bible is very different from books written by human authors. The apostle Paul and the other human authors of the Bible received the words they wrote by receiving revelation that came directly from Jesus Christ. Paul said, "...I want you to know, brethren, that the Gospel which was proclaimed and made known by me is not man's gospel [a human invention, according to or patterned after any human standard]. For indeed I did not receive it from man, nor was I taught it, but [it came to me] through a [direct] revelation [given] by Jesus Christ (the Messiah)" (Galatians 1:11-12).

One way to be absolutely certain that the holy Scriptures are inspired by God is to study prophecies in the Word of God that were later fulfilled. In this chapter I'll briefly share a few examples of prophecy from the Word of God. As you read these examples, you can see for yourself that God really did inspire every word in the Bible. Who else but God could write a Book where so many prophecies were fulfilled exactly as they were prophesied?

Before we look briefly at some examples of biblical prophecy, let's examine a passage of Scripture that tells us that all prophecy in the Bible comes to us from the revelation of the Holy Spirit. "...first [you must] understand this, that no prophecy of Scripture is [a matter] of any personal or private or special interpretation (loosening, solving). For no prophecy ever originated because some man willed it [to do so - it never came by human impulse], but men spoke from God who were borne along (moved and impelled) by the Holy Spirit" (II Peter 1:20-21).

Let's begin our brief study of fulfilled biblical prophecies with a well known biblical truth. Jesus Christ was born in the small town of Bethlehem. We know this historical truth because the Word of God tells us that "...Jesus was born in Bethlehem of Judea..." (Matthew 2:1).

Bethlehem is a small town that is located approximately five miles from Jerusalem. Bethlehem is well known today because it is the birthplace of Jesus Christ. However, several hundred years before Jesus was born, Bethlehem was just one of many small towns surrounding Jerusalem. Anyone who was expecting the Messiah to come to earth probably would have expected Him to come to Jerusalem or to many other places that seemed to be much more logical than Bethlehem.

Jesus Christ was born in Bethlehem because God planned for Him to be born there. Seven hundred years before Jesus was born, a prophet named Micah prophesied that Bethlehem would be the place of His birth. "...you, Bethlehem Ephratah, you are little to be among the clans of Judah; [yet] out of you shall One come forth for Me Who is to be Ruler in Israel, Whose goings forth have been from of old, from ancient days (eternity)" (Micah 5:2).

Seven hundred years is a long time. How could any human being predict seven hundred years in advance that the Messiah would be born in such a small town as Bethlehem? Micah was exactly right when he prophesied that Bethlehem would be the place where the Messiah would be born. Only God could have inspired these words.

Another example of the accuracy of biblical prophecy can be seen in Scripture references pertaining to the virgin birth of Jesus Christ. Virgin birth makes no sense whatsoever to the logical and intellectual thinking of the world. It is an accepted fact that a man and a woman must have a physical relationship to produce a child. However, God's ways are vastly different from the ways of human beings. Jesus Christ had a human mother and a divine Father.

The Messiah had to be born of a virgin because He could not be a descendant of Adam. All descendants of Adam inherit his sinful nature. Several hundred years before Jesus Christ was born to a virgin named Mary, the prophet Isaiah said, "...the Lord Himself shall give you a sign: Behold, the young woman who is unmarried and a virgin shall conceive and bear a son, and shall call his name Immanuel [God with us]" (Isaiah 7:14).

The virgin birth of Jesus Christ was accurately prophesied long before Jesus was born. Many years after Isaiah made this prophecy, God sent an angel to Nazareth to speak to a young woman named Mary who was a virgin. "...the angel Gabriel was sent from God to a town of Galilee named Nazareth, to a girl never having been married and a virgin engaged to be married to a man whose name was Joseph, a descendant of the house of David; and the virgin's name was Mary" (Luke 1:26-27).

The angel Gabriel told Mary that, because of God's grace, she would become pregnant and give birth to a Son Who would be named Jesus. Gabriel said, "...Do not be afraid, Mary, for you have found grace (free, spontaneous, absolute favor and loving-kindness) with God. And listen! You will become pregnant and will give birth to a Son, and you shall call His name Jesus" (Luke 1:30-31).

Mary couldn't understand how she could become pregnant because she had never had an intimate relationship with a man. Gabriel explained to Mary that the Holy Spirit would cause her to become pregnant with the Son of God. "...Mary said to the angel, How can this be, since I have no [intimacy with any man as a] husband? Then the angel said to her, The Holy Spirit will come upon you, and the power of the Most High will overshadow you [like a shining cloud]; and so the holy (pure, sinless) Thing (Offspring) which shall be born of you will be called the Son of God" (Luke 1:34-35).

Only God could have caused prophecy to be given hundreds of years in advance that Jesus Christ, the Messiah, would be born of a virgin in the small town of Bethlehem. The statistical odds of this event taking place are incalculable, but the virgin birth occurred in Bethlehem exactly as the Word of God said it would.

The Bible is filled with many other examples of fulfilled prophecy. All of these documented instances show us that the Bible is exactly what it claims to be – the living, supernatural Word of Almighty God.

The purpose of this book is not to give a detailed explanation of a large number of different prophecies. However, if you would like to check out a few references to other examples of biblical prophecy, look at Hosea 11:1 where it was prophesied that the Messiah would go to Egypt. Matthew 2:14-15 tells us that this prophecy was fulfilled. Exodus 34:28 prophesies that the Messiah would go without food for forty days and forty nights. Matthew 4:2 tells us that this prophecy was fulfilled.

Zechariah 9:9 prophesies that the Messiah would ride into Jerusalem on a donkey's colt. John 12:14-15 tells us that this prophecy was fulfilled. Isaiah 33:3-7 prophesies that the Messiah would remain silent before His accusers when He faced them during His trial. Luke 23:9 tells us that this prophecy was fulfilled.

Psalm 22:18 prophesies that soldiers would throw dice for the clothing of the Messiah. John 19:24 tell us that this prophecy was fulfilled. Both Psalm 34:20 and Zechariah 12:10 prophesied that, even though the legs of the criminals next to Him would be broken, not one of the Messiah's bones would be broken, but His side would be pierced. John 19:31-37 reports the fulfillment of this prophecy.

Anyone who carefully studies these and the hundreds of other biblical prophesies that were fulfilled must come to the inescapable conclusion that the Bible truly is the Word of God. The Bible was written over a period of almost fifteen hundred years by approximately forty human authors who were inspired by Almighty God. Different portions of the Bible were written in Hebrew, Greek and Aramaic. In spite of the fact that the Bible was written at different times by different people in different languages and in different locations, the overall content of the holy Scriptures is remarkably consistent.

Please attempt to visualize forty different human authors of the Bible living in different countries hundreds of years apart. Imagine the tremendous difference in their education, their backgrounds and the way they lived. How can any Book written by so many people over such a long period of time fit together so perfectly unless it truly is inspired by Almighty God?

The Word of God is filled with so much supernatural wisdom and knowledge that we cannot possibly begin to comprehend its depth. The holy Bible isn't just a book. It actually is an entire library of supernatural truth that unfolds thousands of magnificent revelations from Almighty God. The vastness of the holy Scriptures is incomprehensible to the limitations of the human intellect.

The Bible contains more significant information than all of the information that is contained in all of the books in all of the libraries throughout the world. All Christians who can even begin to comprehend the tremendous depth and scope of the Word of God should be highly motivated to study and meditate on God's living Word throughout every day of the remainder of their lives on earth.

The United States of America was founded as a Christian country based upon the principles of the Word of God. George Washington began the custom of the president of our country taking the oath of office with his left hand placed upon the Bible. Every succeeding president has started his term in office in this manner.

Many of the founding fathers of our country have spoken very highly of the holy Bible. George Washington said, "It is impossible to rightly govern the world without God and the Bible." Patrick Henry said, "There is a Book which is greater than all other books which have ever been printed." Andrew Jackson said, "That book, sir, is the rock on which our republic rests."

Thomas Jefferson said, "I always have said and always will say that the studious perusal of the sacred volume will make better citizens, better fathers and better husbands." John Quincy Adams said, "I have for many years made it a practice to read through the Bible at least once each year." Benjamin Franklin said, "Young man, my advice to you is that you cultivate an acquaintance with and a firm belief in the holy Scriptures."

As we read these words from the founding fathers of the United States, we can see how important the Word of God was to them. One of our greatest presidents, Abraham Lincoln, relied on the holy Scriptures consistently throughout his term of office. President Lincoln said, "I am profitably engaged in the Bible. Take all of this book upon reason that you can and the rest by faith, and you will live a better man. This great book is the best gift God has given to man. All the good from the Savior of the world is communicated to us through this great book."

The Word of God is wisdom from heaven that has been given to us here on earth. Can you think of anything besides the Bible that came from heaven that also can be contacted through our senses? Can you name one other thing from heaven that anyone in the world can see, touch or hear?

We can see the wisdom of God with our eyes. We can hear it with our ears. The Bible is a magnificent spiritual "bridge" that connects heaven and earth. The wisdom of heaven will be revealed to us continually if we consistently fill our minds and our hearts with wonderful spiritual truths from the supernatural Word of God.

Chapter 11

We Are Able to Partake of the Divine Nature of God

The holy Bible is the only Book in the world that is able to bring the wisdom and power of God to its readers. It is the only Book in the entire world that is filled with life from God. The Word of God is spiritually alive. Jesus Christ said, "...The words (truths) that I have been speaking to you are spirit and life" (John 6:63).

The tremendous supernatural power of the living Word of God is beyond the limits of our human comprehension. The first chapter of the Bible is devoted entirely to an explanation of how God created everything in the universe with words that came out of His mouth. This same spiritual power has been poured into the pages of the holy Bible. "...the Word that God speaks is alive and full of power [making it active, operative, energizing, and effective]; it is sharper than any two-edged sword, penetrating to the dividing line of the breath of life (soul) and [the immortal] spirit, and of joints and marrow [of the deepest parts of our nature], exposing and sifting and analyzing and judging the very thoughts and purposes of the heart" (Hebrews 4:12).

We have just read two Scripture references that tell us that the Word of God is spiritually alive. We also are told that the Word of God is filled with the power of Almighty God. Our Father wants each of us to learn how to appropriate the power of His living Word in our lives.

The amplification of this passage of Scripture tells us that the Word of God is "active." We need to learn how to activate the enormous power of the Word of God in our lives. We also are told that the Word of God is "operative." It will operate effectively in us and through us if we learn how to appropriate its power and its wisdom.

The Word of God is "energized." It is filled to overflowing with the supernatural energy of Almighty God. Our Father's unlimited energy is available to each of His beloved children. The Word of God is "effective." It can and it will effectively produce God's desired results in our lives if we learn how to bring its power into manifestation.

When this passage of Scripture was written, soldiers carried swords that were honed to razor sharpness. The Word of God is much sharper in the spiritual realm than these swords were in the natural realm. God's Word is able to penetrate into our innermost nature.

Only God can reach deep down inside of us to show us what we truly are like. God accomplishes this goal through His Word. God's Word will reach deep down inside of us if we obey our Father's specific instructions to study and meditate daily on the holy Scriptures. The Word of God has the power to transform our lives far beyond the limits of our human comprehension.

Because we often are weak and inadequate and unable to solve difficult problems by ourselves, we should learn how to fill our minds and our hearts continually with the power of the living Word of God. "...we possess this precious treasure [the divine Light of the Gospel] in [frail, human] vessels of earth, that the grandeur and exceeding greatness of the power may be shown to be from God and not from ourselves" (II Corinthians 4:7).

Our loving Father has made it possible for us to appropriate His mighty power through His Word. If we will obey our Father's instructions to constantly fill our minds and our hearts with His Word, we will find that the power of Almighty God will operate in us and through us as we yield our lives moment by moment to God.

We should thank our Father continually for the gift of His precious Word. We did not earn and we do not deserve this wonderful gift from God. The Word of God is completely different from books written by human beings because it is filled with the power of Almighty God. "...we also [especially] thank God continually for this, that when you received the message of God [which you heard] from us, you welcomed it not as the word of [mere] men, but as it truly is, the Word of God, which is effectually at work in you who believe [exercising its superhuman power in those who adhere to and trust in and rely on it]" (I Thessalonians 2:13).

I pray that no person reading the Scripture references in these chapters will underestimate the awesome power of the living Word of God. The "superhuman power" of the Word of God works effectively in all of God's children "who adhere to, trust in and rely on" the promises of God.

The Word of God contains so much spiritual power that the world we live in and all of the planets, stars and galaxies in the universe are controlled by it. "...upholding and maintaining and guiding and propelling the universe by His mighty word of power..." (Hebrews 1:3).

This passage of Scripture refers to words that were spoken about Jesus Christ. We have seen that Jesus Christ and the Word of God are the same. We are told that the world we live in and all of the planets, stars and galaxies in the universe are held in place by the Word of God. God's Word is so powerful that it is able to hold up everything in the entire universe. The universe would crumble if the Word of God didn't keep everything in place.

We are told that the entire universe is maintained by the Word of God. When something is maintained, it is kept in good working order so that it will operate efficiently. The Word of God is so powerful that it is able to keep everything in the universe in perfect operating order.

We also are told that the Word of God guides the universe. A guide shows us the way, directs us and keeps us on course. The Word of God has the supernatural ability to keep everything in the universe on course and headed in the right direction.

Finally, we are told that the universe is propelled by the Word of God. This word comes from the Latin roots "pro" and "pellere." The prefix "pro" means "forward." The word "pellere" means "to drive." The Word of God is so powerful that it is able to drive everything in the universe forward.

If the Word of God has this much power throughout the universe, we must understand how much power it can have in our individual lives if we will pay the price to learn how to bring glory to God by the demonstration of His power. The Word of God is much more powerful than thermonuclear power or any other power on earth.

The Word of God is so powerful that God actually created heaven by speaking words with His mouth. God also created a great multitude of angels (referred to as host) by words He spoke with His mouth. "By the word of the Lord were the heavens made, and all their host by the breath of His mouth" (Psalm 33:6).

Tremendous blessings of God's nature and character are available to every child of God if we will obey our Father's instructions to constantly fill our minds and our hearts with His living Word. "...He has bestowed on us His precious and exceedingly great promises, so that through them you may escape [by flight] from the moral decay (rottenness and corruption) that is in the world because of covetousness (lust and greed), and become sharers (partakers) of the divine nature" (II Peter 1:4).

Our Father has given us the wonderful promises in His Word to enable us to escape from all of the "moral decay, rottenness and corruption" we see in the world today. These deplorable conditions come from the "covetousness, lust and greed" of people who fail to live their lives in accordance with the specific instructions our Father has given us in the holy Scriptures.

This passage of Scripture then goes on to make a remarkable statement. We are told that, through the Word of God, *we actually can partake of the nature of Almighty God.* We actually will take on more and more of God's nature if we obey our Father's instructions to continually fill our minds and our hearts with His Word.

Our Father has done His part. By His grace He has made His supernatural, powerful Word available to every person in the world. Will we do our part? Our part is to get into the Word of God continually and to stay there. Our part is to learn everything we possibly can about the magnificent instructions in the Word of God and to obey these instructions to the best of our ability.

Our part is to constantly fill our minds and our hearts with the thousands of precious promises in the Word of God because we seek our Father with our whole being and with a deep desire to know Him intimately. Our part is to believe God's promises wholeheartedly as we know our Father more intimately each day that we fellowship with Him by partaking of His living Word.

Everything and every person in the world is dying, but the Bible is life. The Word of God is wonderfully alive. The Bible is in a class by itself. The Word of God is eternal. It is referred to as "...the ever living and lasting Word of God" (I Peter 1:23).

This supernatural Book is spiritually alive because the Bible is the Book with God in it. Even though the words in the Bible were written long ago, the Bible is fresh and new and up to date because it is eternal. "...the Word of the Lord (divine instruction, the Gospel) endures forever..." (I Peter 1:25).

I'd like to share my personal testimony about the Word of God being fresh, new and up to date. I have studied and meditated continually on the promises and instructions in the Word of God for more than twenty-seven years. There is no way I could have spent more than twenty thousand hours during all of these years reading and studying any book written by a human author.

I have read thousands of books written by men and women. Most of these books have been read once. I have read a few of these books two or more times. However, after studying and meditating on the holy Bible continually for more than a quarter of a century, I can tell you that the Word of God is still fresh and vibrant to me. I am never bored by studying and meditating on the holy Scriptures. I am hungrier today for the Word of God than ever before.

Charles Spurgeon, a leading nineteenth century evangelist and teacher, once said, "Nobody ever outgrows the Scriptures; the Book widens and deepens with years." Cecil B. DeMille, a famous Christian movie producer, once said, "After more than sixty years of daily reading of the Bible, I never fail to always find it new and marvelously in tune with the changing needs of every day."

The demand for books written by human authors usually lasts for only a few years. A book that is still in significant demand ten or twenty years after it originally was published is very unique. Only an extremely small percentage of books continue to be in demand from one generation to the next. We call these books classics.

The holy Bible has survived many different generations. What other book was read continually by the founders of the United States and is still avidly read, studied and meditated upon by millions of people throughout the world today?

If we attempt to read books that were written two thousand years ago, we will see how meaningless most of them are to us. Books that were written one hundred years ago are not meaningful to many people today. The Word of God is still alive and up to date and filled to overflowing with the enormous power of Almighty God.

God's Word is so vast that its magnitude is completely beyond the limits of our human comprehension. The vastness of God's Word is compared to the virtually innumerable number of grains of sand on a large beach or in a desert. "How precious and weighty also are Your thoughts to me, O God! How vast is the sum of them! If I could count them, they would be more in number than the sand..." (Psalm 139:17-18).

The Word of God is so powerful that it is able to lift us up spiritually, emotionally and physically. The psalmist knew that God's Word could revive him. He prayed to God saying, "...revive and stimulate me according to Your word!" (Psalm 119:25).

Apparently God answered this prayer quite rapidly. Soon after this prayer, the psalmist went on to say that the Word of God actually had revived him and comforted Him. He said, "This is my comfort and consolation in my affliction: that Your word has revived me and given me life" (Psalm 119: 50).

The Word of God is like a spiritual diamond. Diamonds are multi-faced gems that shine and sparkle from many different angles. As we grow spiritually and continue to study and meditate on God's Word, we will continually see new brilliance and beauty in the holy Scriptures that we couldn't see before.

The Word of God is filled with magnificent spiritual treasure from heaven. The more of this treasure we find, the more we will realize how much additional treasure from God is still available to us. Christians who make the quality decision to continually fill their minds and their hearts with the living Word of God will embark on a lifetime treasure hunt that will make the earthly treasures of gold, silver, diamonds, rubies and other precious gems look like nothing in comparison. The psalmist said, "I rejoice at Your word as one who finds great spoil" (Psalm 119:162).

The word "spoil" in this passage of Scripture refers to treasure that was taken from a defeated foe. When this passage of Scripture was written, victorious soldiers stripped defeated enemies of their treasures. These soldiers looked forward with great anticipation to finding this spoil.

Jesus Christ explained what a treasure actually is. A treasure is anything we desire wholeheartedly. Whatever we want more than anything else is treasure to us. Jesus said, "For where your treasure is, there will your heart be also" (Matthew 6:21).

I can't think of anything in this world that is more of a treasure to me than the Word of God. The holy Scriptures have changed my life significantly. Every aspect of my life revolves around the Word of God that fills my mind and my heart to overflowing.

We should be in absolute awe of the enormity of the Word of God. If we can truly comprehend the tremendous supernatural power of the Word of God, we will be in much more awe of it than we are of anyone on earth, no matter how powerful that person might be. The psalmist said, "...my heart stands in awe of Your words [dreading violation of them far more than the force of prince or potentate]" (Psalm 119:161).

We should have a deep and sincere desire to learn God's instructions throughout every day of our lives. We should be completely dedicated to learning everything we can about how our Father wants us to live our lives. We should be absolutely committed to living our lives in constant obedience to every instruction God has given us in the holy Scriptures.

Unbelievers cannot even begin to comprehend the immense spiritual power of the Word of God. Christians who approach the Word of God each day with reverence and awe will receive great rewards from their loving Father. The holy Scriptures are filled with God Himself. We will be able to know our Father more intimately and receive vitally important information from heaven if we will study and meditate continually on the contents of God's holy Book.

The holy Scriptures are a magnificent means of supernatural communication between heaven and earth. This wonderful Book is filled with precious gems that have been sent to us from God's throne in heaven. These instructions and promises are our lifeline to Almighty God.

We should carefully guard the privilege we have been given to learn from God's Word, to obey God's instructions and to know and believe the thousands of promises our Father has given to us. Our lives actually can depend totally and completely upon our obedience to God's instructions and our unwavering faith in the promises of God.

If we truly desire to receive wisdom from God, we should be absolutely determined to continually hear the instructions our Father has provided for us. We must not neglect the precious privilege we have been given to study and meditate continually on the Word of God. "Hear instruction and be wise, and do not refuse or neglect it" (Proverbs 8:33).

The Word of God is similar to the signs and guardrails that we see along a highway. Our Father has given us specific instructions that will enable us to stay on the narrow spiritual road He wants us to walk on throughout our lives on earth. Unfortunately, some Christians fail to pay close attention to the specific directions their Father has given them. They move onto the broad highways of life where many unbelievers and immature Christians travel.

The Word of God overflows with the wisdom of God. The depth of the Word of God is so great that we cannot even begin to absorb everything our Father has made available to us. I am convinced that we will continue to study and meditate on the holy Scriptures throughout eternity.

The Bible is a precious and wonderful gift from our loving Father to His beloved children. We should open this gift every day of our lives to partake of the inexhaustible supply of magnificent instructions and promises our Father has provided for us. Our Father wants each of us to have a love affair with His Word. We should never be able to get enough of God's precious Word.

I pray that the last two chapters have given you a sincere awe of and appreciation for the supernatural power of the living Word of God. Now that we have established this foundation, we are ready to begin to learn from the holy Scriptures exactly and specifically how to receive manifestation of the wisdom of God.

Chapter 12

Think as God Thinks and Receive God's Wisdom

If we sincerely desire to receive wisdom from God we must learn how to consistently fill our minds with the Word of God. Our Father wants us to think the way He thinks. He wants us to learn how to direct our minds in obedience to the instructions He has given us in His Word. "...be wise, and direct your mind in the way [of the Lord]" (Proverbs 23:19).

As we have seen, everything becomes new deep inside of us when we are born of the Spirit. The spiritual veil that used to blind us from understanding God's ways is removed. We are given the precious opportunity to partake of the wisdom of God.

We must learn how to renew our minds in the Word of God if we want to receive wisdom or any other blessings from our Father. An unrenewed mind cannot think the way God thinks. We cannot receive God's wisdom if our minds are carnal. We will progressively think more and more the way that God thinks if we consistently renew our minds in His Word.

Some Christians seldom, if ever, pay the price of renewing their minds in the Word of God. Other Christians make the quality decision to renew their minds in the holy Scriptures on a daily basis. These Christians are much more likely to receive wisdom from God than Christians who fail to renew their minds in God's Word each day.

We have seen that the Word of God is the Truth (see John 17:17). Our Father wants every one of His children to "...come to know the Truth [that they will perceive and recognize and become accurately acquainted with and acknowledge it]..." (II Timothy 2:25).

God has given us the ability to direct our minds just as He has given us the ability to control our hands, our arms, our feet and our legs. The control of our limbs is essentially automatic. We use our hands, our arms, our feet, and our legs spontaneously throughout each day of our lives.

The control of our minds is not automatic. Our Father wants us to learn to direct our thoughts by continually renewing our minds in His Word. He wants us to progressively think more and more the way He thinks and less and less the way that unbelievers think.

Our Father has given us specific scriptural instructions to obey if we sincerely desire to receive His wisdom. We will stop our Father from empowering us with His wisdom if we disregard His specific instructions to renew our minds in His Word on a daily basis. Renewing our minds each day opens a continually widening spiritual stream through which our loving Father can pour out His wisdom in us, to us and through us.

Our minds are similar to computers. They must be "programmed" in order to operate effectively. If we don't consciously program our minds with the Word of God, our minds will automatically be programmed by the ways of the world and by the influence of Satan and his demons. Many people do not understand how much their minds are programmed by such things as the books they read, the television programs and movies they watch, the computer games they play, the input they receive from the Internet and many other things they have learned over the years from their parents, teachers and peers.

The truth in the Word of God comes to us from heaven. There is no way that heavenly truth can line up with the ways of a world that is dominated by the influence of Satan (see Ephesians 2:2). The Word of God empowers us with the ability to constantly erase the erroneous thinking that comes from the influence of the world.

Some of us have to go through a season of adversity to become awakened to the importance of renewing our minds continually in the Word of God. The psalmist David experienced tremendous blessings from renewing his mind in the Word of God because of the adversity he experienced. David said, "...I delight in Your law. It is good for me that I have been afflicted, that I might learn Your statues. The law from Your mouth is better to me than thousands of gold and silver pieces" (Psalm 119:70-72).

Some people think that adversity is always bad. Adversity can be a tremendous blessing if it causes us to turn to God. David said that it was good for him to go through the adversity he went through because this adversity caused him to learn from the Word of God. David knew that the opportunity to learn from God's Word was much more valuable to him than spending the same amount of time and energy attempting to accumulate wealth.

We now are ready to carefully study one of the most significant passages of Scripture in this book. We cannot expect to receive our Father's wisdom if we ignore the following instructions He has given to us. "Do not be conformed to this world (this age), [fashioned after and adapted to its external, superficial customs], but be transformed (changed) by the [entire] renewal of your mind [by its new ideals and its new attitude], so that you may prove [for yourselves] what is the good and acceptable and perfect will of God, even the thing which is good and acceptable and perfect [in His sight for you]" (Romans 12:2).

This passage of Scripture tells us that we shouldn't be conformed to the "external, superficial customs" of the world. God's wisdom comes from the inside out, not from the outside in. We are told that our lives will be transformed if we renew our minds continually in the Word of God. The word "transformed" is extremely important to each of us.

Soon after Jesus Christ told His disciples that He would be killed and raised from the dead, He led Peter, James and John high up onto a mountain. An amazing event took place on this mountain. "...His appearance underwent a change in their presence; and His face shone clear and bright like the sun, and His clothing became as white as light" (Matthew 17:2).

The Greek word that explains the change that took place during the appearance of Jesus Christ on that mountain is the word "metamorphoo." This transformation is referred to as the transfiguration of Jesus Christ. The Greek word "metamorphoo" that is translated "transformed" in Romans 12:2 is the same Greek word that is used to describe the spectacular transfiguration in Matthew 17:2.

If we obey our Father's instructions to constantly renew our minds in His Word, we will find that our lives will be *completely transformed* just as the appearance of Jesus Christ was transformed on that mountain. The Greek word "metamorphoo" that I mentioned has the same root as the English word "metamorphosis." *Webster's New World Dictionary* describes a metamorphosis as "a complete change of character, appearance or condition."

One of the best examples of a metamorphosis takes place when an ugly caterpillar is transformed into a beautiful butterfly. Our lives will undergo an even more beautiful transformation if we will make the quality decision to renew our minds each day in the Word of God. We'll be able to see things more and more from a heavenly perspective as a wonderful spiritual metamorphosis occurs in our minds over a period of time.

If we consistently renew our minds in the Word of God, our minds will be steadily changed from what they were to what our Father wants them to become. As members of the family of God, we should speak God's language just as naturally as people in the world speak about the things of the world. Jesus Christ wants each of us to die to our old way of thinking just as He died for us. "...our old (unrenewed) self was nailed to the cross with Him..." (Romans 6:6).

Our Father tells us that we should *constantly* renew our minds in His Word. "Strip yourselves of your former nature [put off and discard your old unrenewed self] which characterized your previous manner of life and becomes corrupt through lusts and desires that spring from delusion; and be constantly renewed in the spirit of your mind [having a fresh mental and spiritual attitude]..." (Ephesians 4:22-23).

Our Father wants us to continually "strip ourselves" of the attitude and actions that dominated our lives before we became Christians. Because of the sacrifice of Jesus Christ, we have been given the opportunity to completely transform the carnal thoughts we used to think and the way we used to live. We will accomplish this goal if we constantly renew our minds in the Word of God. This passage of Scripture says that we will "have a fresh mental and spiritual attitude" if we obey our Father's instructions to renew our minds continually in His Word.

The Word of God emphasizes the importance of renewing our minds consistently so that we can be changed into God's image. "...you have stripped off the old (unregenerate) self with its evil practices, and have clothed yourselves with the new [spiritual self], which is [ever in the process of being] renewed and remolded into [fuller and more perfect knowledge upon] knowledge after the image (the likeness) of Him Who created it" (Colossians 3:9-10).

Once again, we are instructed to "strip off" the carnality of our former nature before we were saved. We each must make the decision to constantly turn away from the way we used to be. We are told that we will "clothe" ourselves spiritually as this process takes place. When we put on clothing in the natural realm, we cover ourselves with this clothing. When we clothe ourselves each day in the spiritual realm, we will constantly be "renewed and remolded" to become more and more like God.

Renewing our minds in the Word of God also helps us to overcome discouragement and fear. "...we do not become discouraged (utterly spiritless, exhausted, and wearied out through fear). Though our outer man is [progressively] decaying and wasting away, yet our inner self is being [progressively] renewed day after day" (II Corinthians 4:16).

Have you ever been so discouraged that you were "spiritless, exhausted and weary because of fear?" Some people experience increasing fear and discouragement as they grow older and experience the changes in their minds and in their bodies that are caused by their habits over the years.

This passage of Scripture speaks about "the outer man progressively decaying and wasting away." Our bodies actually decay as we grow older. We should do our very best to keep physically fit. We also can offset many of the problems that are caused by the aging process by renewing our minds in the Word of God on a daily basis.

Some Christians fail to obey God's instructions to renew their minds daily. They are complacent because they don't see any immediate consequences as a result of failing to obey this specific instruction from God. They fail to understand that the penalty for disobedience to God's instructions often is delayed, but this penalty ultimately must be paid.

Renewal is one of God's laws. We are able to renew our bodies each day by eating nourishing food. We can renew our bodies each night by getting a good night's sleep. Our Father wants us to apply this same principle of renewal to our minds. He wants us to strengthen our minds every day of our lives. "...brace up your minds" ... (I Peter 1:13).

A brace is a piece of metal that strengthens something else by supporting its weight. When we brace something, we fortify it. Our Father wants us to fortify our minds each day. The psalmist knew the importance of strengthening himself with promises from the Word of God. He prayed asking God to "...raise me up and strengthen me according to [the promises of] Your word" (Psalm 119:28).

Many Jews converted to Christianity shortly after Jesus Christ ascended into heaven. They were extremely eager to learn everything they could about the things of God. When the apostle Paul spoke about these converts, he described them as having "...inclination of mind and eagerness, searching and examining the Scriptures daily to see if these things were so" (Acts 17:11).

Our Father wants us to have inquisitive minds. We should "search and examine the Scriptures daily" to learn everything we possibly can about the ways of God. We should set aside precious time every day of our lives to study the magnificent Book of Instructions our Father has provided for us.

We should have an earnest desire to see things from God's perspective. We should want so much to become like God that we wouldn't even think of missing thc opportunity to spend time with Him by renewing our minds in His Word each day. We must not waste the precious opportunity we have been given to know God and to become more like Him as we continually renew our minds in His Word.

In the United States young people attend grammar school, middle school and high school for twelve years. Many people invest four more years of their lives to pursue a college education. Some people invest additional years into advanced study. This substantial investment of time is normal, natural and accepted in this country.

If these principles apply in the world today, why would any of us think we can receive wisdom from God if we are unwilling to set aside significant amounts of time each day to fill our minds with wonderful illuminating spiritual truths from God's Book of Instructions? The return on our investment of time studying the Word of God will be infinitely greater than the return on any time we invest in learning worldly principles.

The power and plan of God are available to every child of God. These wonderful spiritual truths won't automatically leap off the pages of the Bible. Our Father wants us to revere His Word. He wants us to appreciate His Word as the precious gift that it is.

We did not earn and we do not deserve the Word of God. Our Father has given us His Word by His grace and by His love. We should not fail to take full advantage of the opportunity we have been given to renew our minds continually in the holy Scriptures.

We should build a solid spiritual foundation if we sincerely desire to receive a continual outpouring of the wisdom of God. Mature Christians pay the price of spending time with God and abiding in His Word daily over a long period of time.

George Mueller was a great Christian leader in the nineteenth century. He once said, "I look upon it as a lost day when I have not had a good time over the Word of God. Friends often say 'I have so much to do, so many people to see, I can't find time for Scripture study.' Perhaps there are many who have more to do than I.

"For more than half a century, I have never known one day when I have not had more business than I could get through. For four years I have had annually about thirty thousand letters and most of these have passed through my own hands.

"Then, as a pastor of a church with twelve hundred believers, great has been my care. Besides, I have had five immense orphanages; also at my publishing depot, printing and circulating of millions of tracts, books and Bibles; but I have always made it a rule never to begin work until I had a great season with God in His Word. The blessing I have received has been wonderful."

This same wonderful blessing is available to every child of God. I pray that the instructions from the Word of God in this chapter will motivate you to enjoy time with God in His Word on a daily basis.

Chapter 13

We Should Take a Daily Spiritual "Bath" in God's Word

Satan and his demons do not want us to receive wisdom from God. They continually try to influence us by attempting to put thoughts and temptations into our minds that are contrary to the instructions and promises from the Word of God. Some Christians who have severe spiritual battles going on in their minds have no conception of the source of these thoughts. Our minds and our hearts should be so full of the Word of God that Satan and his demons cannot get a foothold in our minds and our hearts.

Did you ever wonder why Judas Iscariot, once a beloved disciple of Jesus Christ, turned his back on Jesus? The answer is that Satan was able to get into his heart with the thought of betraying Jesus. "...Satan having already put the thought of betraying Jesus in the heart of Judas Iscariot..." (John 13:2).

Satan obviously was able to put thoughts into the minds and hearts of human beings two thousand years ago. Satan hasn't gone anywhere. We must understand that the atmosphere around us is filled with God's angels and with Satan's fallen angels. Satan and his legions of fallen angels are increasingly active in these last days before Jesus Christ returns. We must learn how "...to keep Satan from getting the advantage over us; for we are not ignorant of his wiles and intentions" (II Corinthians 2:11).

The Word of God explains how Satan and his demons attempt to take advantage of us. We need to learn how to walk in the total, complete and absolute victory Jesus Christ has given us over Satan and his demons. Jesus said, "Behold! I have given you authority and power to trample upon serpents and scorpions, and [physical and mental strength and ability] over all the power that the enemy [possesses]; and nothing shall in any way harm you" (Luke 10:19).

When Jesus speaks of "serpents and scorpions," He is referring to Satan and his demons. Jesus has given us the authority to "trample upon" Satan and his assistants. Satan is under our feet in the spiritual realm. We have been given the ability to walk all over him because of the victory that Jesus Christ won at Calvary.

Jesus Christ has given us an absolute victory over Satan in every way. Nothing that Satan and his demons attempt to do can harm us. The victory that Jesus Christ won over Satan belongs to every child of God, but we must know how to fight and win spiritual battles against Satan and his demons. "...though we walk (live) in the flesh, we are not carrying on our warfare according to the flesh and using mere human weapons. For the weapons of our warfare are not physical [weapons of flesh and blood], but they are mighty before God for the overthrow and destruction of strongholds, [inasmuch as we] refute arguments and theories and reasonings and every proud and lofty thing that sets itself up against the [true] knowledge of God; and we lead every thought and purpose away captive into the obedience of Christ (the Messiah, the Anointed One)..." (II Corinthians 10:3-5).

This passage of Scripture tells us that we should never attempt to fight spiritual battles with human weapons. Jesus Christ has provided us with everything we need to walk in victory over Satan and his demons. However, spiritual battles cannot be won if we attempt to fight them with our flesh and blood.

We have been given the ability to withstand everything that Satan and his demons attempt to do to us. The words "every proud and lofty thing" in Luke 10:19 refer to Satan and his demons. They once were archangels and angels with a high position in the kingdom of God before they fell from heaven because of their pride. They now are busily engaged in attempts to get into our minds and our hearts with thoughts and temptations that go against the knowledge of God.

The words "every thought and purpose" are extremely important. Our Father doesn't want just some of our thoughts or most of our thoughts to be led into obedience to Jesus Christ. He tells us that it is possible for *every* one of our thoughts to be brought into obedience to Jesus Christ.

If we fail to obey our Father's instructions to renew our minds in His Word each day, our disobedience will give Satan's demons the opportunity to get into our minds with thoughts that ultimately could cause severe problems in our lives. Satan and his demons consistently try to get into our minds. We must be more persistent than they are.

We receive a complete spiritual cleansing when we are saved. We cannot receive spiritual cleansing by ourselves. We can only be cleansed through the shed blood of Jesus Christ. "He saved us, not because of any works of righteousness that we had done, but because of His own pity and mercy, by [the] cleansing [bath] of the new birth (regeneration) and renewing of the Holy Spirit…" (Titus 3:5).

By the grace of God and by the magnificent sacrifice of Jesus Christ, we each received a wonderful spiritual cleansing when we were saved. We received and continue to receive wonderful spiritual renewal through the Holy Spirit. This spiritual birth gives us the opportunity to cleanse our minds on a daily basis.

Most of us take a shower or a bath every day to cleanse our bodies. We must understand the importance of taking a refreshing spiritual "bath" in the Word of God every day to cleanse our minds. "How shall a young man cleanse his way? By taking heed and keeping watch [on himself] according to Your word [conforming his life to it]" (Psalm 119:9).

We can cleanse ourselves spiritually by immersing ourselves each day in the Word of God. We cleanse ourselves by conforming our lives to the instructions our Father has given us in His pure and wonderful Word. "The words and promises of the Lord are pure words, like silver refined in an earthen furnace, purified seven times over" (Psalm 12:6).

All of the words in the Bible are "pure words." When this passage of Scripture was written, silver was placed into a furnace on seven different occasions to remove all impurities. If we continually renew our minds in the Word of God, our minds will be purified just as silver is purified.

We must understand the tremendous cleansing power of the holy Scriptures. Jesus Christ loves us so much that He gave His life for us so that we can be cleansed by the Word of God. "...Christ loved the church and gave Himself up for her, so that He might sanctify her, having cleansed her by the washing of water with the Word" (Ephesians 5:25-26).

We must not miss out on the opportunity for daily cleansing that has been made available to us. "...since these [great] promises are ours, beloved, let us cleanse ourselves from everything that contaminates and defiles body and spirit, and bring [our] consecration to completeness in the [reverential] fear of God" (II Corinthians 7:1).

The Bible contains more than seven thousand promises from God. We did not earn these precious promises. Our Father gave us these wonderful promises because He loves us.

We live in evil times. Satan and his demons continually try to influence us. Also, the pull of the world we live in is constant. We cannot live the way our Father wants us to live unless we constantly cleanse ourselves from spiritual contamination by obeying our Father's instructions to take a daily "bath" in His Word.

This passage of Scripture shows us the relationship that exists between continually cleansing ourselves in the great promises in the Word of God and continually living with reverential fear of God. We have learned that the fear of God is the beginning of wisdom. We can see the relationship that exists between receiving the wisdom of God and cleansing ourselves continually in the Word of God.

The supernatural cleansing power of the Word of God is available to every child of God. Our Father won't force us to take a daily spiritual bath. We must make this decision ourselves just as we make the decision to cleanse our bodies each day. When we cleanse our bodies, we cleanse them from the outside in with a shower or a bath. When we cleanse our minds, we cleanse them from the inside out by continually renewing our minds with the magnificent spiritual cleansing power of the Word of God.

We have seen that our Father has made His wisdom available to us through Jesus Christ. If we take a spiritual bath every day of our lives, we will be blessed by the wonderful spiritual truths we are able to tap into as we cleanse ourselves continually from the ways of the world.

Our minds will become more and more like the mind of Jesus Christ if we obey our Father's instructions to renew our minds continually in His Word, "...we have the mind of Christ (the Messiah) and do hold the thoughts (feelings and purposes) of His heart" (I Corinthians 2:16).

The spiritual significance of this promise is overwhelming. Please insert your name where the word "we" is used in this passage of Scripture. Know that *you* have the mind of Jesus Christ because I Corinthians 2:16 says that you do.

We should always be aware that Jesus Christ lives in our hearts. Jesus makes His home in our hearts when we ask Him to be our Savior. "May Christ through your faith [actually] dwell (settle down, abide, make His permanent home) in your hearts!..." (Ephesians 3:17).

We should always be conscious of the indwelling presence of Jesus Christ. Personalize this promise. Know that Jesus Christ is with you every minute of every hour of every day of your life just as the Word of God says He is.

If Jesus Christ lives in us, His mind obviously lives in us. If we have the mind of Jesus Christ always available to us, we also have the wisdom of Jesus Christ available to us at all times.

If we obey our Father's instructions to renew our minds each day in His Word, our minds will become more and more aligned with the mind of Christ that resides in us. All Christians have been given the mind of Christ, but only a small percentage of Christians fully utilize this precious gift. "All who keep His commandments [who obey His orders and follow His plan, live and continue to live, to stay and] abide in Him, and He in them. [They let Christ be a home to them and they are the home of Christ.] And by this we know and understand and have the proof that He [really] lives and makes His home in us..." (I John 3:24).

This passage of Scripture urges us to obey the instructions our Father has given us in His Word. We will abide in Jesus Christ and He will abide in us if we live our lives the way the Word of God instructs us to live. As a result of this obedience, we can be absolutely certain that Jesus Christ really does make His home in us.

There are two kinds of minds – a mind that is being constantly renewed and a carnal, unrenewed mind. We each make the decision on a daily basis how carnal we want our minds to be. We can choose each day to see and understand great spiritual truths that we cannot possibly comprehend if we fail to renew our minds continually in the Word of God.

Our Father wants us to stretch our minds every day of our lives. He wants each of His children to grow spiritually by constantly studying the precious Book of Instructions He has made available to us. We will continually turn away from the ways of the world as our minds are renewed over a period of time.

As our minds are renewed, we will see things more and more from God's perspective. We no longer will listen to some of the things we used to listen to on radio or television. We won't allow our minds to be contaminated by many of the movies that are so evil today. We won't allow the evil contained in many worldly books to get into our minds. We will refuse to allow our minds to be polluted by the influence of Satan and his demons.

Our hunger and thirst for the Word of God will be in direct proportion to the realization of our vital need for the Word of God. We cannot afford to become complacent. We will not ignore these specific instructions if we understand the importance our Father places on continually renewing our minds in His Word.

In the last two chapters we have seen many instructions from God telling us to renew our minds continually in His Word. In the next chapter we will learn *how* to renew our minds in the Word of God. Many Christians want to study the Bible, but they don't know how to study the Bible. I will explain the method I use to study the Bible. I pray that some of these principles for studying God's Word will help you to study the Word of God more effectively.

Chapter 14

How to Study the Bible

Many Christians know that they should study the Bible daily for spiritual nourishment, but they fail to achieve this goal. I believe the primary reason why many Christians fail to study the Bible consistently is that they do not have a proven and effective method to study the Word of God. In this chapter I will share with you the specific techniques I have used to study the Bible for the past twenty-seven years.

I want to begin by emphasizing that there is more than one way to study the Word of God. Christians use many different methods to study the holy Scriptures effectively. Nevertheless, all methods of Bible study have one thing in common – they follow specific *principles* pertaining to the study of the holy Scriptures. Methods change continually, but proven principles never change.

Our Father knew that we would need a Book of Instructions to show us how He wants us to live. Many years ago He made the provision to provide us with the wonderful Bible we have available to us today. "...whatever was thus written in former days was written for our instruction, that by [our steadfast and patient] endurance and the encouragement [drawn] from the Scriptures we might hold fast to and cherish hope" (Romans 15:4).

The Word of God is filled with many specific instructions from our loving Father. The Word of God also is filled with thousands of wonderful promises from God. Our Father has given us these instructions to guide us and these promises to encourage us and to enable us to persevere with faith without giving up hope.

I would like to begin the explanation of the method I use to learn and obey God's instructions and to learn and believe God's promises with the one passage of Scripture that I believe gives us the foundation for effective Bible study. "Study and be eager and do your utmost to present yourself to God approved (tested by trial), a workman who has no cause to be ashamed, correctly analyzing and accurately dividing [rightly handling and skillfully teaching] the Word of Truth" (II Timothy 2:15).

Do you want God to approve of the way you live? This passage of Scripture tells us that we should eagerly present ourselves to our Father for His approval. We should seek this approval based upon our study of God's Word and the practical application of God's instructions and promises when we are tested by trials and tribulations in our lives.

Bible study is hard work. We should make the commitment to diligently study God's Word day after day, week after week, month after month and year after year. I believe we need to understand the difference between *reading* the Bible and *studying* the Bible. I once discussed this subject with Ed Hiers who is a close friend and a mature Christian leader. Ed gave me an example of the difference between studying the Bible and reading the Bible that I have never forgotten.

Ed said that, if a man had a book explaining exactly what to do if he was lost in the woods, he would merely *read* the book if he was casually sitting at home reading the book. On the other hand, Ed said that, if this man actually was lost in the wilderness and happened to have this book with him, he would do much more than just read the book. He would *study* this book as if his life depended upon it.

We should study the Bible as if our life depended upon it. The quality and effectiveness of our lives will be dramatically improved if we continually fill our minds and our hearts with the living Word of God and apply these promises and instructions in the power of God.

Our Father wants us to pay the price of studying His Word each day of our lives. He wants us to learn how He wants us to live. He wants us to make the corrections that must be made if our lives do not line up with His instructions. "Apply your mind to instruction and correction and your ears to words of knowledge" (Proverbs 23:12).

Many Christians start out with a sincere desire to study the Bible, but they fail to consistently follow through on this goal over a long period of time. I don't believe it is a coincidence that the word "discipline" and the word "disciple" come from the same root. If we truly want to be disciples of God, we should discipline ourselves to work hard and to persevere to stick to a proven and effective method of studying the holy Scriptures.

The Bible wasn't written with one specific section dealing with wisdom, another section dealing with love, another section dealing with finances and another section dealing with faith. Throughout the Bible we find wisdom for every area of life. I categorize these areas and bring them together by topic.

I have used a topical method of Bible study for the past twenty-seven years. This method has been extremely fruitful in my life. I also have received many letters from people telling me how much this specific method of Bible study has helped them.

Several years ago I wrote the book, *How To Study The Bible.* I also recorded two cassette tapes on this subject. I have recently re-recorded both of these tapes so that their content will include many additional truths I have learned about Bible study and Scripture meditation.

In this chapter I will give you a very brief summary of the contents of this book and these tapes. You might want to purchase the book and the cassette tapes to learn more about this topical method of studying the Bible if the following comments and the contents of this chapter are of interest to you.

"I have read almost all of your books and they are outstanding. The one that blessed me the most was *How to Study the Bible.* The studying part was excellent, but the meditation chapters were very, very beneficial. I'm indebted to you for sharing these. I purchased 30 copies to give to friends. Every earnest student of God's Word needs a copy." (Tennessee)

"My wife and I are utilizing the Bible study method that you explained in *How to Study the Bible.* We are really growing spiritually as a result. Our old methods of study were not nearly as fruitful. Thanks for writing about your method." (Idaho)

"Your book, *How to Study the Bible,* has helped me very much. I am an organized person and I like to write down and file information. This method is exactly what I've been praying for. Thank you for writing this book." (Mississippi)

"I must say after reading Jack Hartman's book, *How to Study the Bible,* that I felt like I am starting all over again. Wow!! May God's rich blessings be yours." (Louisiana)

"My wife and I are presently rereading together *How to Study the Bible* as part of our daily devotional time together following private devotions. We are impressed with the practical approach. Please send us 10 copies to distribute to our friends." (Ontario, Canada)

"I have just finished your book, *How to Study the Bible.* Mr. Hartman certainly has a gift for simple but dynamic Bible teaching. Please send me 20 more copies." (Texas)

I was on the verge of financial bankruptcy and a nervous breakdown when I became a Christian. I studied the Bible to find everything I could about the subjects of finances, overcoming worry and fear and increasing my faith in God. The precious "nuggets" I found in the Word of God at that time have formed the foundation for the comprehensive system of topical Bible study I have used ever since I began to study God's Word.

I currently have several hundred file folders that are filled with Scripture references and other material based upon specific topics. The following list of potential topics for Bible study is merely a brief summary of the hundreds of different topics I have studied:

Anger
Death
Faith
Finances
God
Holy Spirit
Jesus Christ
Children
Evangelism
Fear and worry
Forgiveness
Heaven and hell
Humility and pride
Joy

Love
Patience
Perseverance
Satan
Strength and weakness
Wisdom and knowledge
Marriage
Peace
Prayer
Spiritual growth
Victory

Most of these topics can be broken down into numerous subtopics. For example, I probably have had forty or fifty different file folders pertaining to the subject of faith in God. In addition, I have compiled many other file folders that contain subtopics on such subjects as fear and worry, finances, patience, perseverance and peace. I am absolutely exhilarated by the tremendous amount of material I have accumulated after all of these years devoted to studying the Word of God.

I would like to compare the method I use to study the Bible to putting together a very large jigsaw puzzle. I am *not* saying that the Bible is a puzzle. Our Father's instructions are not puzzling – they are very clear. However, I believe that putting together the various "pieces" of God's Word is quite similar to fitting together the pieces of a jigsaw puzzle.

If you spread out all of the pieces of a large puzzle on a table and then put this puzzle together one piece at a time, you often will experience a feeling of satisfaction as this puzzle takes shape. One piece of the puzzle leads to another. This piece leads to another piece. Eventually, everything fits together. This same principle applies to studying the Bible topically. It is very exciting to see how all of the different pieces of Scripture on a given topic fit together into a cohesive whole.

If you would like to study the Bible topically, I recommend that you begin by highlighting, underlining or drawing a rectangle around the meaningful passages of Scripture you come across each time you use your Bible. I recommend that you write a one or two word topical heading in your Bible next to the passages of Scripture you have identified. Don't be afraid to mark up your Bible. I believe that Bibles are made to be written upon.

You can continue to identify topics in your Bible as the Holy Spirit leads you. The possibilities are endless. As your number of topics grows, you may want to put them on file cards, put them in file folders or type these topical Scripture references into a computer categorized by topic.

If you will give this system of topical Bible study a fair trial and stick with it, I believe you will be excited to see how the Word of God will come together in your mind and in your heart. As you dig deeply into God's Word over a period of time, I believe you will receive more and more comprehensive insight into the ways and purposes of God which is the definition of the wisdom of God we are using in this book.

I believe you will find that this topical method of studying the Bible will become one of the most rewarding things you do. You must be patient. Results will not come overnight. If you persist, you will find that your Bible study will become more effective as good habits of Bible study become more firmly established.

I recommend that you always start your daily Bible study with prayer. Ask God to reveal wonderful and meaningful spiritual truths as you study His Word. You might want to pray something similar to what the psalmist prayed when he said, "Open my eyes, that I may behold wondrous things out of Your law. I am a stranger and a temporary resident on the earth; hide not Your commandments from me" (Psalm 119:18-19).

In my book on studying the Bible, I explain the use of several Bible study aids such as a topical Bible, a chain reference Bible and a Bible dictionary. Also, as you have seen in this book, I prefer *The Amplified Bible* for my personal Bible study. The shades of meaning of the original Greek and Hebrew have opened the Word of God tremendously to me during the years I have studied and meditated on Scripture references from this version of the Bible.

If you would like to share in the fruit of the labor I have done over the years, I recommend that you carefully review the list of books, Scripture Meditation Cards and cassette tapes in the back of this book. I believe you will find that I have done a lot of the work for you in finding, studying and explaining many different topics from the Word of God. All of our books, Scripture Meditation Cards and cassette tapes are filled to overflowing with the Word of God.

I urge you to commit yourself to a definite and specific program of Bible study – the system I use or any other system that works effectively for you. Persevere on a daily basis throughout the remainder of your life. Our Father doesn't want us to take His Word lightly. He said, "Take firm hold of instruction, do not let go; guard her, for she is your life" (Proverbs 4:13).

Our Father wants us to hold tightly to the wonderful instructions He has provided for us. He doesn't want us to let go of these instructions. Our Father urges us to carefully guard the instructions He has given to us. We must not miss out on the tremendous opportunity we have been given to learn from the holy Scriptures.

We should never allow anything to distract us from studying the Bible effectively on a daily basis. The Word of God is life-changing. I urge you to be absolutely determined to take full advantage of the opportunity you have been given to study the Word of God effectively throughout every day of your life.

If you persist in your Bible study, I believe you will find so much spiritual treasure that you will be overwhelmed by the magnitude of what our Father has made available to us through the holy Scriptures. Our Father wants us to dig deeply into the awesome depth of His Word. There is no limit to what we can learn from the Word of God. We will be much more receptive to guidance from the Holy Spirit as we learn more and more from God's Word.

In the last three chapters we have discussed the importance of renewing our *minds* in the Word of God. In the next chapter we'll discuss the importance of God's Word living in our *hearts.* In subsequent chapters we'll discuss *how* to get the Word of God to drop from our minds down into our hearts through consistent meditation on the holy Scriptures.

Chapter 15

The Word of God Should Live in Our Hearts

Our Father wants us to learn how to get the truth from His Word up off the printed pages of the Bible into our minds and then down into our hearts. The psalmist said, "Behold, You desire truth in the inner being; make me therefore to know wisdom in my inmost heart" (Psalm 51:6).

We need to learn how to continually plant seeds of truth from the Word of God into our hearts if we want to receive a harvest of God's wisdom. The world's wisdom comes from the outside in. God's wisdom comes from the inside out because it already resides in us.

I believe that we begin the process of receiving wisdom from God by renewing our minds in God's Word on a daily basis. I have learned that the Word of God will drop from our minds down into our hearts if we meditate continually on the holy Scriptures. Some Christians only know God in their minds.

Our Father wants each of us to know Him intimately in our hearts. We *think* with our *minds* and we *believe* with our *hearts.* "...with the heart a person believes..." (Romans 10:10).

This passage of Scripture refers to receiving eternal salvation through Jesus Christ by believing in our hearts that He died for our sins and that God raised Him from the dead. I believe this biblical principle of believing in our hearts that is required when we first become Christians applies throughout the remainder of our lives after we are saved. We must understand how important it is to continually fill our hearts with God's living Word.

We now are ready to learn how to increase our faith in God to the point where we will be absolutely certain deep down inside of our hearts that we will receive the manifestation of the wisdom our Father has promised to us. "...faith is the assurance (the confirmation, the title deed) of the things [we] hope for..." (Hebrews 11:1).

Our Father doesn't want His Word to have its home on a desk or a bookshelf. He doesn't want His Word to have its home only in our minds. Our Father wants His Word to have its home in both our minds and our hearts. "Let the word [spoken by] Christ (the Messiah) have its home [in your hearts and minds] and dwell in you in [all its] richness..." (Colossians 3:16).

The word "let" in this passage of Scripture is very important. We each should continually make the decision that the Word of God will live in our minds and in our hearts. The Word of God will not force its way into our minds and our hearts. We must do what our Father tells us to do so that His instructions and His promises will come up off the printed pages of the Bible into our minds and than drop down into our hearts. We are told that Jesus Christ wants His Word to "dwell in us in all its richness."

Whenever we are in a crisis situation, we always will react based upon whatever we truly believe deep down in our hearts. We cannot change our deeply held core beliefs quickly. We can only make this change over a period of time as the Word of God comes alive in our hearts. "… as he thinks in his heart, so is he…" (Proverbs 23:7).

Our Father wants us to study and meditate on His Word on a daily basis. The words in the following passage of Scripture refer to Scripture references. King Solomon said, "My son, let them not escape from your sight, but keep sound and godly Wisdom and discretion, and they will be life to your inner self…" (Proverbs 3:21-22).

If we want to receive manifestation of a continual flow of wisdom from God, we cannot afford to let the Word of God escape from our sight, even for one day. The problems we face will not be able to bring us down if our hearts are filled to overflowing with the supernatural power of the living Word of God. "The law of his God is in his heart; none of his steps shall slide" (Psalm 37:31).

When we are faced with difficult circumstances, we are in a precarious position if we have disobeyed our Father's instructions to continually fill our minds and our hearts with His Word. If we ignore these instructions, we can put ourselves in a position where we have to be "pruned" by learning what we have to learn as a result of going through a season of adversity. In many cases, this adversity is caused by wrong choices we have made.

When plants or trees are pruned, they are cut so the unnecessary portions are removed. This pruning enables a plant or a tree to grow properly. We may not have to be pruned by the problems we face if we obey our Father's instructions to continually fill our minds and our hearts with His Word.

We can be like the disciples of Jesus Christ who were "already cleansed and pruned" because He continually taught them from the Word of God. Jesus told His disciples, "You are cleansed and pruned already, because of the word which I have given you [the teachings I have discussed with you]" (John 15:3).

We each make constant choices that will have a significant ultimate impact upon our lives. Will we obey our Father's instructions to fill our minds and our hearts daily with His Word? If we obey these instructions from God, we often will receive the cleansing and pruning we need because our minds and our hearts are continually being filled with our Father's instructions and with His wonderful promises.

We have seen that God emphasizes His instructions to us through repetition. If our loving Father gives us the same instruction repeatedly, we can be assured that He wants us to pay close attention to what He is telling us. God repeatedly tells us to store up His Word in our minds and in our hearts. "...you shall lay up these My words in your [minds and] hearts and in your [entire] being..." (Deuteronomy 11:18).

Our faith in God will increase steadily if we humble ourselves before God by constantly filling our hearts with His Word. Job said, "Receive, I pray you, the law and instruction from His mouth and lay up His words in your heart. If you return to the Almighty [and submit and humble yourself before Him], you will be built up..." (Job 22:22-23).

The Word of God is a precious treasure. Instead of focusing continually on storing up treasure on earth by attempting to accumulate earthly wealth, we can invest this time and energy much more profitably by storing up the treasure of God's Word in our hearts. We should follow the wise advice King Solomon gave to his son. "My son, keep my words; lay up within you my commandments [for use when needed] and treasure them" (Proverbs 7:1).

If we are truly wise, we won't be preoccupied with storing up earthly treasures in the form of wealth and property. Instead, we'll obey our Father's repeated instructions to store up knowledge from His Word in our minds and in our hearts. "Wise men store up knowledge [in mind and heart]...." (Proverbs 10:14).

We have just seen four different Scripture references where our Father tells us to "lay up" or "store up" His Word in our minds and in our hearts. This repeated emphasis shows us the priority our Father places on our minds and our hearts being filled with His Word.

Any accumulation of worldly riches is only temporary. If we continually store the truth of God's Word in our hearts, we will be blessed forever because the Word of God in our hearts will remain with us throughout eternity. The Bible speaks of "...the Truth which lives and stays on in our hearts and will be with us forever..." (II John 2).

I believe our hearts are somewhat similar to a bank account. Our Father wants us to continually make "deposits" of His Word into our hearts. One of the greatest assets any Christian can have is a heart that is filled with thousands of promises and instructions from the Word of God. No one can ever take this wonderful treasure from God away from us.

If our hearts are filled with the Word of God, we will have a tremendous reservoir of spiritual truth to draw upon whenever we need it. When we are faced with a difficult problem, we will be able to make "faith withdrawals" from the Word of God that we have "deposited" into our hearts over a period of time.

Have you ever had a heavy heart? The Word of God tells us that heavy hearts are caused by anxiety. Our Father wants us to have glad hearts. Our hearts will sing with joy if we continually fill them with encouragement from the living Word of God. "Anxiety in a man's heart weighs it down, but an encouraging word makes it glad" (Proverbs 12:25).

Some people overreact emotionally to the circumstances in their lives. They are happy if the circumstances are favorable. They are unhappy if the circumstances are unfavorable. If we continually fill our hearts with the Word of God, we will be filled with God's joy regardless of the circumstances we face. "...he who has a glad heart has a continual feast [regardless of circumstances]" (Proverbs 15:15).

We should never allow ourselves to be controlled by the circumstances in our lives. What happens in our lives is not important - the important thing is how we *react* to what happens to us. Our hearts will rejoice if they are filled with the Word of God. We will react with absolute faith in the reliability of God's promises and God's power instead of reacting to the circumstances we face. "The precepts of the Lord are right, rejoicing the heart..." (Psalm 19:8).

We should obey the following instructions from Jesus Christ if we want to be set free from the influence of circumstances in our lives. Jesus said, "...If you abide in My word [hold fast to My teachings and live in accordance with them], you are truly My disciples. And you will know the Truth, and the Truth will set you free" (John 8:31-32).

Jesus instructs us to "abide" in His Word. When we abide in the Word of God, we focus on God's Word continually. Our lives are controlled by the amount of God's Word that lives in our minds and our hearts. Jesus instructs us to "hold fast to His teachings and to live in accordance with them." If we truly want to be disciples of Jesus Christ, we should hold tightly onto the Word of God and live our lives in accordance with its instructions.

I have pointed out previously that the words "disciple" and "discipline" have the same root. We will "know the Truth" of God's Word if we have the discipline to fill our hearts continually with the Word of God. This magnificent Truth is so powerful that it can and will set us free from the effect of circumstances in our lives. We will be ready to serve as soldiers in the army of Jesus Christ.

In this chapter we have seen that our Father definitely wants us to store up His Word in our minds and our hearts. I have referred briefly to meditating on the Word of God in order to fill our hearts with God's promises and instructions. In the next five chapters we'll study the holy Scriptures in detail to see exactly what it means to meditate on the Word of God, why we should meditate continually on the Word of God and how to meditate successfully on the Word of God.

Chapter 16

Scripture Meditation and the Wisdom of God

Now that we have seen the importance of God's Word living in our hearts, we are ready to learn *how* to fill our hearts with the Word of God. We can achieve this desirable goal by meditating continually on the holy Scriptures. In the following chapters I will explain a system of Scripture meditation that will require some hard work on your part.

Our Father wants us to work diligently at whatever we do. "Whatever your hand finds to do, do it with all your might..." (Ecclesiastes 9:10). Whenever we undertake any project, we should work hard at whatever we are doing as if this project was being performed for the Lord. "Whatever may be your task, work at it heartily (from the soul), as [something done] for the Lord and not for men..." (Colossians 3:23).

If you believe what you will read about Scripture meditation in these chapters and if you are willing to pay the price you are required to pay, I believe you will find that your efforts will enable you to draw much closer to the Lord. I believe you will find that you will be able to trust the Lord much more than you trusted Him before. You also will "program" yourself to live your life in obedience to the specific instructions our Father has given us in His Word.

I have learned that Scripture meditation is a vitally important spiritual key that allows us to receive manifestation of the power, ability and wisdom of God. I believe that we must obey our Father's instructions to meditate continually on His Word if we want to fully partake of His wisdom and the many other blessings He has made available to us.

We will start these five chapters on Scripture meditation with what I believe are two of the most important passages of Scripture in the Bible. I often brought up these two passages of Scripture in the form of a quiz when I used to give seminars throughout the United States and Canada. I was surprised to find that less than 10% of the Christians in the audiences were obeying God's instructions in these two passages of Scripture.

I believe that Joshua 1:8 and Psalms 1:2-3 are two of the most significant passages of Scripture in this book. Most of the other scriptural concepts in this book revolve around these two passages of Scripture. Let's begin our study of these passages of Scripture by recreating exactly what transpired when the Book of Joshua was written.

God selected Joshua to replace Moses after he died. God knew that Joshua would be overwhelmed as he attempted to follow in Moses' footsteps as the leader of Israel. God assured Joshua that He would be with him and that He would not fail him or forsake him. God urged Joshua to be strong, courageous and single-minded.

God then told Joshua exactly what He wanted him to do to be successful in his new position. God said, "This Book of the Law shall not depart out of your mouth, but you shall meditate on it day and night, that you may observe and do according to all that is written in it. **For then you shall make your way prosperous, and then you shall deal wisely and have good success"** (Joshua 1:8).

These instructions that God gave to Joshua apply to each of us today. I'd like to explain the last part of this passage of Scripture first to emphasize the wonderful blessings our Father has promised to us. I have emphasized the blessings that God promised to Joshua by putting them in bold print. Please study the words in bold print so that you can clearly see the blessings your Father promises to give to *you* if you will obey the specific instructions He has given in the first part of this passage of Scripture.

First, God promises that we will be able to "make our way prosperous." Spiritual prosperity refers to much more than financial prosperity. The Hebrew word that is translated "prosperous" in this passage of Scripture (and also in Psalm 1:3) means "to live in a godly way, to push forward, to break through, to overcome." We should meditate continually on the Word of God if we truly want to break through to become what our Father wants us to become.

The second promise that God gave to Joshua is that he would be able to "deal wisely." These words give us an important scriptural key to receiving the wisdom of God. We must obey God's instructions in the first portion of this passage of Scripture if we want to "have good success" in receiving the wisdom of God and the other blessings our Father wants to give us.

What exactly does God tell us to do to receive these blessings of prosperity, wisdom and success? First, our Father says that He does not want His Word to "depart out of our mouths." Our Father wants us to speak His Word continually throughout every day of our lives. Next, He tells us that we should meditate on His Word throughout the day and night. Finally, God says that, as a result of this constant meditation, we should carefully observe what His Word tells us to do. Then, our Father wants us to do exactly what His Word instructs us to do.

Do you sincerely desire to receive the prosperity, wisdom and success your Father promises to give to you? Can you honestly say that you are obeying the three specific instructions your Father instructs you to carry out to receive these magnificent blessings? Are you meditating throughout the day and night on God's Word, speaking God's Word continually and obeying the specific instructions you have learned as a result of continual meditation?

We now are ready to look at the second passage of Scripture that I believe is vital to receiving wisdom from God and the other blessings our Father wants to give us. "...his delight and desire are in the law of the Lord, and on His law (the precepts, the instructions, the teachings of God) he habitually meditates (ponders and studies) by day and by night. And he shall be like a tree firmly planted [and tended] by the streams of water, ready to bring forth its fruit in its season; its leaf also shall not fade or wither; **and everything he does shall prosper [and come to maturity]" (**Psalm 1:2-3).

Once again, let's look at the last portion of this passage of Scripture first to see exactly what our Father promises to us. I also have put these blessings in bold print so that you can clearly see the blessings your Father has promised to give to *you.*

Once again, your Father promises that you will prosper (live in a godly way, push forward, break through and overcome) in everything you do. God also promises that everything you do will "come to maturity." You will become spiritually mature and successfully complete your endeavors if you obey these specific instructions from God.

This promise from God is preceded by our Father telling us that we should delight in His Word and that we should have a deep and sincere desire to obey His instructions. If we truly delight in God's Word and if we desire to do what our Father instructs us to do, we will obey His instructions to meditate on His Word throughout the day and night.

This passage of Scripture is similar to Joshua 1:8. If we sincerely desire to be mature and for everything we do to prosper, we should obey our Father's instructions to meditate throughout the day and night on the instructions and promises He has given to us. Can you honestly say that you are obeying God's instruction to meditate on His Word throughout the day and night?

If we meditate constantly on His Word, our Father says we will be like trees that are planted next to a stream of water. He promises that we will bring forth fruit in season in our lives. He also says that we will be like leaves on trees that do not fade and wither.

What is God referring to in this comparison to trees that are planted next to a stream of water? Please visualize an orchard of fruit trees that has experienced a tremendous drought. Visualize the grass on the ground around these trees being brown instead of green. Visualize the leaves on most of the trees in this orchard being brown. Visualize that most of the trees in the orchard are not bearing fruit. Then, please visualize that the one row of trees that is next to the stream of water is green and lush and producing an abundant harvest of fruit.

Why does this one row of trees produce its fruit in season in spite of the drought? When rain fails to come down from the sky, each of the trees next to the stream can reach down with its roots to bring up water from the stream so that it will not wither. These trees still are able to produce fruit in season, regardless of external conditions.

Everything we do will prosper if we will faithfully obey these instructions from God. We will be like trees planted next to a stream of water that are able to bear fruit in a drought. We will be able to receive manifestation of this wonderful promise from God if we habitually meditate throughout the day and night on the Word of God. You will experience godly success if you obey your Father's specific instruction in this area.

Dear reader, if you do not receive anything else from this book, please be determined to obey the instructions in these two passages of Scripture. Please understand that only a small percentage of Christians are receiving manifestation of these conditional promises from God because very few Christians obey God's instructions to meditate constantly on His Word throughout the day and night.

Now that we have seen the importance of meditating continually on the Word of God, we are ready to begin to learn exactly what we should do when we meditate on the Word of God. I have explained Scripture meditation for many years by saying that we meditate on the Word of God by doing everything that chronic *worriers* do. However, instead of meditating on the potential problems that worriers think about constantly, we should meditate continually on God's promises and instructions. "Your mind will meditate on the terror…" (Isaiah 33:18).

What do chronic worriers do when they are faced with a potentially severe problem? They "meditate on the terror." They think continually about what they are afraid will happen to them. They are consumed by the potential problems they face. They turn these problems over and over in their minds. They look at them from every conceivable angle. They magnify these problems. They talk a lot about these potential problems. They visualize these problems coming into manifestation in their lives.

The preceding paragraph is an exact description of what we should do when we meditate on the Word of God except that our Father wants us to meditate continually on His promises and instructions instead of meditating continually on potential problems. When we meditate on the Word of God, we should focus constantly on specific promises and instructions our Father has given to us.

We should turn these promises and instructions from God over and over in our minds throughout the day and night. We should look at these promises and instructions from every possible angle. We should personalize these promises and instructions. We should magnify these promises and instructions. We should be determined to obey God's instructions. We should constantly visualize God's promises coming into manifestation in our lives. We should verbalize these promises and instructions.

If you truly want to receive manifestation of God's wonderful promises in Joshua 1:8 and Psalm 1:2-3, will you make the decision to meditate continually on the holy Scriptures? Will you give Scripture meditation a fair trial over a period of time to see for yourself that you will receive manifestation of these wonderful promises from God? Our Father always does what He says He will do. Will we do what He instructs us to do?

Most Christians have experienced great encouragement from hearing a powerful and encouraging message from a person who is preaching enthusiastically under a powerful anointing of the Holy Spirit. Most of us have experienced the exhilaration of walking out of a church service filled with faith and enthusiasm because we have heard the anointed Word of God preached in a powerful way.

We all would like to be able to sustain the enthusiasm we receive at these times. However, we can't bring these anointed preachers to be with us for twenty-four hours a day to preach to us continually, to motivate us, to encourage us and to help us to increase our faith in God. Our Father knew we would need to receive these blessings. He told us how to receive continual motivation and encouragement and how to increase our faith in Him by meditating on His supernaturally powerful Word throughout the day and night, every day of our lives.

When we meditate on God's Word, we should open our mouths and talk about whatever we are meditating upon. Our Father wants our ears to hear His Word being spoken continually. If we can't hear the Word of God being spoken by an anointed preacher, we can hear ourselves speaking the Word of God throughout the day and night.

Tests have indicated that most people forget approximately 90% of what they hear within thirty days. We cannot possibly receive everything we need from one or two church services a week. We should add to what we learn in church by faithfully obeying our Father's instructions to meditate continually on His Word.

Our Father wants us to learn from Him throughout the day and night. He wants us to consistently fill our eyes, our ears, our minds, our hearts and our mouths with His Word throughout every day of our lives. If we obey these instructions from God, we will constantly experience the wonderful spiritual uplifting that we experience when we hear anointed preaching of the Word of God.

In this first chapter pertaining to meditation on the holy Scriptures we have established a scriptural foundation that hopefully will motivate and encourage you to meditate continually on God's Word. Please review this chapter carefully before proceeding. If you haven't already done so, please underline or highlight God's specific instructions and promises pertaining to meditating on His Word.

I believe that your life will be changed beyond comprehension if you will give daily Scripture meditation a fair trial over a reasonable period of time. I have not found anything else in all of my years as a Christian that is more beneficial to me than continual meditation on the Word of God.

Chapter 17

Specific Instructions on Scripture Meditation

As we prepare to learn more about meditation on the Word of God, I would like to begin this chapter by explaining what meditation is *not.* Satan and his demons often try to influence us to duplicate godly principles with an inferior substitute. We see an example of this satanic influence in the significance that many eastern religions place upon meditation.

We must understand the major difference between meditation on the Word of God and the meditation of eastern religions. Many people are deceived by Satan through transcendental meditation and similar forms of meditation that are emphasized by eastern religions. Some of these eastern religions focus on the necessity of "nothingness" in our minds when we are meditating. Our Father never intended for us to meditate upon "nothing." Our Father wants us to meditate continually on His living Word.

We play right into Satan's hands if we empty our minds during meditation. Satan and his demons are looking for empty minds that can be influenced by the deceptive thoughts they attempt to put into these minds.

Satan and his demons are powerless against Christians who faithfully obey God's instructions to meditate continually on His Word. They know that Christians whose minds and hearts and mouths are filled with the Word of God will consistently walk in the victory Jesus Christ won for them.

Next, I want to comment on what I perceive to be the difference between memorization of the holy Scriptures and meditation on the holy Scriptures. I am *not* saying that Scripture memorization isn't beneficial. Memorization leads to meditation. I believe that memorization takes place in our *minds*. I believe that consistent meditation on the holy Scriptures causes the Word of God to drop from our minds down into our *hearts*.

We do not know if one day we may not have Bibles, as is the case for many Christians today. When our hearts are filled with the Word of God, no one can ever take the power of God and His Word from our hearts. Continual meditation on the Word of God is an investment of time that will result in eternal blessings.

Whenever we meditate on a passage of Scripture, we should personalize what we are meditating on as a specific instruction or promise from Almighty God that is directed to each of us individually. We should reflect quietly, deeply and thoroughly over a period of time on the specific instructions and promises we are meditating on.

As you meditate, I recommend that you insert your name whenever possible into every Scripture reference. Speak this passage of Scripture out loud again and again and again. Verbalize the promises and instructions from the Word of God repeatedly until they are planted in your heart.

Dig deeply into the Word of God. Search. Probe. Explore. Ask for guidance from the Holy Spirit as you examine each passage of Scripture thoroughly. Realize that each passage of Scripture is filled with wonderful spiritual treasure that comes to us from heaven.

Whenever you meditate on a passage of Scripture, turn that passage of Scripture over and over in your mind throughout the day and throughout the night. Look at it from every possible angle. Be determined to obey God's instructions. Visualize God's promises being manifested in your life. Boldly speak the specific promises from God that you believe will be manifested in your life.

I have mentioned previously that a friend led me to Jesus Christ when I was on the verge of bankruptcy and a nervous breakdown. My friend told me that every word in the Bible was inspired by God. He told me that the only way I could escape from the problems I faced was to continually "saturate" myself in the Word of God.

As the weeks and months went by, I found myself "awash in a sea of Scripture." I continually filled my mind and my heart with the Word of God. I didn't understand the principles of Joshua 1:8 and Psalm 1:2-3 at that time but, by the guidance of the Holy Spirit, I did what they instructed me to do anyway. I wasn't a Bible scholar, but I was determined to believe my Father's promises and to obey His instructions.

I will never forget what I did during these discouraging times with Philippians 4:13, my favorite passage of Scripture. At that time I was meditating on the King James version of the Bible.

This passage of Scripture in that version of the Bible says, "I can do all things through Christ which strengtheneth me."

I remember sitting at the desk in my small office downstairs in our home in New Hampshire continually speaking this magnificent promise from God out loud one hundred times. I used to sit at my desk and say over and over again, "I *can* do *all* things through the strength of Jesus Christ." I would say these words boldly and emphatically. I often would add to these words as I personalized this promise while I meditated on it. Each time I spoke this passage of Scripture, I wrote the number down on a pad of paper.

On many different occasions I continued this process until I had verbalized from Philippians 4:13 one hundred times. I can clearly recollect how much my faith in God increased when I was able to look at my pad of paper and see that I had personalized, meditated upon and verbalized this wonderful promise from God one hundred times.

As the weeks and months went by, I began to write in longhand the observations I received as a result of continually meditating on Philippians 4:13 and many other passages of Scripture. I hired a woman who was able to read my handwriting to type these meditations.

Over the past twenty-seven years several other Christian women have typed these meditations which I now dictate on tape instead of writing longhand. These tens of thousands of typed meditations have grown to the point where I have more than twenty large file cabinet drawers that are filled to overflowing with hundreds of files filled with material I have written as a result of meditating on the Word of God for more than a quarter of a century.

By God's grace our business did not fail. I no longer head up this business, but I am still quite active in it. This business has grown and prospered. Many of the more than one hundred people who are associated with this organization are Christians. We have two prayer meetings and one Bible study each week in one of our conference rooms.

I can tell you from personal experience that constant meditation on the Word of God works. I can tell you from my experience and from many testimonies I have received that your life will be transformed. You will be amazed by the changes that will take place in your life if you will persevere in renewing your mind daily in the Word of God and meditating throughout the day and night on the holy Scriptures over a period of several months and, then, several years.

How many times have you found yourself humming a song that you heard several hours before? This same principle applies to meditating on the Word of God. If you will constantly fill your mind and your heart with the holy Scriptures, you will find that these promises and instructions from Almighty God will remain at the forefront of your consciousness.

Some people who read these recommendations will say, "I'm too busy to do this meditation throughout every day and night." Do you think your Father would have instructed you to do something that is impossible for you to do? Make the quality decision to obey the instructions from your Father who knows exactly how busy you are.

I believe we should study the Word of God every morning and then meditate on specific passages of Scripture throughout the day and night. I believe that our morning Bible study gives us a solid foundation for the upcoming day. We can't carry our Bibles with us to meditate on them throughout every day and night of our lives. However, we can carry small cards with passages of Scripture to meditate on them continually.

I have spent many hours meditating on the Word of God by placing Scripture cards on the dashboard of my automobile. I also kept several Scripture references on 3" by 5" file cards under a plastic cover on my desk when I was a self-employed businessman. I meditated continually on these promises that were always in front of me.

Whenever I was faced with an extremely difficult problem, I asked my secretary to hold all calls. I closed the door to my office. I turned away from the problems that seemed to be so overwhelming. Instead of dwelling on the problems I faced, I meditated continually on the promises of God from the Scripture meditation cards on my desk.

At various times in my life I have had Scripture cards stuck upon the walls of our home, on the mirror in our bathroom and on our refrigerator. A housewife working in her home can keep Scripture cards on a kitchen counter, a stove, a dishwasher or a washing machine. Many people can place individual Scripture cards on a desk or a work table at their place of employment.

We are only limited by the limitations of our creativity. If it is impossible for you to meditate during your workday, you can always meditate on your breaks, during your lunch hour and while you drive to and from work. Most people have some discretionary time during the evening hours. We can meditate effectively on the Word of God during this time. If we really want to meditate throughout the day and night on the Word of God, we will find a way to accomplish this goal.

Many of us have more discretionary time than we realize. If we sleep eight hours each day and if we work eight hours each day, we have the remaining eight hours to use at our discretion. Also, many of us have a large portion of the day on Saturday available to us. We *can* find ample time to meditate continually on the holy Scriptures *if* we truly want to obey God's specific instructions in this area.

The Word of God is the wisdom of God. You cannot even begin to comprehend the magnificent wisdom of God you will be able to tap into if you will obey your Father's instructions to meditate continually on His Word. Unfortunately, many Christians fail to dig deeply into the Word of God. They go through the motions of studying the Word of God without actually extracting the enormous amount of wisdom and power that is contained in the holy Scriptures. We cannot grow in Christ unless we obey our Father's instructions to study and meditate on His Word continually.

We will begin to understand the vastness of the holy Scriptures as we meditate continually on God's Word. We'll understand that we can spend every day of our lives saturating ourselves in God's Word. We'll know that we will never even begin to scratch the surface of the enormity of the living Word of God.

In this chapter we have laid an additional foundation for meditating on the holy Scriptures. I believe the Holy Spirit will speak to you as each of the chapters about meditating on the Word of God unfolds. I believe you will become increasingly more convinced of the importance of meditating constantly on the holy Scriptures.

Chapter 18

Additional Instructions on Scripture Meditation

I don't believe we can meditate effectively on the holy Scriptures unless we constantly open our mouths and speak about the passage of Scripture we are meditating upon. The Hebrew word "hagah" that is translated "meditate" in both Joshua 1:8 and Psalm 1:2 means "to murmur." When we meditate on the Word of God, we should always "murmur" – we should speak about what we are meditating on.

We saw in Joshua 1:8 that this important passage of Scripture begins with the words, "This Book of the Law shall not depart out of your mouth." Our Father obviously wants us to speak His Word continually throughout the day and night. We obey God's instructions when we speak His Word with faith while we meditate. "...he who has My word, let him speak My word faithfully..." (Jeremiah 23:28).

Our faith in God will grow as we continually speak the Word of God with faith when we meditate. God created us so that our faith in Him would increase when we *hear* His Word being spoken with faith. "...faith comes by hearing [what is told]..." (Romans 10:17).

Our ears enable us to plug into the supernatural power of the living Word of God. We must hear the Word of God to receive the manifestation of God's promises. Our Father didn't make a mistake when He said that faith comes by hearing His Word.

I believe that our Father wants our ears to constantly hear our mouths speaking His Word. We give substance to our meditation when we open our mouths and verbalize what we are thinking. The Word of God enters our hearts the same way it comes out of our hearts – through our mouths.

The Word of God is God speaking to us. We should speak God's Word back to Him. When we meditate continually on God's Word, we speak His Word back to Him. We will find that the Word of God is always fresh and new when we continually speak the wonderful promises and instructions our Father has given to us.

Our Father wants us to open our mouths continually to say what He says. The Word of God is voice activated. I believe that we activate the promises of God by continually speaking the Word of God with bold faith. Speaking clarifies the Word of God and makes it more distinct and sharply defined. Our meditation becomes more real and meaningful when we verbalize the seeds of God's Word that we are planting into our hearts.

Several of the books I have written have emphasized the importance of meditating on the Word of God. If you read some of my earlier books, you will see that I recommended that readers copy Scripture references onto 3" by 5" file cards so they could carry these cards with them continually. I have received many comments over the years from people who told me how much they have benefited from the 3" by 5" cards they have carried with them.

Several years ago I received a life-changing telephone call from Terry Lemerond, the man to whom we have dedicated this book. Terry had been blessed by meditating on the 3" by 5" Scripture cards he made. However, Terry significantly changed my life and the lives of many other people when he telephoned that day suggesting some changes in using cards to meditate on the Word of God.

Terry said, "Jack, very few people will actually take the time to write down Scripture references on a 3" by 5" card. The people who write these cards will soon find that the cards become dog-eared and crumpled through use. I believe you should write the Scripture cards yourself, have them printed and put them in a container that is easy to carry. I believe many lives will be changed if you do this. Please pray and see if God speaks to you as I believe He has spoken to me in regard to this concept."

I prayed and I immediately knew that God wanted me to write these Scripture Meditation Cards. As a result, I have stopped writing Christian books for the past five years. Instead, I devoted my efforts to co-authoring the following ten sets of Scripture Meditation Cards with my wife, Judy.

1. *Financial Instructions from God*
2. *Freedom from Worry and Fear*
3. *A Closer Relationship with the Lord*
4. *Receive God's Blessings in Adversity*
5. *Our Father's Wonderful Love*
6. *Enjoy God's Wonderful Peace*

7. *Find God's Will for Your Life*
8. *Receive Healing from the Lord*
9. *Continually Increasing Faith In God*
10. *God Is Always with You*

Each of these sets of fifty-two Scripture Meditation Cards contains approximately seventy-five Scripture references. Each card contains at least one Scripture reference. Several cards have two Scripture references. By God's grace these Scripture cards have encouraged thousands of people all over the world.

These cards are the size of business cards – 2 ½" by 3 ½". We have placed each set of 52 cards in dark blue vinyl cardholders. These cards are small enough to easily fit into a pocket or a purse. I believe you will draw closer to God if you will carry these Scripture Meditation Cards with you to meditate continually on the Word of God throughout the day and night.

Please go back and review the ten titles I have listed. Which of these subjects are of interest to you? Would you like to take advantage of the thousands of hours Judy and I have spent researching the Word of God to provide ready-made Scripture Meditation Cards for your daily meditation? You will see in the back of this book that we offer you a quantity discount if you order several sets of these cards.

I also have dictated a cassette tape that is approximately eighty-five minutes long to go with each set of Scripture Meditation Cards. We have seen that our faith in God increases by *hearing* the Word of God. I believe you will be blessed if you will add the "rhema" of the spoken Word of God to the "logos" of the written Word of God in these Scripture cards.

I urge you to purchase the Scripture cards with the cassette tapes. The size limitations of these 2½" by 3½" cards prohibit the inclusion of the substantial amount of additional explanation that is contained on the cassette tapes.

For the past four years I have taught at the River Bible Institute in Tampa, Florida. I have been blessed by the response of the students to our Scripture Meditation Cards. I'd like to briefly share a few of the responses we have received from these students who so eagerly seek God's will for their lives.

"I received the Lord just two months before I came to Bible school. My life is 180 degrees from what it was. I was bound by fear. I began to go over the *Freedom from Worry and Fear* Scripture Meditation Cards in the daytime and I listened to the tape at night. The verses jumped off the card and into me! They became part of me. It was awesome. It was really a blessing!"

"My back was hurting so badly that I couldn't get comfortable. I was miserable whether I sat or stood or laid down. I didn't know what to do. Suddenly, I thought of the Scripture cards on healing that my husband had purchased. I decided to meditate on the Scripture in these cards. I was only on the second card when, all of sudden, I felt heat go from my neck down through my body. The Lord had healed me. I never knew it could happen so fast. The pain has not come back."

"Your Scripture cards have been very helpful to my wife and myself. We have taped them to the walls in our home and we meditate on them constantly. I also take four or five cards with me every day when I go to work. I meditate on them while I drive. The Scripture on these cards is a constant source of encouragement to us."

"I was recently involved in an automobile accident that was so severe that my car spun 360 degrees. While this was happening, I was amazed at how calm I was because I had just been meditating on one of the cards from *Freedom from Worry and Fear* with the Scripture reference, 'Fear not. I am with you always.' I wasn't afraid. I knew the Lord was with me."

"The result of meditating on these cards is amazing. I accomplished several times as much work as usual. In addition to increased energy, I was accurate and made no mistakes. My employer has noticed and favorably commented. These cards are also resulting in peaceful sleep each night. This is only the first week!"

Old habits of thinking are hard to break. We cannot break deeply rooted thought patterns with occasional Bible study and meditation. We can and will transform our lives if we will obey God's instructions to study and meditate on His Word on a *daily* basis.

Our Father wants us to give His Word first place in our lives. We should honor and revere the precious gift our Father has given us in the holy Scriptures. We should never miss out on the opportunity we have been given to study the Word of God daily and to meditate on it throughout the day and night.

The rewards of meditating on as few as two Scripture references per week are enormous. You will "deposit" more than one hundred passages of Scripture into your heart each year if you meditate on only two passages of Scripture a week. In ten years you will have more than one thousand Scripture references living in your heart.

You obviously can meditate on more than two passages of Scripture per week. The cumulative results of meditating on Scripture over a period of time are enormous. I have been filling my mind and my heart with the Word of God for more than a quarter of a century. I often find myself speaking Scripture that I didn't know was living inside of me.

We learn best through repetition. Repetition is extremely powerful. Water dripping continually on a rock will wear the rock away over a period of time. This principle of repetition is very important in the area of Scripture meditation. Scientific studies have proven that we need to listen to the same message several times in order to retain it.

The Word of God doesn't sink into our hearts when we first meditate on it. Our Father has told us that He wants us to develop a habit pattern of studying and meditating on His Word on a daily basis. We must meditate continually on the Word of God. I have explained that studies have shown that we quickly forget much of what we hear only one time.

Our Father doesn't want us to "stop and start" in our spiritual growth. We should obey our Father's instructions to study and meditate on His Word daily if we truly want to receive wisdom from Him. We never stand still in the spiritual realm. We are either moving forward or moving backward. Jesus said, "...whoever has [spiritual knowledge], to him will more be given and he will be furnished richly so that he will have abundance; but from him who has not, even what he has will be taken away" (Matthew 13:12).

We all know that bad habits can get a foothold in our lives through repetition. This same principle applies to the good habit of renewing our minds daily and meditating throughout the day and night on the Word of God. This repetition will become a good habit if we obey these instructions from God.

Our Father wants us to meditate on His Word early in the morning, throughout the day and again in the evening. He promises to reward us bountifully if we focus our thoughts diligently on His Word. "The thoughts of the [steadily] diligent tend only to plenteousness..." (Proverbs 21:5).

We should follow the example of the psalmist who started meditating on the holy Scriptures early in the morning. He said, "…I am awake before the cry of the watchman, that I may meditate on Your word" (Psalm 119:148). We should love God's Word so much that we will meditate on it throughout the day. The psalmist said, "Oh, how love I Your law! It is my meditation all the day" (Psalm 119:97).

I believe it is very important to meditate on the Word of God at night. Many Christians watch the news on television at night just before they go to bed. *Why* would we ever want to fill our minds at bedtime with the bad news of the world unless we spend even more time meditating on the good news of the holy Scriptures? We should follow the example of the psalmist when he served as a watchman throughout the night. He said, "…I remember You upon my bed and meditate on You in the night watches" (Psalm 63:6).

The Word of God instructs us to meditate on the holy Scriptures "day and night." I believe we will receive tremendous blessings when we wake up if we meditate on the Word of God at night. "…they [the words of your parents' God] shall lead you; when you sleep, they shall keep you; and when you waken, they shall talk with you" (Proverbs 6:22).

I celebrated my seventieth birthday a few months before this book was published. As I have grown older, I find that I awaken a lot more during the night than I used to. I often use the time that I am awake during the night to fill my mind and my heart with the holy Scriptures.

I urge other people who are awake during the night to take advantage of this precious opportunity to saturate themselves in the Word of God. Even if you sleep through the night, you will find that the Scripture references you meditated on will speak to you when you wake up in the morning.

In this chapter we have learned more scriptural principles pertaining to Scripture meditation. In the next chapter we will see what the Word of God says about the Word of God being our spiritual food. We also will learn how God's laws of sowing and reaping apply to meditating on His Word.

Chapter 19

We Receive Spiritual Nourishment from the Word of God

We have learned that we are able to receive spiritual cleansing by taking a "bath" in the Word of God each day. The Word of God also provides us with the spiritual nourishment our Father wants us to have. When God created us, He made provision for us to feed spiritual food into our minds and our hearts just as He made provision for us to feed our bodies with the natural food we put into our mouths.

In this book we are using the words "comprehensive insight into the ways and purposes of God" as our definition of the wisdom of God. What better way is there to receive more comprehensive insight into the ways and purposes of God than to feed ourselves continually with the Word of God? Job said, "...I have esteemed and treasured the words of His mouth more than my necessary food" (Job 23:12).

Our spiritual food is *more important* than the food we put into our mouths. Our hearts will sing with joy if we learn how to feed ourselves spiritually with the Word of God. "Your words were found, and I ate them; and Your words were to me a joy and the rejoicing of my heart…" (Jeremiah 15:16).

If we have a deep and sincere desire to receive comprehensive insight into the ways and purposes of God, we should be determined to feed ourselves each day with the wonderful spiritual food our Father has provided for us. Jesus said, "…Man shall not live and be upheld and sustained by bread alone, but by every word that comes forth from the mouth of God" (Matthew 4:4).

Most people nourish their bodies with breakfast, lunch and dinner each day. This food is translated into physical energy. In the spiritual realm, if we feed ourselves continually with spiritual food from the Word of God, this food will be transformed into spiritual energy.

Jesus said, "Give us this day our daily bread" (Matthew 6:11). I believe this statement can apply to spiritual food as well as natural food. Jesus didn't say, "Give us this week our weekly bread." Our Father wants us to feed ourselves spiritually each day.

Our Father didn't place any limit on the amount of spiritual food we can consume. There are no restricted diets with our spiritual food. We have been given the privilege of nourishing ourselves with an unlimited amount of the wonderful spiritual food our Father has made available to us. Our Father wants us to feast throughout the day and night on the extremely potent spiritual nutrition that is contained in His Word.

God's Word nourishes our minds and our hearts. It helps us to settle our emotions. We will be able to tune in to God's voice and to draw closer to Him if we feed ourselves with the living Word of God each day. Our lives will be transformed if we continually feed ourselves with wonderful spiritual food from the holy Scriptures.

Our appetite for spiritual food will increase as we continually study and meditate on the Word of God. We soon will find that we can't get enough of God's Word. We will be consumed by our desire to draw closer and closer to God by continually feeding ourselves the spiritual food our loving Father has provided for us.

I believe that Christians who do not have a deep hunger to learn from the Word of God suffer from spiritual malnutrition. We wouldn't experience good health in the natural realm if we didn't constantly put living food into our mouths and if we didn't exercise our bodies vigorously. This same principle applies in the spiritual realm. The apostle Paul told Timothy that he should be "...ever nourishing your own self on the truths of the faith..." (I Timothy 4:6).

We feed ourselves spiritually by studying and meditating on the holy Scriptures each day. We exercise ourselves spiritually by obeying our Father's instructions and by stepping out in faith on His promises.

I believe that we *eat* our spiritual food by *studying* the Word of God. I believe that we *digest* our spiritual food by *meditating* on the Word of God. When we digest natural food, this food goes from our mouths into our stomachs. When we digest spiritual food, this food drops from our minds into our hearts.

Our Father wants us to learn how to chew our spiritual food. We cannot properly digest food for our bodies without chewing this food thoroughly. This same principle applies in the spiritual realm. We digest our spiritual food by "chewing" on it as a result of meditating on the Word of God. We are able to extract vital spiritual nourishment by meditating on the holy Scriptures.

We receive energy in the natural realm from the food we digest. We are able to receive wonderful spiritual energy by digesting our spiritual food. There is no "junk food" in the Word of God. Every morsel of spiritual food our Father has provided for us is very nutritious.

We should never rush when we meditate on the Word of God. Our Father doesn't want us to "gulp down" our spiritual food. He wants us to chew our spiritual food slowly. It is possible to meditate too quickly on the Word of God, but I don't believe it is possible to meditate too slowly on the holy Scriptures.

Sometimes we should meditate on only one passage of Scripture for an entire day or maybe even longer than one day. We shouldn't move on to another passage of Scripture until we have extracted every possible bit of spiritual nourishment from the Scripture we are meditating on. The Word of God is alive. The Holy Spirit will quicken God's living Word to us if we abide each day in the wonderful promises and instructions our loving Father has given to us.

We have just seen that the Word of God is our spiritual food. The Word of God also is a spiritual seed. Jesus said, "...The seed is the Word of God" (Luke 8:11). We have seen previously that our Father wants us to plant the seeds of His Word in the spiritual soil of our minds and our hearts. "...you shall lay up these My words in your [minds and] hearts and in your [entire] being..." (Deuteronomy 11:18).

Many Christians have no comprehension of the awesome spiritual power that is contained in the Word of God. As we continually plant the seed of God's Word in our minds and in our hearts, we are planting magnificent supernatural spiritual seeds that will enable us to extract a harvest of more and more of God's wisdom, power and ability from deep down inside of ourselves.

Our Father wants the spiritual seeds that we plant each day to continually take root and grow. As we plant these seeds over a period of weeks, months and years, our minds and our hearts will be filled with many different spiritual seeds at various stages of development.

In the natural realm farmers don't always plant just one kind of seed. Farmers with large farms continually plant different kinds of seeds at different times. They often have different crops at various stages of development. This same principle applies in the spiritual realm. We will progressively understand great spiritual truths if we continually study and meditate on the Word of God.

Seeds have enormous multiplying power. In the natural realm a very small seed is able to multiply itself many times over to produce a substantial harvest. We are planting spiritual seeds that will multiply greatly when we continually meditate throughout the day and night on the Word of God.

We will speak words of worry, fear, doubt and unbelief if we focus continually on the problems we face. These negative words plant negative seeds in the spiritual realm. We plant powerful spiritual seeds when we speak God's promises with bold faith as we meditate daily on the holy Scriptures. Our Father wants us to plant positive spiritual seeds as we continually meditate on His Word.

We wouldn't expect to receive a harvest in the natural realm if we didn't plant seeds. This same principle applies in the spiritual realm. If we want to receive a harvest of God's wisdom and other blessings from God, we need to continually plant the appropriate seeds. This book is filled with hundreds of "spiritual seeds" pertaining to the wisdom of God. You can plant these seeds in your mind and in your heart by continually studying and meditating on these Scripture references. If you do, you will receive a bountiful harvest of the wisdom of God.

In the natural realm a seed is placed in the ground and, by a process that many of us do not understand, these seeds take root and grow and ultimately break through the surface of the earth to produce a harvest. The Word of God works in a similar manner. The Word of God is spiritually alive just as seeds in the natural realm are alive. When we continually plant the living Word of God in our minds and in our hearts, it comes alive on the inside of us just as seeds in the ground come alive to produce a harvest.

In the natural realm we know that we have to weed out our gardens and fields of crops to receive an abundant harvest. This same principle applies in the spiritual realm. Satan and his demons continually try to get into our minds and, from there, down into our hearts. Each day we must "weed out" the thoughts that Satan's demons attempt to put into our minds and our hearts by filling our minds and our hearts continually with the purity of seeds from God's Word (see II Corinthians 10:5).

In this chapter we have learned important truths about God's spiritual food. We have learned that the Word of God is a spiritual seed that we should plant continually in our minds and in our hearts. In the next chapter we will conclude our study of the wonderful blessings our Father has made available to us if we will meditate continually on His Word.

Chapter 20

Final Thoughts on Scripture Meditation

In this final chapter pertaining to Scripture meditation I will pull together the remaining material I have accumulated on this subject. I have so much additional material that this chapter will be one of the longest and most comprehensive chapters in this book. Let's begin by looking at another important area of Scripture meditation – continual meditation on God's faithfulness.

In addition to believing God for manifestation of His promises in the present and in the future, another way to meditate effectively is to focus continually on God's faithfulness in the past. God has proven Himself faithful in my life on many different occasions. I also have observed His tender and loving care in the lives of many other people. When I'm going through difficult times, I often reflect upon the many times God has faithfully delivered me and other people I know from adversity.

I believe we all should keep a list of God's faithfulness in our lives. I suggest that you pray asking God to bring to your remembrance all of the times He has been faithful to you in the past. Write these instances down. Put this list in a place where it is readily available.

Get out this personal history of God's faithfulness whenever you are faced with severe problems. Meditate continually upon God's faithfulness in your life. Open your mouth and thank your Father repeatedly for all of the times He has brought you safely through adversity. Then, speak words of faith that clearly indicate your unwavering conviction that your loving Father will once again bring you safely through your current problems.

When I'm faced with severe problems, sometimes I talk with other Christians who have been helped by God. I ask them to tell me what God did for them during difficult seasons in their lives. My faith in God invariably increases as I listen to the testimony of God's faithfulness in their lives. I know that God will see me through the problems I face just as He has faithfully carried my bothers and sisters in the Lord through the storms in their lives.

I also have found that it is extremely helpful to meditate on the great works of God that are described in the Bible. The psalmist expressed this principle when he said, "I will meditate also upon all Your works and consider all Your [mighty] deeds" (Psalm 77:12).

The Bible is filled with numerous examples of God delivering people from seemingly impossible situations. If you need encouragement, you might want to meditate on the tremendous victory David won over the giant Goliath (I Samuel 17:1-58), on the deliverance of Daniel in the lion's den (Daniel 6:1-28) and on the miraculous escape of Shadrach, Meshach and Abednego from the fiery furnace (Daniel 3:1-30).

The Book of Job is a tribute to God's faithfulness in the face of many seemingly impossible situations. If you face a severe problem, you might want to meditate on God's faithfulness to Joshua and his followers when the walls of Jericho miraculously came tumbling down (Joshua 6:1-21), upon the miracle of Moses and the Israelites as they were brought safely across the Red Sea (Exodus 14:1-31) and upon God's grace in sparing the life of Abraham's son, Isaac (Genesis 22:1-18).

If you need deliverance from a seemingly impossible situation, you might want to meditate on the miraculous conversion of Saul of Tarsus who once hated Jesus Christ passionately only to later become the beloved apostle Paul by a mighty act of God (Acts 9:1-31). You might want to meditate on the story of the disciples of Jesus Christ who were exhausted after fishing all night with no results. They then found that their nets were filled to overflowing with fish when they acted in faith upon the specific instructions Jesus gave them (Luke 5:1-11).

Be encouraged by meditating on the ability of Jesus Christ to successfully feed five thousand men and their wives and children with five loaves of bread and two fish (Mark 6:32-44) and by a second occasion where Jesus performed a similar miracle (Mark 8:1-9). Know that Jesus is the same today as He was then (see Hebrews 13:8). Trust Him to bring you safely through the adversity you face today just as He helped these people in the past.

We must not allow the problems we face to seem to be more powerful than God. Some Christians look at their problems as big, big problems and they look at God as a little, little God. Our Father wants us to do just the opposite. No matter how difficult our problems might seem to us, He wants us to know that He is Almighty God. Our seemingly unsolvable problems are not difficult for Him to solve.

Our Father wants us to take our attention off the problems in our lives. He wants us to focus instead on the promises He has given to us. He has instructed us to meditate continually on His great promises. He wants our minds and our hearts to be *so full* of His promises that thoughts about the problems we face *cannot* get into our minds and our hearts.

We should never give up hope when we are faced with adversity. Through the resurrection power of Jesus Christ, our Father will give us hope when the situation we face seems to be hopeless. We will receive great blessings from our loving Father if we continually draw closer to Him by meditating throughout the day and night on His Word.

We have read several passages of Scripture from the Psalms that show us the deep desire the psalmist David had to meditate continually on the Word of God. We should have the same delight in God's Word that David had. He said, "I will meditate on Your precepts and have respect to Your ways [the paths of life marked out by Your law]. I will delight myself in Your statutes; I will not forget Your word" (Psalm 119:15-16).

We should be so committed to the Word of God that we will keep God's promises in front of us at all times. We should meditate continually on God's promises because we delight in Him. "Delight yourself also in the Lord, and He will give you the desires and secret petitions of your heart" (Psalm 37:4).

This passage of Scripture explains the relationship between delighting in the Lord and receiving the desires of our hearts. Our loving Father wants to give each of us the desires of our hearts. He even wants to give us the secret desires we have never told anyone about. He will give us these desires when our desires are the same as His desires.

The Word of God is a spiritual mirror. The Lord will reveal Himself more and more to us as we study and meditate daily on the holy Scriptures over a period of time. We will become more like He is as we see Him in His Word. "...[because we] continued to behold [in the Word of God] as in a mirror the glory of the Lord, we are constantly being transfigured into His very own image in ever increasing splendor..." (II Corinthians 3:18).

Our Father wants to come alive to us when we are faced with severe problems. He will come alive to us, in us and through us if His Word fills our minds and our hearts. Our Father wants us to reveal His glory to us as we constantly meditate on His Word and draw closer to Him as a result of this meditation. As this process continues, we will be "transfigured" into the image of God.

When we behold something, we are able to see it clearly. We will be able to see our Father more clearly if we obey His instructions to renew our minds in His Word daily and to meditate throughout the day and night on the holy Scriptures. Our character will change as this process continues over a period of time. Our nature will become more like God's nature.

We must not take the Word of God lightly. Some of God's children live at a level of faith that is far below where their Father wants them to be. The reality of the numerous promises pertaining to God's power, ability and wisdom will explode on the inside of us if we will pay the price of obeying our Father's instructions to continually fill our minds and our hearts with His Word.

Most Christians will say they believe that the Bible is divinely inspired, but their words and actions in a crisis situation often show otherwise. Why wouldn't we study the holy Scriptures constantly and meditate on God's Word throughout the day and night if we are absolutely convinced that every word in the Bible really is inspired by Almighty God?

Our loving Father will never force us to do anything. He has given each of us the freedom to choose. Our Father has told us exactly what He wants us to do in the area of Bible study and meditation. We each must decide whether we will obey God's specific instructions in this area or whether we will disregard these instructions to live our lives the way we want to live them.

We live in a generation where many things are "instant" – fast food restaurants, microwave ovens, cameras that produce pictures immediately, one hour dry cleaning, rapid oil changes for our automobiles, money machines at banks, fax machines, cellular telephones and the Internet. Many of us are impatient. We are always looking for "a quick and easy fix."

I have explained that meditating on the Word of God is hard work. Scripture meditation requires the expenditure of a great deal of time and effort day after day, week after week and month after month. We will only spend large amounts of time on activities that are meaningful and important to us. I pray that the emphasis in this book on Scripture meditation will motivate you to do exactly what your Father has instructed you to do in this vitally important area in your life.

Our loving Father is no different from loving parents here on earth except that His love for us is much, much greater than the love that any human parents have ever had for their children (see our Scripture Meditation Cards, *Our Father's Wonderful Love).* I pray that you will be completely secure in your knowledge of your Father's wonderful love for you.

Human parents receive great enjoyment from seeing their children grow and mature and develop. We should give our heavenly Father the enjoyment of seeing us meditating constantly upon His Word as we continually draw closer to Him and walk and talk with Him throughout every day of our lives. "May my meditation be sweet to Him; as for me, I will rejoice in the Lord" (Psalm 104:34).

Our Father loves to fellowship with us. He wants us to lift our eyes from the printed pages of the Bible to look into His eyes. He wants us to know Him personally because we abide in His Word and because His Word abides in us. We will know our Father much more intimately if we obey His instructions to meditate constantly on His Word.

The Bible repeatedly tells us of the emphasis the psalmist David put on meditating on the Word of God. David had a sincere desire for the thoughts of his heart and the words he spoke to be acceptable to the Lord. He said, "Let the words of my mouth and the meditation of my heart be acceptable in Your sight, O Lord, my [firm, impenetrable] Rock and my Redeemer" (Psalm 19:14).

David lifted his hands in praise and thanksgiving because of his love for God and for God's Word. He meditated continually on the Word of God because of his fervent love for the holy Scriptures. "My hands also will I lift up [in fervent supplication] to Your commandments, which I love, and I will meditate on Your statutes" (Psalm 119:48).

David knew from many past experiences that God had given Him tremendous revelation as a result of meditating on His Word. These same blessings are available to us today. I believe that we will receive increasing manifestation of the wisdom our Father has put within us if we obey His instructions to meditate constantly on His Word.

Our Father will unfold wonderful spiritual truths to us if we continually study and meditate on His Word. He will reveal more and more of the meaning of His Word to us. "The sum of Your word is truth [the total of the full meaning of all Your individual precepts]; and every one of Your righteous decrees endures forever" (Psalm 119:160).

God's Word is infinite and eternal. We will never learn everything we can learn from God. I believe that our Father will continue to teach us throughout eternity. I believe He has given each of us the precious opportunity to get a head start on this eternal revelation by studying and meditating daily on His Word while we are here on earth.

The entire world would change dramatically if a significant percentage of Christians faithfully obeyed God's instructions to renew their minds in God's Word daily and to meditate throughout the day and night on the holy Scriptures. I pray that you will be determined to experience this dramatic transformation in your life.

I'd like to close these chapters on Scripture meditation with a subject that is near and dear to my heart. Cassette tapes enable us to learn from anointed preachers and teachers throughout every day of our lives. I have been blessed repeatedly for more than a quarter of a century as the Holy Spirit has ministered to me from many anointed preachers and teachers I have heard on cassette tapes.

The wealth of anointed teaching and preaching that is available to us through cassette tapes is incredible. I purchase a large number of cassette tapes by mail each year. I want to learn from God constantly. I pass these tapes on to others when I am finished with them.

We have seen that the Bible tells us that faith comes from *hearing* the Word of God. My faith soars when I meditate continually on preaching and teaching from these anointed servants of God. I can't get enough of the things of God. I search continually for new cassette tapes from preachers and teachers who are tuned in to the Holy Spirit and speak continually under His anointing.

As the years have gone by, I have found many people whose anointed messages have continually witnessed to my spirit. As I have found these "cassette tape mentors," I have purchased more and more of their tapes to learn everything I can as the Holy Spirit ministers through them. Some of the greatest spiritual truths I have learned have come from these cassette tapes from anointed men and women of God.

I have compiled a comprehensive list of ministries that provide what I believe are anointed messages on cassette tapes. If you would like a free copy of this list, please write to me and enclose a stamped return envelope. A wide variety of cassette tapes are available from these ministries at a nominal charge.

After you receive this list, you simply need to write one letter asking these ministries to send you their catalog of cassette tapes and to add you to their mailing list. You can either photocopy this letter or print duplicates on a printer attached to a computer. Soon after mailing these letters you will receive catalogs of some of the most anointed preaching and teaching you will ever hear.

I am not saying that listening to cassette tapes is a substitute for personal Bible study and meditation. I am saying that learning from these cassette tapes is a wonderful supplement to our personal Bible study and meditation. As I have listened to many cassette tapes over the years, I have learned great spiritual truths that have caused me to turn to the Word of God with new understanding. The preaching and teaching on these cassette tapes have been catalysts that have moved me into new plateaus of spiritual growth I never could have experienced otherwise.

Cassette tapes are a blessing because they are so flexible. I can listen to them during many hours of the day when I'm doing routine things such as shaving, dressing, opening my mail and driving my automobile. I utilize every moment I can to renew my mind and to meditate on the holy Scriptures.

When my wife edited this paragraph she said, "I keep the Bible on tape in my car at all times. I listen to these Bible cassettes over and over. I continually hear things that quicken my heart. I visualize the descriptions as if they were a movie and as if I was there while these things were happening. I especially listen to the gospels again and again. I walk with Jesus each day as I listen to what He did and said. I carry the Old Testament in my car and I listen to the New Testament in our house when I exercise on the mini-trampoline."

Thank you for bearing with me during this long final chapter about meditating on the Word of God. I pray that these five chapters on Scripture meditation have been a blessing to you. I believe these chapters are the heart of this book. I do not believe we can be transformed into God's image and receive an outpouring of God's wisdom without saturating ourselves continually in His living Word.

Chapter 21

We Can Release God's Wisdom through Our Mouths

We have learned what the holy Scriptures say about getting the Word of God up off the printed pages of the Bible into our minds. We have learned what the holy Scriptures say about getting the Word of God from our minds down into our hearts. In this chapter we will learn about the importance of the Word of God flowing continually from our hearts out of our mouths.

One of the most significant passages of Scripture we have been studying begins by explaining the importance of speaking God's Word constantly. We have seen that Joshua 1:8, the foundation of our teaching on meditating on the Word of God, begins with the words, "This Book of the Law shall not depart out of your mouth..."

If we want to grow and mature in the Lord, we must understand that we are able to release immense spiritual power by the words we speak. Our words are so important that they actually can cause life or death. "Death and life are in the power of the tongue, and they who indulge in it shall eat the fruit of it [for death or life]" (Proverbs 18:21).

God, in His wisdom, only created human beings with the ability to express the thoughts in their minds and the beliefs of their hearts with their mouths. The words we speak are so important that we can be spiritually imprisoned or set free by these words. Jesus Christ said, "...by your words you will be justified and acquitted, and by your words you will be condemned and sentenced" (Matthew 12:37).

Even though our spoken words are very powerful, we must understand that we *cannot* control our tongues through sheer willpower. "...the human tongue can be tamed by no man. It is a restless (undisciplined, irreconcilable) evil, full of deadly poison" (James 3:8).

At one time or another we all have had the experience of hearing words come out of our mouths that we immediately wished we had not said. If the words that we speak are as important as the Bible says they are, *how* can we control these words?

The Word of God says that the key to the words that come out of our mouths is what we truly believe deep down in our hearts. Jesus explained this principle when He said, "...out of the fullness (the overflow, the superabundance) of the heart the mouth speaks. The good man from his inner good treasure flings forth good things, and the evil man out of his inner evil storehouse flings forth evil things" (Matthew 12:34-35).

Whenever we are in a crisis situation, the words that come out of our mouths will always reveal whatever we truly believe deep in our hearts. The supernatural power of the Word of God will flow out of our mouths continually if we have obeyed our Father's instructions to fill our hearts to overflowing with the holy Scriptures.

Our words are spiritual containers that have the ability to release immense spiritual power. Since the Word of God is the wisdom of God, we can see that the wisdom of God can be released out of our mouths in direct proportion to the amount of God's Word that lives in our hearts.

We have seen the scriptural relationship that exists between the words we speak and what we truly believe deep in our hearts. This spiritual principle of our heartfelt beliefs controlling the words that come out of our mouths is very important. This principle can be used to significantly affect the quality of our lives from the time that Jesus Christ becomes our Savior until we go to heaven. "...The Word (God's message in Christ) is near you, on your lips and in your heart; that is, the Word (the message, the basis and object) of faith ..." (Romans 10:8).

This passage of Scripture explains that the Word of God in our hearts and our mouths is the basis of our faith in God. Let's look again at a passage of Scripture we studied in a previous chapter "...if you acknowledge and confess with your lips that Jesus is Lord and in your heart believe (adhere to, trust in, and rely on the truth) that God raised Him from the dead, you will be saved. For with the heart a person believes (adheres to, trusts in, and relies on Christ) and so is justified (declared righteous, acceptable to God), and with the mouth he confesses (declares openly and speaks out freely his faith) and confirms [his] salvation" (Romans 10:9-10).

We must understand that we cannot go to heaven when we die through good works because all human beings, with the exception of Jesus Christ, are sinners (see Romans 3:10 and Romans 3:23). We cannot receive eternal salvation until we open our mouths and acknowledge that we are sinners. We must repent of our sins if we desire to live eternally in heaven (see Luke 13:5).

Jesus Christ became sin for us (see II Corinthians 5:21). He died a horrible death on a cross at Calvary to pay the price for the sins of every person. God then raised Jesus from the dead. We cannot be saved unless we believe in our hearts and confess with our mouths that Jesus Christ came down from heaven to take the sins of all mankind upon Himself (see John 1:29).

We are justified and made righteous before God when we believe in our hearts that Jesus Christ paid the price for our sins. We then must open our mouths to confirm our salvation by openly declaring our faith in the sacrifice Jesus Christ made for us and our assurance that God raised Him from death. This *same* principle of believing in our hearts and speaking what we believe with our mouths should be manifested throughout the remainder of our lives on earth as evidence of our unwavering faith in Almighty God.

We can see additional examples of believing in our hearts and speaking what we believe with our mouths in both the Old Testament and the New Testament. The psalmist said, "I believed (trusted in, relied on, and clung to my God), and therefore have I spoken…" (Psalm 116:10). The apostle Paul repeated this thought when he said, "…I have believed, and therefore have I spoken…" (II Corinthians 4:13).

Our Father wants words of faith from hearts that are filled to overflowing with His precious promises to continually pour out of our mouths. Our Father will rejoice when the words we speak come from hearts that are filled with the power and the wisdom of His Word just as King Solomon rejoiced when his son spoke words of wisdom. "My son, if your heart is wise, my heart will be glad, even mine; yes, my heart will rejoice when your lips speak right things" (Proverbs 23:15-16).

The apostle Paul warned Timothy against speaking words that have no eternal significance. The precious privilege we have been given to speak words with our mouths can lead us away from God just as these words can lead us toward God. Paul said, "...avoid all empty (vain, useless, idle) talk, for it will lead people into more and more ungodliness" (II Timothy 2:16).

Many people speak thousands of words each day that have absolutely no eternal significance. They speak "empty, vain, useless and idle words." A majority of the words that we speak throughout every day of our lives should be eternally significant because these words should flow out of the abundance of God's Word living in our hearts. Our hearts will be filled with spiritual treasure if we have paid the price over a period of years of filling our hearts with the Word of God through continual meditation.

We all have been given the opportunity to deposit large amounts of God's Word into our minds and our hearts. Unfortunately, many Christians fail to take advantage of this privilege that has been given to us by our loving Father. If we have taken full advantage of this precious opportunity, the words that come out of our mouths will line up with God's Word. The cumulative effect of these words of faith spoken over a period of years will change the quality of our lives to a much greater degree than most of us can ever begin to comprehend.

Christians who obey God's instructions to renew their minds daily in His Word and to meditate on the holy Scriptures throughout the day and night will find an increasing flow of God's wisdom and power pouring out of their mouths. Our Father gives us increased understanding and comprehension when we meditate continually on His Word. "My mouth shall speak wisdom; and the meditation of my heart shall be understanding" (Psalm 49:3).

The Word of God is much greater than any earthly treasure. We are speaking the most precious words we could possibly speak when our spoken words line up with God's Word. "There is gold, and a multitude of pearls, but the lips of knowledge are a vase of preciousness [the most precious of all]" (Proverbs 20:15).

The Bible explains the contrast between the words of believers whose minds and hearts are filled with God's Word and the words of unbelievers who do not have this solid spiritual foundation. "The words of a wise man's mouth are gracious and win him favor, but the lips of a fool consume him. The beginning of the words of his mouth is foolishness, and the end of his talk is wicked madness. A fool also multiplies words..." (Ecclesiastes 10:12-14).

We will receive favor from God if we speak words of wisdom that come out of minds and hearts that are filled with God's Word. If we speak foolish words that have no spiritual significance, we will be consumed by these words. We must not make the mistake of speaking many foolish words that have absolutely no eternal significance.

We can see an example of God's wisdom operating in the lives of mature believers by the way we yield our mouths and our emotions to the Holy Spirit when we are tempted to be angry. Immature people allow their anger to pour out of their mouths. Mature Christians who are wise in the Lord are able to restrain their anger. "A [self-confident] fool utters all his anger, but a wise man holds it back and stills it" (Proverbs 29:11).

Angry words "pour fuel on the fire" of a relationship between people. If we are wise in the ways of God, we will speak softly when someone is angry with us. A situation that could be very volatile will immediately become calm if we respond to angry words with a soft voice. "A soft answer turns away wrath, but grievous words stir up anger" (Proverbs 15:1).

We have learned a lot about the wisdom of God. We now are ready to see what the Word of God has to say about receiving wisdom from God in direct proportion to our faith in God.

Chapter 22

The Wisdom of God and Our Faith in God

All of us who faithfully and consistently obey our Father's instructions to feed His Word into our eyes, our ears, our minds, our hearts and our mouths will find that our faith in God will increase significantly as a result. We should pay this price on a daily basis if we truly want to receive manifestation of God's wisdom in our lives. The holy Scriptures explain that a definite relationship exists between receiving wisdom from God and our faith in God.

In the first chapter of this book I purposely referred to James 1:5 without including verses 6-8. At that time I was merely trying to explain the theme passage of Scripture for this book. We saw then that our Father promises to give His wisdom liberally to any of His children who ask for it.

If we read on after this promise, we will find that this promise from God is a *conditional* promise. If we truly desire to receive wisdom from God, we are required to meet specific conditions in regard to our faith in God. In this chapter we will examine what James 1:6-8 says about the relationship between our faith in God and receiving the wisdom of God that has been placed within us. We now are ready to look at all four of the verses in James 1:5-8 together:

"If any of you is deficient in wisdom, let him ask of the giving God [Who gives] to everyone liberally and ungrudgingly, without reproaching or faultfinding, and it will be given him. Only it must be in faith that he asks with no wavering (no hesitating, no doubting). For the one who wavers (hesitates, doubts) is like the billowing surge out at sea that is blown hither and thither and tossed by the wind. For truly, let not such a person imagine that he will receive anything [he asks for] from the Lord, [for being as he is] a man of two minds (hesitating, dubious, irresolute), [he is] unstable and unreliable and uncertain about everything [he thinks, feels, decides]" (James 1:5-8).

As we look at this portion of Scripture in its entirety, we should briefly review some biblical principles that we covered in the first chapter of this book. First, please underline or highlight the words "any of you" in James 1:5. Personalize this promise. Know that God is referring to *you*.

If you are faced with a difficult problem, ask God with faith for His wisdom. You can be certain that your Father will give His wisdom to "everyone liberally and ungrudgingly." Know that this word "everyone" includes *you*.

As we have discussed previously, God gives the precious gift of His wisdom to "everyone without reproaching or faultfinding." Our Father puts no restrictions on receiving His wisdom. He wants to give His wisdom to every one of His children regardless of any personal shortcomings we have or mistakes we have made.

Even though our Father gives us this all-inclusive promise, we must not think we are worthy of receiving His wisdom. We did not earn the wisdom of God. We do not deserve the wisdom of God. Jesus Christ paid the full price for us to receive God's wisdom. Our Father has offered to give us His wisdom because He loves us.

Immediately after God's promise that we have just reviewed in James 1:5, the next verse begins with the conditional word "only." If we want to receive God's wisdom, we can *only* receive His wisdom "in faith with absolutely no wavering, hesitating or doubting." *We must know that wavering faith will block us from receiving the precious wisdom from God that has been made available to us.*

If our faith wavers, we are told that we should "not imagine that we will receive anything from the Lord." Our Father doesn't want us to doubt Him at any time. Our Father wants us to be absolutely certain that He means exactly what He says when He promises to give us His wisdom.

If we waver, hesitate or doubt, we are told that we will be like a "billowing surge out at sea that is blown hither and thither and tossed by the wind." Our Father wants our faith in Him to be steady and consistent *regardless of the circumstances in our lives.* We are told that anyone who is "a man of two minds" (someone who goes back and forth between faith in God and doubt and unbelief) should not expect to receive wisdom from God.

Our Father wants us to be unwavering in our faith that He will give us His wisdom. Instead of being "unstable and uncertain," our Father wants our faith in Him to be firm, stable and unwavering. If our faith does waver, our Father wants us to repent of this lack of faith and to ask Him for forgiveness. We then should begin once again to consistently express our unwavering faith in God by our words and by our actions.

Our Father doesn't want us to wonder if He will give us His wisdom (or anything else He promises to give to us). He doesn't want us to merely hope He will give us His wisdom. He wants us to *know* absolutely and unequivocally that He will give us His wisdom.

None of us would openly call our Father a liar. If we know that God has definitely promised to give us His wisdom, do our words and our actions in a crisis situation clearly indicate that we unequivocally believe this promise? If our words and actions indicate that we do not believe God will keep His promise to give us His wisdom, don't these words and actions actually indicate that we believe God is a liar? "...He who does not believe God [in this way] has made Him out to be and represented Him as a liar..." (I John 5:10).

If you are a parent, wouldn't you be deeply concerned if you promised to do something for one of your children and your child's reaction to your promise showed that he or she thought you were a liar? Our heavenly Father is no different. He wants us to pay the price of studying and meditating on His Word daily so that we will know exactly what He has promised to do for us. He wants us to believe each of His precious promises with unwavering faith in His reliability.

The Word of God, speaking about the unbelieving Israelites in the desert, explained why they failed to receive manifestation of the promises God made to them. "...the message they heard did not benefit them, because it was not mixed with faith (with the leaning of the entire personality on God in absolute trust and confidence in His power, wisdom, and goodness)..." (Hebrews 4:2).

We must understand that we can only benefit from the promises our Father makes to us if we receive these promises with deep and unwavering faith. The amplification of this passage of Scripture defines faith as "the leaning of the entire personality on God with absolute trust and confidence in His power, wisdom and goodness."

This excellent definition of faith clearly indicates that our Father does not want our faith in Him to waver at any time. We see a good example of unwavering faith by observing Abraham's reaction when God told him when he was almost one hundred years old that his elderly wife was going to have a baby. Even though Abraham could not intellectually comprehend that a woman of that age could have a baby, his faith in God did not waver:

"He did not weaken in faith when he considered the [utter] impotence of his own body, which was as good as dead because he was about a hundred years old, or [when he considered] the barrenness of Sarah's [deadened] womb. No unbelief or distrust made him waver (doubtingly question) concerning the promise of God, but he grew strong and was empowered by faith as he gave praise and glory to God, fully satisfied and assured that God was able and mighty to keep His word and to do what He had promised" (Romans 4:19-21).

Our Father doesn't want our faith in Him to be weak just because we face a seemingly impossible situation. He doesn't want our faith in Him to waver because of doubt and unbelief. If our Father says He will do something, we should know that He always does exactly what He promises to do.

We should be absolutely certain that our Father will keep His promises, regardless of the seeming difficulty of any circumstances we face. God's promises are *much more powerful* than *any* problems in our lives. Our Father wants us to react to every circumstance with absolute and unwavering faith in Him. He wants us to praise Him and give Him glory because we honor Him and because we trust Him completely.

Our Father wants us to be single-minded in regard to our faith in Him. He tells us exactly what He wants us to do so that we will be single-minded in our faith. "Let your eyes look right on [with fixed purpose], and let your gaze be straight before you. Consider well the path of your feet, and let all your ways be established and ordered aright. Turn not aside to the right hand or to the left; remove your foot from evil" (Proverbs 4:25-27).

When we are faced with difficult problems, our Father does not want us to focus on these problems. He wants us to look straight ahead at all times instead of dwelling on the problems we face. He doesn't want us to turn to the right. He doesn't want us to turn to the left. He wants us to keep moving forward because we trust Him completely.

God tells each of us to remove our feet from evil. If we are not single-minded and if we don't keep moving straight ahead, we give Satan's demons an opportunity to come into our minds in an attempt to weaken our faith in God. "Leave no [such] room or foothold for the devil [give no opportunity to him]" (Ephesians 4:27).

Now that we have examined what the Bible says about being single-minded in regard to our faith in God, we are ready to learn the relationship between justification before God and our faith in God. We become justified before God when we ask Jesus Christ to be our Savior. When we are justified before God, we are treated by God just as if we had never sinned.

We have seen that God often emphasizes the spiritual principles He wants us to understand through the use of repetition. Consider the repeated emphasis in the following four passages of Scripture:

"...the [rigidly] just and the [uncompromisingly] righteous man shall live by his faith and in his faithfulness" (Habakkuk 2:4).

"...The man who through faith is just and upright shall live and shall live by faith" (Romans 1:17).

"...The man in right standing with God [the just, the righteous] shall live by and out of faith..." (Galatians 3:11).

"...the just shall live by faith [My righteous servant shall live by his conviction respecting man's relationship to God and divine things, and holy fervor born of faith and conjoined with it]; and if he draws back and shrinks in fear, My soul has no delight or pleasure in him" (Hebrews 10:38).

Our Father places a very high priority on our faith in Him. There is absolutely no doubt that our Father wants us to *live our lives with unwavering faith in Him*. Our Father is pleased when our faith in Him is tested to see if it is real and it is found to be so.

When we are faced with difficult problems and our faith in God is tested, we must understand that our faith in God is much more precious to Him than gold is to people on earth. "...you may be distressed by trials and suffer temptations, so that [the genuineness] of your faith may be tested, [your faith] which is infinitely more precious than the perishable gold which is tested and purified by fire..." (I Peter 1:6-7).

Our Father has not put any limitations on the availability of His wisdom to each of His beloved children. Any limitation to receiving the wisdom of God has to be a limitation that *we set* either through lack of knowledge of God's promise in James 1:5 or through lack of deep and unwavering faith in the reliability of this promise. If we pray with unwavering and persevering faith based upon God's specific promise to give us wisdom, we can be absolutely assured that our Father will honor this request if we really believe He will keep this promise. Jesus Christ said, "...it shall be done for you as you have believed..." (Matthew 8:13).

The power of Almighty God is the greatest power in the universe. As great as God's power is, we must understand that *we actually are able to block the mighty power of God through doubt and unbelief.* We can see the truth of this remarkable statement by looking at the following example in the life of Jesus Christ.

Jesus was brought up in the town of Nazareth. He lived in Nazareth for many years. We know that Jesus was a loving person because God is love. We can assume that He loved everyone in His home town. As Jesus traveled around the countryside healing multitudes of people, He must have looked forward with great anticipation to returning to Nazareth. He must have wanted very much to lay His hands on sick people in Nazareth to give them the great miracles of healing that so many other people received.

However, when Jesus returned to Nazareth He was not treated with awe and respect. "...on the Sabbath He began to teach in the synagogue; and many who listened to Him were utterly astonished, saying, Where did this Man acquire all this? What is the wisdom [the broad and full intelligence which has been] given to Him? What mighty works and exhibitions of power are wrought by His hands! Is not this the Carpenter, the son of Mary and the brother of James and Joses and Judas and Simon? And are not His sisters here among us? And they took offense at Him and were hurt [that is, they disapproved of Him, and it hindered them from acknowledging His authority] and they were caused to stumble and fall" (Mark 6:2-3).

This passage of Scripture tells us that the people of Nazareth were astonished by the wisdom of Jesus Christ. Instead of receiving the blessings that flowed to people everywhere else, the people of Nazareth doubted His mighty power because He had lived among them for so many years. They failed to acknowledge His authority. We are told that they stumbled and fell as a result of their unbelieving attitude toward Jesus.

The next three verses of Scripture explain a very important spiritual truth. "...Jesus said to them, A prophet is not without honor (deference, reverence) except in his [own] country and among [his] relatives and in his [own] house. And He was not able to do even one work of power there, except that He laid His hands on a few sickly people [and] cured them. And He marveled because of their unbelief (their lack of faith in Him)..." (Mark 6:4-6).

We must not make the same mistake the people of Nazareth made. This passage of Scripture doesn't say that Jesus didn't want to perform healing miracles in Nazareth. It says that "*He was not able* to do even one work of power there." The doubt and unbelief of the people of Nazareth blocked the healing power of Jesus Christ. Jesus was amazed at the lack of faith the people in His home town had in Him.

In this book we are studying about the wisdom of God. We must not block our Father from giving us His wisdom because of doubt and unbelief. We have been assured that we can place absolute trust in every promise from God. "...Know in all your hearts and in all your souls that not one thing has failed of all the good things which the Lord your God promised concerning you. All have come to pass for you; not one thing of them has failed" (Joshua 23:14).

This emphatic statement that Joshua made to the Israelites applies to each of us today. We can be absolutely certain that none of God's promises has ever failed. Our Father always does exactly what He promises to do. "...let us seize and hold fast and retain without wavering the hope we cherish and confess and our acknowledgement of it, for He Who promised is reliable (sure) and faithful to His word" (Hebrews 10:23).

This passage of Scripture refers to eternal salvation, but this spiritual principle applies to every promise in the Word of God. We can always rely totally, completely and absolutely on every promise from God. If we are tempted to doubt that God will give us His wisdom, we should "hold fast" to our Father's promise that He will give us His wisdom.

We should open our mouths and boldly say that we know God will give us His wisdom. We must not allow our faith in this promise to waver. Our Father stands behind every one of the thousands of promises in the Bible. His integrity cannot be questioned.

We should absolutely refuse to allow any thoughts to enter our minds that are contrary to the undeniable fact that our Father has unequivocally promised to give us His wisdom. Our Father doesn't want us to make the mistake of turning away from Him because of doubt and unbelief. "...brethren, take care, lest there be in any one of you a wicked, unbelieving heart [which refuses to cleave to, trust in, and rely on Him], leading you to turn away and desert or stand aloof from the living God" (Hebrews 3:12).

In this chapter we have seen that our Father wants us to receive His wisdom with unwavering and single-minded faith in the promise He has given us. In the next chapter we will look further into the holy Scriptures to learn how to receive God's wisdom through simple childlike faith.

Chapter 23

Receive God's Wisdom With Simple Childlike Faith

We must turn away from the ways of the world if we want to receive our Father's wisdom by faith as He has instructed us to do. The world's belief system is anchored upon the sensual perception of human beings. Unsaved people react based upon what they observe through their senses. These people only believe what they can see. They "walk by sight."

Our Father wants us to do exactly the opposite. He wants us to put the circumstances in our lives in last place. He wants us to put our faith in Him in first place. "For we walk by faith [we regulate our lives and conduct ourselves by our conviction or belief respecting man's relationship to God and divine things, with trust and holy fervor; thus we walk] not by sight or appearance" (II Corinthians 5:7).

This passage of Scripture tells us that we should "walk by faith." Our Father wants every aspect of our lives to revolve around our absolute and unwavering trust in Him. We all have heard people say, "I'll believe it when I see it." This statement is exactly the opposite of what the Word of God teaches. From God's perspective, *first we believe. Then we see.*

God's ways are the opposite of the ways of the world. Sight is the enemy of faith. If we are faced with a very difficult problem that seems to have no solution, we must not focus on that problem. We will become extremely discouraged if we continually focus on the problems we face.

Instead of dwelling upon any problems, we should obey our Father's instructions to continually fill our minds and our hearts with His promises. Our Father wants the good news of His Word on the inside of us to be predominant over any bad news we receive. "...the [uncompromisingly] righteous (the upright, in right standing with God) shall be in everlasting remembrance. He shall not be afraid of evil tidings; his heart is firmly fixed, trusting (leaning on and being confident) in the Lord. His heart is established and steady, he will not be afraid..." (Psalm 112:6-8).

If we walk by sight, we very well might be "afraid of evil tidings" - the bad news we hear about a particular situation. However, if we walk by faith, our minds and our hearts will be "in everlasting remembrance" of God's promises. We will always be focused on our Father's promises if we obey His instructions to continually meditate on His Word throughout the day and night.

Our eyes, our ears, our minds, our hearts and our mouths should be so filled with powerful promises from God that we will not allow bad news to get inside of us. We should guard our hearts vigilantly (see Proverbs 4:23). Our hearts should be focused constantly upon God's indwelling presence and on

God's promises. If we do these things, our hearts will be "established and steady. We will not be afraid."

If we want to receive wisdom or any other blessing from God, every aspect of our lives should revolve around our Father's love for us, our love for Him and our unwavering faith in Him. The Bible emphatically tells us that we shouldn't rely on our human insight and understanding. "Lean on, trust in, and be confident in the Lord with all your heart and mind and do not rely on your own insight or understanding. In all your ways know, recognize, and acknowledge Him, and He will direct and make straight and plain your paths. Be not wise in your own eyes; reverently fear and worship the Lord and turn [entirely] away from evil" (Proverbs 3:5-7).

This passage of Scripture doesn't mean that we should completely throw out common sense and all of the academic and scientific knowledge we have accumulated in our lives. However, we never should allow the limitations of our human insight and understanding to come ahead of our faith in specific promises from God. We are instructed to acknowledge the Lord in all of our ways. We should always put God first and keep Him first. If we obey these instructions, our Father promises to direct our paths.

Our Father promises to do His part, but we must do our part. If we want to receive wisdom from God, we shouldn't "be wise in our own eyes." Instead of trusting in the limitations of human wisdom, we should "turn away from evil." If we refuse to give in to fear, Satan and his demons will not be able to get a foothold in our minds and our hearts. We should "reverently fear and worship the Lord" instead of being afraid of the problems we face. We have seen previously that the fear of the Lord is the starting point to receiving wisdom from God.

Our faith in God will increase if we truly fear Him and hold Him in reverent awe at all times. We can only enter into God's kingdom and receive wisdom and other blessings from our Father through simple childlike faith. Jesus said, "...whoever does not receive and accept and welcome the kingdom of God like a little child [does] positively shall not enter it at all" (Mark 10:15).

When we first become Christians, we receive our salvation by coming to God with the faith of little children. We ask Jesus Christ to be our Savior because we have simple childlike faith that He died on the cross at Calvary to pay the price for all of our sins. This same spiritual principle applies throughout our lives on earth.

If you are a parent, think of your children. If you are not a parent, think of children you have observed as they have grown up. During the first few years of children's lives, these children are completely dependent upon their parents. They look to their parents with total, complete and absolute trust that their parents will provide all of their needs.

As children grow older and reach adolescence, they usually forget how simple things were when they were little children. They begin to complicate their lives. Their growing intellectual knowledge often overrides the simple childlike trust they had in their parents when they were very young.

Faith in God requires us to return to the simplicity of our childhood. Our Father Who loves us with love that is beyond human comprehension wants us to trust Him with unwavering faith to provide manifestation of His wisdom and all of His other promises. He wants us to trust Him with the same simple trust that little children have in their loving parents.

Some of us fail to receive manifestation of God's promises because of fear. We are afraid because we know deep down inside of ourselves how weak and inadequate our limited human abilities are. We're afraid because we know that the difficult problems we face are far beyond our human ability to solve these problems. The apostle Paul said, "...for the sake of Christ, I am well pleased and take pleasure in infirmities, insults, hardships, persecutions, perplexities and distresses; for when I am weak [in human strength], then am I [truly] strong (able, powerful in divine strength)" (II Corinthians 12:10).

Instead of being afraid because of our human weakness and inadequacy, we actually are instructed to "take pleasure" in adversity. God's ways certainly are different from our ways. We should rejoice when we are faced with problems we cannot solve with our limited human abilities. We should rejoice because we know that *the mighty strength of God is available to us when our human strength and ability are woefully inadequate.*

Personalize this wonderful promise. Refuse to give in to doubt and unbelief because of any human weakness and inadequacy you have. The power, ability and wisdom of Almighty God are available to every child of God through faith in God. The power of God will guard us if we have unwavering faith in God. The Bible speaks of Christians "...who are being guarded (garrisoned) by God's power through [your] faith..." (I Peter 1:5).

Our Father wants us to turn away from our problems. He promises to bless us if we take refuge in Him because we trust Him completely. "...blessed (happy, fortunate, and to be envied) are all those who seek refuge and put their trust in Him!" (Psalm 2:12).

Please underline or highlight the word "all" in this passage of Scripture. Personalize this promise. Know that the word "all" in this promise applies to *you.* Know that your faith in God will bring you into God's glory. Jesus said, "...Did I not tell you and promise you that if you would believe and rely on Me, you would see the glory of God?" (John 11:40).

Every problem in our lives gives us an opportunity to trust God. When we are in a crisis situation, our Father wants us to refuse to give up because we believe wholeheartedly that He can and will give us the answers we have to have.

Our Father always wants to help us. He has assured us that He will never desert us when we are faced with difficult problems. "...He [God] Himself has said, I will not in any way fail you nor give you up nor leave you without support. [I will] not, [I will] not, [I will] not in any degree leave you helpless nor forsake nor let [you] down (relax My hold on you)! [Assuredly not!]" (Hebrews 13:5).

Repeat this powerful promise again and again and again. Speak this promise boldly. Refuse to give up. Our Father has promised that He will never fail us or leave us without His support. The amplification of this promise repeats the words "I will not" three times to emphasize that God will never leave us. We can place complete faith in God.

Now that we have laid a spiritual foundation to receive the wisdom of God through our faith in God, we are ready to learn about receiving revelation knowledge from the Holy Spirit. Because of the price that Jesus Christ paid for us at Calvary, we are not limited to the sense knowledge that unsaved people have to depend upon. I believe you will be very excited about the information you are about to read pertaining to the magnificent revelation knowledge that is available by faith to every one of God's children.

Chapter 24

We Can Receive Revelation Knowledge from the Holy Spirit

Christians who live in these last days before Jesus Christ returns should learn how to receive the spiritual knowledge, wisdom, guidance and understanding that is available to us. I believe that we receive spiritual knowledge by studying the Word of God. I believe that we are able to tap into God's wisdom, guidance and understanding when we meditate continually on the holy Scriptures. I believe that we need the solid foundation of minds and hearts that are filled with the Word of God to receive revelation knowledge from the Holy Spirit.

I believe that knowledge of God without receiving revelation from the Holy Spirit can be compared to owning a powerful automobile without possessing the key that is required to turn on the ignition. I believe that a heart filled with the Word of God is an important spiritual "key" that we must have to consistently and effectively receive revelation knowledge from the Holy Spirit.

Before we are born spiritually we receive worldly knowledge through our senses. When we are born spiritually we are given the spiritual capacity to receive revelation knowledge from the Holy Spirit. The Holy Spirit wants to reveal revelation knowledge to us that transcends our senses. When the Holy Spirit reveals these great spiritual truths to us, this process is similar to turning on a light. We are able to see truths that were there all the time, but we could not see them before.

We see an example of the manifestation of revelation knowledge when Jesus Christ asked His disciples who people thought He was. "...they answered, Some say John the Baptist; others say Elijah; and others Jeremiah or one of the prophets" (Matthew 16:14). Jesus then asked a question that could only be answered by revelation knowledge. "He said to them, but who do you [yourselves] say that I am?" (Matthew 16:15).

At that very moment God spoke the answer to this question into the heart of Simon Peter. God told Peter that Jesus was His beloved Son. "Simon Peter replied, You are the Christ, the Son of the living God" (Matthew 16:16).

Jesus immediately responded by telling Peter that He had just received knowledge that was not the flesh and blood knowledge that is available to us through our senses. "Then Jesus answered him, Blessed (happy, fortunate, and to be envied) are you, Simon Bar-Jonah. For flesh and blood [men] have not revealed this to you, but My Father Who is in heaven" (Matthew 16:17).

We can learn about revelation knowledge by studying the Bible to see how Jesus Christ received revelation knowledge during His earthly ministry. Although Jesus was and is the Son of God, He conducted His earthly ministry as the Son of Man. The four gospels are filled with references to the Son of Man such as "...Foxes have holes and the birds of the air have lodging places, but the Son of Man has nowhere to lay His head" (Matthew 8:20).

Jesus did not perform any miracles until after He received the Holy Spirit. We must understand that Jesus Christ did not do what He did during His earthly ministry only because He was the Son of God. He did what He did because He came to earth as the Son of Man who received revelation knowledge from the same Holy Spirit Who will give us revelation knowledge today.

The earthly ministry of Jesus Christ began when John the Baptist received revelation knowledge pertaining to Jesus. When John the Baptist saw Jesus for the first time, he immediately knew that God had sent Him to earth to pay the price for the sins of the world. "The next day John saw Jesus coming to him and said, Look! There is the Lamb of God, Who takes away the sin of the world!" (John 1:29).

John the Baptist could not have known through his senses that the man who approached him on the bank of the Jordan River was Jesus Christ. His eyes and his ears could not give him this information. John only knew this great spiritual truth because he received it as revelation knowledge from God.

Shortly after that, John the Baptist actually saw the Holy Spirit descend from heaven to live in the heart of Jesus Christ throughout His earthly ministry. John said, "...I have seen the Spirit descending as a dove out of heaven, and it dwelt on Him [never to depart]" (John 1:32).

Jesus began to perform magnificent miracles shortly after John the Baptist saw the Holy Spirit enter into Him. These miracles continued throughout His earthly ministry. As Jesus neared the end of His earthly ministry, He knew that His disciples would need guidance from the Holy Spirit after He ascended into heaven. Because of this knowledge, Jesus told His disciples that it was *good* for them that He was going away.

This statement couldn't have made any sense to the disciples. From their perspective they couldn't understand how they could possibly benefit if Jesus left them. Jesus explained why it was beneficial to His disciples for Him to leave them. He said, "...it is profitable (good, expedient, advantageous) for you that I go away. Because if I do not go away, the Comforter (Counselor, Helper, Advocate, Intercessor, Strengthener, Standby) will not come to you [into close fellowship with you]; but if I go away, I will send Him to you [to be in close fellowship with you]" (John 16:7).

Jesus explained that, after He went away, the Holy Spirit would come to them to be with them. The amplification of this passage of Scripture explains the many different benefits the Holy Spirit is able to provide for us. He is referred to as our "Counselor, Helper, Advocate, Intercessor, Strengthener and Standby."

The same Holy Spirit Who was made available to the disciples of Jesus Christ is available to all of God's children today. We became children of God when we were born spiritually. Our Father loves us so much that He has made provision for the Holy Spirit to live in our hearts. "...because you [really] are [His] sons, God has sent the [Holy] Spirit of His Son into our hearts, crying, Abba (Father)! Father!" (Galatians 4:6).

The Holy Spirit gives us the ability to know that God truly is our loving Father. The word "Abba" in this passage of Scripture is similar to the word "Daddy" in the English language.

The Holy Spirit comes to life inside of us when we receive Jesus Christ as our Savior.

Refuse to complicate this statement of fact. *Know* by faith that *you* have the Holy Spirit living in your heart because the Word of God says that you do. Jesus Christ confirms the fact that the Holy Spirit lives in your heart. Jesus spoke of "The Spirit of Truth, Whom the world cannot receive (welcome, take to its heart), because it does not see Him or know and recognize Him. But you know and recognize Him, for He lives with you [constantly] and will be in you" (John 14:17).

Unbelievers cannot receive the Holy Spirit. They "do not see Him, know Him or recognize Him." All Christians are given the ability to "know and recognize" the Holy Spirit. We can learn how to hear His voice. He is "the Spirit of Truth" and we can hear Him speaking to us when our hearts are filled with the Truth of God's Word (see John 17:17).

Earthly parents have a desire to give good gifts to their children. We are assured that our heavenly Father will give the gift of the Holy Spirit to every one of His children who asks Him for this gift. Jesus said, "If you then, evil as you are, know how to give good gifts [gifts that are to their advantage] to your children, how much more will your heavenly Father give the Holy Spirit to those who ask and continue to ask Him!" (Luke 11:13).

We have just seen three passages of Scripture that promise *you* that the Holy Spirit lives within you. Receive the power of the Holy Spirit in your life by faith. We live in the last days before Jesus Christ returns. Our Father has promised a huge outpouring of the Holy Spirit during these last days. "And it shall come to pass in the last days, God declares, that I will pour out of My Spirit upon all mankind..." (Acts 2:17).

We are able to receive tremendous power from the Holy Spirit when we know by faith that He lives inside of us. I believe that the words "power, ability, efficiency and might" in the following passage of Scripture include the knowledge, wisdom, guidance and understanding from God that are available to us from the Holy Spirit. "...you shall receive power (ability, efficiency, and might) when the Holy Spirit has come upon you, and you shall be My witnesses in Jerusalem and all Judea and Samaria and to the ends (the very bounds) of the earth" (Acts 1:8).

The Holy Spirit hasn't changed since this passage of Scripture was written. He is available to every Christian today by faith. I pray that you, dear reader, will live yielded to God through the Holy Spirit Who resides in you. I pray that the Holy Spirit will light a fire in you that will transform your life.

We live in uncertain times. Many people are concerned about the future. The Holy Spirit knows what will happen in the future. He knows exactly what we should do to prepare for the future. He will tell us how to prepare for the future if we learn how to hear His voice and if we obey the instructions He gives to us.

Christians don't have to judge everything by their senses. Magnificent revelation knowledge from the Holy Spirit is available to give us the understanding we have to have. The Holy Spirit can and will guide us, help us and lead us. Now that we have studied this basic information pertaining to revelation knowledge, we are ready to learn additional facts from the Word of God. In the next chapter we will see that the Holy Spirit is our teacher. We will learn how to receive instruction from Him.

Chapter 25

The Bible Is Our Textbook and the Holy Spirit Is Our Teacher

I believe that the Holy Spirit speaks to each of us continually. We must learn how to tune in to His voice so that we can learn from Him. I believe that hearing the voice of the Holy Spirit is somewhat similar to tuning in to a radio station here on earth.

Many radio stations are broadcasting on different AM and FM frequencies in the atmosphere around us. We cannot hear at one time all of the voices that are speaking on these radio stations. However, if we want to tune in to a particular radio station, we need to tune our radio to the designated frequency of that station. We then will be able to hear the programming from that station that we couldn't hear until we tuned in to the proper frequency.

If we want to hear what the Holy Spirit is saying to us, we need to learn how to "tune in" to His voice. In several of my books and cassette tapes I have said that I believe we are able to tune in to the voice of the Holy Spirit through the "spiritual radio station, WORD." Our minds and our hearts will be filled to overflowing with the Word of God if we obey our Father's instructions over a period of time to renew our minds daily in His Word and to meditate throughout the day and night on the holy Scriptures. Jesus Christ said, "...Everyone who is of the Truth [who is a friend of the Truth, who belongs to the Truth] hears and listens to My voice" (John 18:37).

The Word of God is referred to as "the Truth" in several passages of Scripture. Jesus explained that we must be "a friend of the Truth" if we desire to hear His voice. Our minds and our hearts should be filled with the Word of God if we expect to hear His voice.

The apostle Paul explained to the Corinthians that he and the other human authors of the sixty-six books of the Bible actually were writing words that were taught to them by the Holy Spirit. Paul said, "...we are setting these truths forth in words not taught by human wisdom but taught by the [Holy] Spirit, combining and interpreting spiritual truths with spiritual language [to those who possess the Holy Spirit]" (I Corinthians 2:13).

This passage of Scripture tells us that the human authors of the Bible were given anointed words that were written for Christians - "those who possess the Holy Spirit." We saw in the last chapter that all children of God have the Holy Spirit.

All Christians have been give the ability to hear the voice of the Holy Spirit, but many Christians do not understand how to hear what the Holy Spirit is saying to them. I believe Christians whose hearts are filled with the Word of God as the result of continual meditation will find that they are able to tune in to the voice of the Holy Spirit. The Author of the

Word of God Who lives in their hearts will enable them to hear His voice speaking to them.

The Bible is our Book of Instructions. The Holy Spirit is our Teacher. Our Father wants each of us to attend the School of the Holy Spirit daily. The Holy Spirit wants to reveal great spiritual truths to each of us in our hearts. Our hearts are His classroom.

Every day of our lives we should voluntarily "go to school" to receive the wonderful revelation knowledge from the Holy Spirit that our Father has made available to each of His beloved children. The Holy Spirit is ready, willing and able to teach us throughout every day of our lives.

In addition to using the Word of God as His textbook, the Holy Spirit can teach us from the circumstances that take place in our lives by giving us revelation knowledge pertaining to these circumstances. The Holy Spirit also anoints human teachers and preachers so that we can learn from them as they speak to us under His anointing.

Our Father watches over each of His children throughout every day of our lives. He knows where every person on earth is at all times. He knows exactly what each of His children needs to learn from Him. He will teach us everything we need to know. "I [the Lord] will instruct you and teach you in the way you should go; I will counsel you with My eye upon you" (Psalm 32:8).

We have seen that the Holy Spirit is the Comforter Who was sent to take the place of Jesus Christ with His disciples. Jesus explained to His disciples that the Comforter would teach them everything they needed to know just as He had taught them throughout His earthly ministry. Jesus said, "...the Comforter (Counselor, Helper, Intercessor, Advocate, Strengthener,

Standby), the Holy Spirit, Whom the Father will send in My name [in My place, to represent Me and act on My behalf], He will teach you all things..." (John 14:26).

Unfortunately, many Christians have absolutely no awareness of the constant outpouring of teaching that is available to them from the greatest Teacher in the universe Who lives in their hearts. We make a big mistake if we fail to take full advantage of the precious opportunity we have been given to learn from the teaching of the Holy Spirit.

Many Christians unknowingly fall far below the level of revelation knowledge that is available to them. They make the mistake of trying to do by themselves with their limited human abilities what can and should be done in them and through them under the guidance of the Holy Spirit.

We must not make the mistake of limiting the One Who knows no limits. Our Father wants each of His children to be filled with the Holy Spirit. We aren't filled with the Holy Spirit on an occasional basis. The infilling of the Holy Spirit is a continual process. We should "...ever be filled and stimulated with the [Holy] Spirit" (Ephesians 5:18).

The word "ever" in this passage of Scripture indicates that we should constantly be filled with the Holy Spirit. *How* are we filled with the Holy Spirit? I believe we are filled with the Holy Spirit to the degree we are *empty of self*. Instead of pursuing selfish goals, our Father wants us to humbly, fearfully, willingly and continually yield control of our lives to the Holy Spirit.

The Holy Spirit will never force Himself upon us. He wants to control our lives, but we must continually of our own free will make the decision to yield control of our lives to Him. "...walk and live [habitually] in the [Holy] Spirit [responsive to and controlled and guided by the Spirit]..." (Galatians 5:16).

We would never attempt to control our lives if we could even begin to comprehend the magnitude of the wisdom, power and ability of the Holy Spirit that is available to us. We would gladly yield control of our lives to the Holy Spirit if we could see how ineffectual we are and how magnificent He is. We should trust the Holy Spirit to give us revelation knowledge throughout every day of our lives as He teaches, guides, instructs and empowers us.

We are the hands, the feet and the mouth of the Holy Spirit Who always points to Jesus Christ. The Holy Spirit is inside of us to empower us to carry out God's plan for our lives. He will use us as His vessels if we will constantly turn to Him for revelation and guidance by submitting humbly to Him and trusting completely in Him.

In the next chapter we'll study the holy Scriptures in detail to see how the Holy Spirit actually will speak through our mouths. He will speak through us if we yield our mouths to Him with faith that He will fill them with words that are infinitely superior to any words we can speak out of the limitations of our human understanding.

Chapter 26

The Holy Spirit Will Speak Through Our Mouths

When God created us He gave us minds to think with, hearts to believe with and mouths to speak with. Our Creator didn't give these capabilities to any of the other creatures He created. Our Father wants us to use our minds, our hearts and our mouths for His glory. He has made provision to speak through our mouths to the degree we will yield our mouths to Him because we have absolute faith that He will speak through us.

The Bible is filled with numerous examples of this spiritual principle. We see an example of God speaking through a man when Moses went to God to express apprehension of his ability to speak eloquently. "…Moses said to the Lord, O Lord, I am not eloquent or a man of words, neither before nor since You have spoken to Your servant; for I am slow of speech and have a heavy and awkward tongue" (Exodus 4:10).

Moses felt totally incapable of leading the people he was called to lead. He knew that he had many shortcomings. The Lord assured Moses that He would be with him and that He would teach him what to say. He said, "Now therefore go, and I will be with your mouth and will teach you what you shall say" (Exodus 4:12).

The Lord will speak through each of us today just as He spoke through Moses. When Jesus Christ sent His disciples out to minister, He warned them that men who opposed God would take them to court. Jesus said, "Be on guard against men [whose way or nature is to act in opposition to God]; for they will deliver you up to councils and flog you in their synagogues, and you will be brought before governors and kings for My sake, as a witness to bear testimony before them and to the Gentiles (the nations)" (Matthew 10:17-18).

Most of the disciples were unlearned men. They couldn't be expected to know what to say when they were brought before government leaders who were opposed to God. Jesus told His disciples that they shouldn't be anxious about what they would say. He promised that the Holy Spirit would speak through them when they needed Him. Jesus said, "...when they deliver you up, do not be anxious about how or what you are to speak; for what you are to say will be given you in that very hour and moment, for it is not you who are speaking, but the Spirit of your Father speaking through you" (Matthew 10:19-20).

In this chapter we will see several examples to show us that our Father doesn't want us to worry in advance about what we are going to say. He doesn't want us to depend upon ourselves to say the right thing. He is pleased to speak through us by the Holy Spirit if we will yield our voices to Him because we trust Him to speak through us.

Our Father doesn't want us to struggle and strain as we try to figure everything out with our human intellectual ability. He wants us to have absolute faith that He will speak through us. He wants us to believe wholeheartedly that He will give us the specific words we need exactly when we need them.

Jesus warned His disciples against overpreparing. He said, "Resolve and settle it in your minds not to meditate and prepare beforehand how you are to make your defense and how you will answer. For I [Myself] will give you a mouth and such utterance and wisdom that all of your foes combined will be unable to stand against or refute..." (Luke 21:14-15).

When we are faced with a difficult situation we should never worry in advance about what we should say. Instead, we should have faith that the Lord will give us such words of wisdom that our opponents will not be able to come back with an effective response.

If we are determined to serve the Lord we can expect to find ourselves in many difficult situations where we will be asked questions we cannot answer. We can trust the Lord to speak through us. These same words of revelation that were given to Moses and to the disciples of Jesus Christ many years ago apply to us today. We should believe with simple childlike trust that the Lord will always give us the words we need to say when we need to say them.

Jesus was asked many difficult questions by the Scribes and Pharisees who often tried to trick him. Jesus invariably responded with simple and effective answers that baffled the people who questioned Him. Jesus knew that He wasn't speaking these words Himself. He said, "...What I am telling you I do not say on My own authority and of My own accord; but the Father Who lives continually in Me does the (His) works (His own miracles, deeds of power)" (John 14:10).

The Bible gives us an example of a person being given anointed words to speak when he was under severe pressure. A man named Stephen was made a disciple of Jesus Christ. After having hands laid on him, Stephen was sent out to minister. When some Jewish leaders in a synagogue disputed what he had to say, Stephen was able to respond with words of wisdom that were given to him by the Holy Spirit. "...they were not able to resist the intelligence and the wisdom and [the inspiration of] the Spirit with which and by Whom he spoke" (Acts 6:10).

Would you like to be given words of wisdom under the inspiration of the Holy Spirit when you speak? Know that the same Holy Spirit who spoke through Stephen will speak through you. The Holy Spirit can and will speak through us if we are humble and turn to Him with simple childlike trust.

We must understand that our logical, orderly and intellectual minds will not be able to give us the words we need when we are faced with a crisis situation. We can trust the Lord to give us the words we need when we require an answer that is above and beyond our human capacity to respond. His wisdom is always available to us. "The plans of the mind and orderly thinking belong to man, but from the Lord comes the [wise] answer of the tongue" (Proverbs 16:1).

No matter how gifted any of us might be, our persuasive ability cannot begin to compare to the power of the Holy Spirit. The apostle Paul told the Corinthians that he depended upon the Holy Spirit to speak persuasive words through him. Paul said, "...my language and my message were not set forth in persuasive (enticing and plausible) words of wisdom, but they were in demonstration of the [Holy] Spirit and power [a proof by the Spirit and power of God, operating on me and stirring in the minds of my hearers the most holy emotions and thus persuading them]..." (I Corinthians 2:4-5).

The apostle Paul was a gifted and talented man. Nevertheless, he didn't trust in his human ability to give him the words he needed. Paul trusted completely in the Holy Spirit to give him the words of wisdom he needed to persuade the people who were listening to him.

The ability to have the Holy Spirit speak through us is not limited to pastors, teachers, evangelists and missionaries. God will speak through any of His children who are humble, who will yield themselves to Him and have unwavering faith that He will give them the words they need.

We should open our mouths with absolute faith that the Holy Spirit will fill them with the words we need. We should start on a small scale to see that the Holy Spirit really will speak through us. I believe that, whenever we do something successfully for the first time, we can do it a second time. When we are able to do anything twice, we can keep on doing it.

Dare to believe that the Holy Spirit will speak through *your lips*. I believe an important foundation to receive the anointing of the Holy Spirit is a heart that is filled to overflowing with God's Word. Hearts that are filled with the Word of God will give us simple childlike faith that the Holy Spirit will speak to us, in us and through us.

I'd like to share a little more of the personal testimony I have given previously to explain what the Lord has done in this area in my life. As I have explained previously, I was on the verge of bankruptcy and a nervous breakdown when I became a Christian. The man who led me to Christ told me that the only way I could get out of the mess I was in was to "saturate" myself in the Word of God. I followed his instructions. I filled my mind and my heart constantly with the Word of God. I have continued to fill my mind and my heart with the Word of God since that time.

I received much more than the solution to my problems. I came to know God Himself. I came to understand that life is about much more than solving problems. It is about becoming whole and well through a relationship with our Father God through His Son, Jesus Christ.

I was asked to teach a small Bible study group only sixteen months after I became a Christian. My mind and my heart were filled with the Word of God. I was absolutely amazed to hear the words that came out of my mouth the first night I spoke to this group. I believe God gave me this anointing because I had diligently studied and meditated on His Word.

By God's grace this original group of eight people grew to thirty-five people in just a few weeks. The small conference room in our office building was inadequate. We moved four times in a little over a year to a Holiday Inn, a Sheraton hotel, a large junior high school cafeteria and a large auditorium in a high school. When we were in the high school auditorium, more than three hundred people came every Tuesday night to these Bible study classes in Manchester, New Hampshire. That original Bible study grew into a church of approximately one thousand people, a large Christian school and a strong missions outreach. Praise the Lord!

What God has done for me, He can and will do in your life in whatever area He has called upon you to represent Him. I cannot explain what a thrill it is to know that the Lord is speaking through me. I have repeatedly heard words come out of my mouth that I knew were being spoken through me, not by me. On many occasions I have found myself eagerly anticipating to hear what would come out of my mouth next because I knew the Lord was using me.

I don't know anything that is more satisfying and fulfilling to any Christian than to know that we are being used by the Lord. If we want the Lord to use us as His vessels, we need to get out of the way and trust Him. I believe that the primary requirements for being used by the Lord are to stay close to Him on a daily basis, to fill our minds and our hearts continually with His Word, to always be humble and teachable and to have simple childlike trust that He will speak through us and use us in any way He desires.

If you will step out in faith, I believe you will find that the Holy Spirit will speak through you. You may find that you start slowly but, if you are humble and if you persevere with faith, I believe you will be deeply touched by what the Lord will do through you that you cannot possibly do by yourself.

As this process continues over a period of time, I believe you will find that the ministry the Lord has given you will continue to grow. When we are used by the Lord a first time, a second time and a third time, and if we have a deep, sincere and humble desire to continue to be used by Him, He will use us repeatedly to carry out His assignment for our lives.

Pray continually asking the Lord to use you and to anoint you. Dedicate your life to sincerely and humbly desiring to serve Him in whatever area He has called you to serve Him. Readily admit that you do not have the ability to do yourself what you are trusting the Lord to do through you.

I cannot contemplate ever writing, preparing to teach or giving advice to another person without first praying to God asking for the anointing of the Holy Spirit. I know how inadequate I am. I know that I will fall flat on my face if I try to do myself what only can be done if the Holy Spirit does it through me.

On thousands of occasions over the years I have opened my mouth and humbly and faithfully asked the Lord to give me the words I needed at that particular time. Every chapter of every book I write is written in this way. I have taught over 900 Bible study classes. Each time I have prayed as I have prepared Bible studies and as I taught from the Word of God.

Dare to believe that the Lord will use you in spite of your human inadequacies. Once again, I want to emphasize that the Lord is looking for our availability, not our human abilities. Go back through this chapter and carefully meditate on the Scripture references. Step out in faith and believe that the Lord will use you. Praise the Lord.

This chapter has been longer than usual because my testimony was added to the Scripture references that clearly indicate what the Holy Spirit will do through us if we humbly yield to Him and trust in Him with simple childlike faith. The next chapter is the longest chapter in this book because it is filled with many exciting additional testimonies of the Holy Spirit giving magnificent guidance to several different people.

Chapter 27

We Can Receive Continual Guidance from the Holy Spirit

The same Holy Spirit Who will speak through our mouths when our words are insufficient also is available to guide us in many other areas. Those of us who are earthly parents have guided our children while they were growing up. We should believe that our heavenly Father also wants to provide guidance for each of His beloved children.

God created us. He knew that we would be faced with many situations where we would need His guidance. Guidance from the Holy Spirit is available to us when we need to make difficult decisions and our human understanding is inadequate. Our Father has provided guidance for us in decisions concerning our families, our ministry, our occupations, our health and every other area of our lives.

In this chapter we will study several specific promises from the Word of God pertaining to the guidance that has been provided for us. However, this guidance from God is not automatic. We must learn how to yield to God to receive this guidance. We must have strong and unwavering faith that God will give us this guidance.

God has provided guidance for other living creatures. God has guided salmon to know exactly when to spawn in fresh water and when to live in salt water. He teaches birds how to build nests and when and where they should go during a period of migration. "Is it by your wisdom [Job] that the hawk soars and stretches her wings toward the south [as winter approaches]? Does the eagle mount up at your command and make his nest on [a] high [inaccessible place]? On the cliff he dwells and remains securely, upon the point of the rock and the stronghold. From there he spies out the prey; and his eyes see it afar off" (Job 39:26-29).

Birds don't need a calendar. God gives certain species of birds the guidance they need to know when winter is approaching and they should fly to the south. God shows eagles exactly where to make nests so they can feed their eaglets. If God gives this guidance to birds, fish and animals, *can't we trust Him to provide the guidance we need in our lives?*

Our Father created us to love Him, to serve Him and to obey Him. He is omnipotent, omniscient and omnipresent. There is no better guidance than the guidance that is available to us from God Who has all power, Who knows everything and Who can be in an infinite number of different places at the same time.

I believe the guidance we are able to receive from God is enhanced by the amount of God's Word that lives in our minds and in our hearts. When the psalmist prayed for guidance from God, he asked for guidance from His Word. He said, "Establish my steps and direct them by [means of] Your word..." (Psalm 119:133).

We have seen that God has instructed us to renew our minds in His Word daily. We have seen that God has instructed us to meditate on the holy Scriptures throughout the day and night. Doesn't it make sense that Christians who obey these specific instructions from God will be able to hear God's voice more clearly than Christians who fail to obey these instructions?

Our Father wants us to learn how to hear His voice. He doesn't want us to be deceived by the voices of Satan and his demons. Our Father wants us to make decisions that are biblically sound. If we sincerely want to receive the guidance our Father has provided for us, we should fill our minds and our hearts with His Word so that we can clearly see the path He wants us to follow. "Your word is a lamp to my feet and a light to my path" (Psalm 119:105).

Our ministry, Lamplight Ministries, Inc., is founded upon this passage of Scripture. Our Father has given us a "lamp" to shine light on the path He wants us to follow throughout our lives on earth. This lamp is the Book of Instructions our Father has given to us to tell us exactly how He wants us to live our lives. Our Father also has put the Holy Spirit in us to guide us to obey His instructions. "...I will put My Spirit within you and cause you to walk in My statutes, and you shall heed My ordinances and do them" (Ezekiel 36:27).

God has plans for us that require supernatural power. If we yield control of our lives to the Holy Spirit, He will control our lives to the degree that we let go, one step at a time, one day at a time. "If we live by the [Holy] Spirit, let us also walk by the Spirit. [If by the Holy Spirit we have our life in God, let us go forward walking in line, our conduct controlled by the Spirit]" (Galatians 5:25).

God will be God throughout eternity. He will guide us continually right up until the day we die and go to be with Him in heaven. "For this God is our God forever and ever; He will be our guide [even] until death" (Psalm 48:14).

We have seen that the Word of God is referred to as "the Truth" (see John 17:17). The Holy Spirit is referred to as "the Spirit of Truth." When our minds and our hearts are filled with the Word of God, we have provided an excellent foundation to receive guidance from the Spirit of Truth. Just before His crucifixion Jesus Christ said, "...when He, the Spirit of Truth (the Truth-giving Spirit) comes, He will guide you into all the Truth (the whole, full Truth)..." (John 16:13).

Jesus spoke these words to explain to His disciples that they would continue to receive guidance after He was crucified. The same guidance that was provided by the Holy Spirit to the disciples of Jesus Christ is available to each of us today. We know if we truly are God's children if we willingly allow ourselves to be guided by the Holy Spirit. "...all who are led by the Spirit of God are sons of God" (Romans 8:14).

When we learn how to tune in to the voice of the Spirit of God, we often will hear Him speaking softly to us. He will say such things as, "Do this." "Do that." "Go here." "Go there." "Turn right." "Turn left." "...your ears will hear a word behind you, saying, This is the way; walk in it, when you turn to the right hand and when you turn to the left" (Isaiah 30:21).

In the Old Testament guidance from the Lord on this occasion was referred to by saying that we would "hear a word behind us." In the New Testament this same principle applies except that we are told that we will hear a voice within us telling us exactly what we should do.

I first became aware of these spiritual principles pertaining to guidance shortly after I became a Christian. At that time I read a book titled *God's Smuggler* by Brother Andrew with John and Elizabeth Sherill (Spire Books, Copyright 1967). In this book I was thrilled to read many true stories about the activities of Brother Andrew, a missionary from Holland. Brother Andrew served behind the Iron Curtain that divided the free world from Communist countries at that time.

I read about a trip that Brother Andrew took to Yugoslavia to meet with a Christian leader. When Brother Andrew arrived in the town where this man lived, he found that the man had moved from his previous address. Brother Andrew was in a Communist country where he knew no one and did not speak the language. What could he do?

God knew exactly what to do. The Christian leader Brother Andrew was looking for had previously received a letter telling him that Brother Andrew was coming. At the very moment that Brother Andrew was looking for him, God led this man to return to the apartment building where he used to live. This man did what God told him to do. He met Brother Andrew and, even though they had never met, they each knew the other person. They left together to do what God had called them to do.

This book is filled with many other exciting stories about the guidance Brother Andrew received from God. On several occasions God "made seeing eyes blind" as Brother Andrew was able to bring suitcases filled with Bibles and tracts through checkpoints at the Iron Curtain where his luggage was inspected.

On another occasion Brother Andrew went to a church in Moscow to meet a man who would receive some Bibles Brother Andrew had smuggled into Russia. When Brother Andrew arrived at the church where he was instructed to go, he found about twelve hundred people attending an evening service. He looked into one face after another asking God for guidance.

God ultimately showed Brother Andrew the man He wanted him to see. This man had been told by God in a dream to go to this church in Moscow. He obeyed God's instruction. He was rewarded for his faith by receiving the Bibles God had provided for his church.

I was a new Christian at the time I read this book. I was thrilled and greatly encouraged by what I read. Several years later I read a similar book, *Mission Possible,* by Hans Kristian with Dave Hunt (MP Publications, copyright 1975). This book told the story of Hans Kristian, a man from Denmark, who also smuggled Bibles behind the Iron Curtain. The book is filled with thrilling true stories of God guiding Hans Kristian when he faced seemingly impossible situations in Communist countries.

One story that particularly impressed me told about Hans Kristian and another man trying to find an underground church in Romania to deliver money to the pastor of this church. The only information they had was the street address of this church. They attempted to find the street on a map, but they were unable to understand their Romanian map.

Just as their situation seemed to be hopeless, a young lady came up to the two men and asked if she could help them. They were suspicious because they thought she might be a Communist. They told her the name of the street they were looking for. She asked what number they were looking for on that street. Hans Kristian at first refused to give her the street address. He suddenly felt led of the Lord to give her the number, so he did.

The woman immediately explained that she was praying at home and the Lord told her where to go to lead two men to her church. She obeyed these instructions. She knew these were the men she was looking for because they gave her the street address of her church. She then led them to the meeting place that didn't look any different from the buildings surrounding it. The men were able to give the funds to the pastor because of the supernatural guidance this woman received from the Lord.

This book also is filled with other remarkable stories of guidance from God. *God's Smuggler* and *Mission Possible* probably are out of print today. I can tell you, though, that these two books had a tremendous effect upon me when I read them.

As I was writing this chapter my wife, Judy, and I happened to have dinner with Norwegian evangelist, Rolf Auke, and his wife, Ann. Judy knew what I was writing in this chapter. She asked Rolf if he had ever had an experience where God spoke to him to give him specific guidance.

Rolf told us about an event that happened when he was fifteen years old. He had recently asked Jesus Christ to be his Savior. Rolf lived in Drammen, Norway at that time. One cold winter night, God awakened Rolf at 3:00 a.m. God told him to get out of bed and to walk down to the railroad station. Rolf hesitated because the weather was so cold, but he was certain that God had spoken to him. He was too young to drive an automobile. He got up, dressed warmly and walked to the railroad station.

Just before Rolf got to the railroad station he crossed a bridge where a man was standing. Rolf stopped to talk to this man. The man told him that his wife had kicked him out of their home a few days earlier. The man had been sleeping in his car. He was so discouraged by the problems with his marriage and with the extremely cold weather that he had decided to jump off the bridge that night to take his life.

Rolf knew then why God had awakened him. He encouraged the man. Rolf shared Jesus Christ with him. The man did not jump off the bridge. Instead, when Rolf explained the gospel, the man received Jesus Christ as his Savior. This man then faithfully attended the same church that Rolf attended.

God honored Rolf's obedience. Rolf began preaching in his church at the age of fifteen. He became a traveling evangelist at the age of seventeen. Since that time, Rolf has traveled all over the world as an evangelist. He also has founded a Christian church, a Bible college and a Christian radio station.

I personally have received guidance from God on many occasions over the years. I never attempt to make a decision without praying to God for guidance. My wife, Judy, also has had many similar experiences of receiving guidance from the Lord. I'd like to share one of these experiences with you.

Four years ago Judy was attending a missions conference at a local church. Judy had a luncheon ticket for each day of the conference. She normally enjoyed going to lunch because she shared our publications with many missionaries from all over the world. On this particular day Judy felt led of the Lord to skip lunch. She walked out into the parking lot in front of the church.

At this very moment a man drove an automobile into the church parking lot. He got out and walked over to Judy. Judy asked if he was from India. He said that he was. They began to talk. He told her that his name was Rev. Ebenezer Moses. He said he was just leaving Florida to attend a Christian seminar in Dallas, Texas.

Rev. Ebenezer said that he was driving down a street and the Lord impressed upon him to turn right into the driveway of the church he was passing. He turned right just as Isaiah 30:21 says we should do. There is no question that Ebenezer Moses and Judy Hartman met by divine appointment in front of that church.

As they talked, Judy asked Eb if she could pray for him. Eb said he would like her to pray. Judy was very impressed with Eb's humble demeanor and his sincere desire to serve the Lord. She gave him a copy of our book, *Trust God For Your Finances.* Judy also felt led of the Lord to give Eb $200.

Eb had not said anything to Judy about his financial need. She found out later that he had no money to go to Texas. He only had his airline ticket. He was trusting the Lord completely to provide the remaining money he needed.

In addition to the money she gave Eb, Judy looked at our ministry mailing list to find someone who lived in the Dallas area. She called a man she did not know. This man was led of the Lord to be hospitable to Eb. He also provided additional financial assistance after Eb arrived in Dallas.

Judy wrote down Eb's address, his telephone number and his email address. They have stayed in touch since then by mail, telephone and email. This initial meeting set into action a remarkable series of events that were unquestionably orchestrated by the Lord.

Shortly after Judy met Eb I taught a series of classes at the River Bible Institute in Tampa, Florida. At the beginning of the first class I handed out some reference material on our ministry to each student. This material included a current copy of our newsletter, *The Lamplighter*. In this particular issue Judy had written about Rev. Ebenezer Moses. She suggested to readers of the newsletter that anyone who was interested in India could contact Rev. Ebenezer. She included his address and telephone number in the newsletter.

One of the students in the class was Jim Eilers. Neither Judy or I knew Jim at that time. We later found out that Jim had been led of the Lord to sell his farm in Illinois to move to Florida. Shortly after arriving in Florida Jim enrolled as a student in the River Bible Institute.

Jim knew he was called to be an evangelist. He was interested in India. When he saw what Judy had written in our newsletter, Jim picked up his telephone and called Eb in India. We knew nothing about this telephone call until Judy received an email from Eb asking if she knew Jim Eilers who had called him.

We subsequently met Jim and his wife, Robin. We were impressed by the calling of the Lord upon their lives. Several times after that first meeting we went out to eat after church with Jim, Robin and their children. We often talked about the common interest we all had to reach around the world to serve the Lord.

At that time Jim was just starting as an evangelist. Lamplight Ministries has been used as a bridge to connect Jim with crusades in Russia, Zambia and India. Approximately two years after Judy and Eb met in the church parking lot Judy joined Jim and Robin and their son, Nicholas, on a missionary trip to India.

God moved in a mighty way as Jim, Eb, Robin, Judy and other team members conducted a series of crusades. More than ten thousand people accepted Jesus Christ as their Savior during the five night crusade. The Lord performed mighty healing miracles each night of the crusade.

A four year old girl who had been crippled since birth walked for the first time. Several blind people testified that they were able to see. A deaf boy said that he was able to hear. Each night of the crusade approximately twenty to twenty-five people stood in line to give testimonies of the miraculous healing they had received. Praise the Lord!

Since that time Jim has gone back to India for another crusade with Eb. Thousands of additional people gave their lives to Christ. Many other healing miracles were reported.

Rev. Ebenezer was impressed with my book, *Trust God For Your Finances,* that Judy gave him when they first met. He translated this book into the Tamil dialect of southern India. Lamplight Ministries was able to provide the funds to print five thousand copies of *Trust God For Your Finances* in the Tamil dialect.

Eb is the founder of the India Gospel Fellowship and the Shepherd's Council of India. He has distributed free copies of *Trust God For Your Finances* to many pastors who are members of the Shepherd's Council. These pastors in turn teach these biblical principles pertaining to finances to members of their churches. Judy returned to India recently to speak through an interpreter at a pastors' conference on the subject of God's financial instructions. These pastors had just received their free copies of the translation of *Trust God For Your Finances.*

Isn't God awesome? Because He told Eb to turn into a driveway, Judy to skip lunch and to walk outside of the church and Jim to sell his farm in Illinois and move to Florida, the stage was set for the Lord to move in many different ways to change the eternal destiny of tens of thousands of people. Praise the Lord!

I believe the preceding illustrations have given you practical examples of the guidance of the Holy Spirit. He will give us specific and exact guidance when we need it. Dare to believe that the Holy Spirit will guide *you* just as He has guided the people you have just read about.

When we were little children we felt secure when our parents guided us across a busy street by holding one of our hands and showing us exactly how to proceed. This same principle applies to each of us today. The psalmist explained how God held his hand to guide him. He said, "...I am continually with You; You do hold my right hand. You will guide me with Your counsel..." (Psalm 73:23-24).

Our loving Father wants each of us to believe that He will hold one of our hands today just as He held the hand of the psalmist many years ago. He wants us to be absolutely certain that He is always with us. He wants us to trust Him for guidance the same way that little children trust their loving parents.

When we were little children and we fell down, our parents often picked us up. The Lord will help us today when we fall. "The steps of a [good] man are directed and established by the Lord when He delights in his way [and He busies Himself with his every step]. Though he falls, he shall not be utterly cast down, for the Lord grasps his hand in support and upholds him" (Psalm 37:23-24).

Personalize this promise from the Lord. Believe totally, completely and absolutely that the Lord will direct your steps when He is delighted because you are doing your best to live a life of uncompromising righteousness. The Lord promises to busy Himself with every step you take. Know that the Lord will reach down and pull you up if you fall. Receive by faith the wonderful guidance and help the Lord promises to those who trust Him and obey His instructions.

Our Father wants us to willingly yield control of our lives to the Holy Spirit Who lives in our hearts. He wants us to allow the Holy Spirit to control our lives. "...you are not living the life of the flesh, you are living the life of the Spirit, if the [Holy] Spirit of God [really] dwells within you [directs and controls you]..." (Romans 8:9).

I pray that the Scripture references and the testimonies in this long chapter have encouraged you to trust the Lord completely to guide you as you seek to find and carry out His plan for your life. Our hearts must be right before God if we truly want to receive guidance from the Holy Spirit. In the next chapter we will look into God's Word to see what it says about the relationship between the condition of our hearts and receiving guidance from the Holy Spirit.

Chapter 28

Our Hearts Are the Key to Receiving Guidance from God

The Bible compares us to sheep. Sheep in a flock listen continually for the voice of their shepherd. Jesus Christ is our Shepherd. Jesus said, "...they will listen to My voice and heed My call..." (John 10:16).

Unfortunately, some Christians fail to hear the Lord's voice. If we do not hear the voice of the Lord we fail to receive a tremendous blessing that has been made available to us. In this chapter we will discuss exactly what we should do if we have a deep and sincere desire to hear the Lord's voice continually.

Once we understand that we have been given the opportunity to hear God's voice, we should have a fervent desire to hear God speak to us. Once again, I want to emphasize that I believe a direct relationship exists between the amount of God's Word living in our hearts and our ability to hear God's voice.

We have seen previously that Jesus Christ said, "...Your Word is Truth" (John 17:17). Jesus explained the relationship between loving the Truth of God's Word and hearing His voice. Jesus said, "...Everyone who is of the Truth [who is a friend of the Truth, who belongs to the Truth] hears and listens to My voice" (John 18:37).

Please underline or highlight the word "everyone" in this passage of Scripture. Believe that Jesus Christ is speaking to *you*. Are you "a friend of the Truth?" Have you faithfully obeyed God's instructions to renew your mind daily in His Word (see Romans 12: 2, II Corinthians 4:16 and Ephesians 4:23)? Have you obeyed God's instructions to meditate continually on the holy Scriptures (see Joshua 1:8 and Psalm 1:2-3)? If you can't answer these questions affirmatively, are you now willing to pay the price to renew your mind in God's Word daily and to meditate continually on the holy Scriptures?

Some Christians are complacent. They don't have a deep and sincere desire to hear God's voice. They don't "saturate" themselves in the Word of God on a daily basis. Our Father wants us to hear what He has to say to us, but first we must learn how to hear His voice.

Some of us fail to hear God's voice because we are so preoccupied with worldly activities that we fail to set aside precious time each day to be alone with the Lord. I believe we are able to hear God's voice when we are humble and teachable and when we obey our Father's instructions to live in His presence daily and to study and meditate continually on His Word. We will miss the opportunity to hear God's voice if we fail to spend precious quiet time alone with Him each day.

I believe that revelation knowledge from God bypasses our minds and comes directly to our hearts. We have seen that we fill our hearts with God's Word by meditating continually on the holy Scriptures. I have heard accounts of people in Third World countries who have no Bibles who heard from God. However, I believe that the ability for people to receive revelation knowledge from God is significantly increased by turning away from all of the distractions that are caused by the pull of the world to meditate constantly on the holy Scriptures.

Once we begin to actually receive revelation knowledge from God we will understand wonderful spiritual truths that were previously hidden from us. As God gives us continued revelation our awareness of His presence will increase. We'll yearn to turn away even more from the superficial things of the world to draw closer to God.

The Bible teaches us that our hearts are the key to our lives. Our Father wants us to be very careful about what we allow to come into our hearts. "Keep and guard your heart with all vigilance and above all that you guard, for out of it flow the springs of life" (Proverbs 4:23).

The words "the springs of life" refer to everything that comes from God to us through the Holy Spirit. Our Father wants us to live our lives from the inside out. Most unsaved people and immature Christians are externally oriented. They live their lives from the outside in. They are more concerned with people, places, things and events than they are with the spiritual condition of their hearts. "...the Lord sees not as man sees; for man looks on the outward appearance, but the Lord looks on the heart" (I Samuel 16:7).

Our Father doesn't see things from the same perspective that human beings do. Many of us are unduly concerned about our physical appearance, the clothes we wear and the impression we hope to make on other people. Although many people focus on external appearance, the Lord looks at our hearts.

God says that true beauty is "...the inward adorning and beauty of the hidden person of the heart..." (I Peter 3:4).

We have seen that we have been given the ability to feed upon the Word of God. The "hidden person of the heart" is the "real us" – who we truly are deep down inside of ourselves. The hidden person of the heart needs spiritual food just as much as our bodies need natural food. Our bodies are fed with food that goes into our mouths. The "hidden person of the heart" is fed with spiritual food that goes into our eyes and our ears as a result of continually feeding ourselves the Word of God through constant study and meditation.

We will be spiritually malnourished if we fail to feed the Word of God into our minds and our hearts on a regular and consistent basis. We won't be able to hear the Holy Spirit giving us revelation knowledge if we fail to nourish ourselves continually with the wonderful spiritual food God has provided for the "hidden person of the heart."

We cannot hear God's voice if we do not live in expectation of His unlimited power at work in our lives. "...What eye has not seen and ear has not heard and has not entered into the heart of man, [all that] God has prepared (made and keeps ready) for those who love Him [who hold Him in affectionate reverence, promptly obeying Him and gratefully recognizing the benefits He has bestowed]" (I Corinthians 2:9).

This passage of Scripture explains that no human being can grasp everything our Father wants to reveal to His grateful children who love Him wholeheartedly, revere Him continually and sincerely desire to obey His instructions. We can only comprehend these great spiritual truths as the Holy Spirit reveals them to us. "Yet to us God has unveiled and revealed them by and through His Spirit, for the [Holy] Spirit searches diligently, exploring and examining everything, even sounding the profound and bottomless things of God [the divine counsels and things hidden and beyond man's scrutiny]. For what person perceives (knows and understands) what passes through a man's thoughts except the man's own spirit within him? Just so no one discerns (comes to know and comprehend) the thoughts of God except the Spirit of God" (I Corinthians 2:10-11).

The Holy Spirit lives inside of us. Christians have been given the opportunity to understand great spiritual truths that unbelievers cannot understand because the Holy Spirit will reveal these truths to us. The Holy Spirit knows everything. He is like a large and extremely effective computer, but He is much, much greater. The Holy Spirit can provide us with whatever information we need whenever we need it. He is the Spirit of Truth.

We must understand the tremendous amount of revelation knowledge that our Father has made available to us through the Holy Spirit. The Bible tells us that God is able to "...grant you a spirit of wisdom and revelation [of insight into mysteries and secrets] in the [deep and intimate] knowledge of Him, by having the eyes of your heart flooded with light..." (Ephesians 1:17-18).

Please underline or highlight the words "you" and "your" in this passage of Scripture. Personalize this promise from God. Believe that God will flood *your* heart with light as the Holy Spirit continually reveals more and more magnificent spiritual truths to *you*.

Please notice that this passage of Scripture says that God gives this revelation knowledge to our hearts. We are told that our hearts have "eyes." Our Father wants to reveal Himself to the hearts of His loving children who enjoy a close and intimate relationship with Him.

In this chapter we have seen that we will be able to hear God's voice and receive revelation knowledge from God if our hearts are properly prepared. In the next chapter I will share with you several practical concepts I have learned over the years that have helped me to receive wonderful revelation knowledge from the Holy Spirit.

Chapter 29

Practical Concepts Pertaining to Revelation Knowledge

Our Father doesn't want us to go through our lives on earth devoting our energy to pursuing selfish goals. God created us to serve Him and to serve other human beings. Jesus Christ told His disciples, "...whoever desires to be great among you must be your servant, and whoever wishes to be most important and first in rank among you must be slave of all. For even the Son of Man came not to have service rendered to Him, but to serve, and to give His life as a ransom for (instead of) many" (Mark 10:43-45).

God's ways are very different and much higher than our ways (see Isaiah 55:8-9). If we truly want to be great from God's perspective, we will devote our lives to being a servant instead of desiring to have other people serve us. We are told that we "must be slave of all." If we truly have a deep and sincere desire to serve God, our Father will speak to us constantly to give us ideas on how to serve Him effectively. I have written thousands of pages of notes from thoughts that the Holy Spirit has put into my mind over the years.

In this chapter I will share with you several practical lessons I have learned about receiving revelation knowledge from God. First, I want to emphasize that I have learned on many occasions that God often speaks to me at times when I least expect to hear from Him. Revelation knowledge cannot be coaxed or earned. God gives us revelation knowledge in His unique way and in His unique timing.

On many occasions God has dropped wonderful ideas into my mind when I was taking a shower. He has given me wonderful revelation knowledge when I had shaving lather all over my face. He has given me concepts to serve Him when I was driving my automobile. Sometimes God gives me revelation when my schedule is extremely full and I don't seem to have a minute to spare.

I have learned from experience that, when I know God is speaking to me, I must stop whatever I am doing to immediately write down what I am hearing. On numerous occasions I have stepped out of a shower to write down what God has put into my heart. Many times the shaving lather has dried on my face and I have had to lather up again because I stopped to write what I was hearing from God. I have written many notes in my automobile and at many other times and in many other places when it was not particularly convenient to write down the creative ideas I was receiving from God.

I learned many years ago that I have to have a pad and a pen with me at all times. I have pads and pens in my office, in my bedroom, in my bathroom and in my automobile. I also carry a small memo pad and a small ballpoint pen with me at all times. I am never under any circumstances in a position where I am unable to write down whatever the Holy Spirit reveals to me.

I can tell you from long experience that revelation knowledge has a very short life span. I have often found that information I received from God that seemed to be perfectly clear when I received it was hazy and fuzzy just a few minutes later. I have learned the hard way that I cannot postpone writing down what I hear. Revelation knowledge is usually only a fleeting glimpse. We cannot run the risk of losing the precious gems that God drops into our hearts.

Our Father is looking for His children who are totally receptive to Him at all times and in all places. I believe He is pleased when He sees instant responsiveness regardless of the circumstances. I believe that receiving revelation knowledge from God through the Holy Spirit is similar to popping popcorn. When revelation knowledge starts "popping," it often keeps on "popping and popping and popping." Sometimes I have written several pages of notes because I was willing to start writing immediately and I didn't stop until I had learned everything God chose to reveal to me at that particular time.

At the end of almost every day of my life I come home at night with several notes I have written at different times during the day. Each night I put all of these notes on my desk. The next day I rewrite these scribbled notes in handwriting I can read. I then file everything I have written in an appropriate place for future use.

I have received many wonderful ideas from God in the middle of the night. I wouldn't think of going to bed at night without having a blank pad and a pen next to me. Sometimes I awaken, receive a brief revelation from God, write it down and go back to sleep. On other occasions I get up in the middle of the night and go to my desk and work there for hours based upon what God is revealing to me.

I understand that many people cannot spend these hours in the middle of the night because of occupational commitments the following day. Nevertheless, I believe we should always be prepared to get at least some revelation from God if He chooses to give it to us in the middle of the night.

I also recommend to anyone who sincerely desires to receive revelation knowledge to always take a pen and pad to weekly worship services or any other Christian meeting. I would no more think of going to a Christian meeting without a pad and a pen than I would think of going to that meeting without wearing clothes. I'm not saying that everything we hear in our worship services or at Christian meetings is revelation knowledge. On the other hand, I can testify that, on hundreds of different occasions, I have received wonderful creative ideas when I heard an anointed servant of God speaking.

My friend, Charlie Jones, who has spoken to thousands of audiences all over the world, once said, "Don't write down what I say. Write down what you think as a result of what I say." I have followed Charlie's advice many times over the years.

On several different occasions I have listened to anointed speakers and I have written down exactly what they said. However, at other times I have found that what a particular speaker said stimulated me to write down something that was quite different from what that person said. I have often found that the anointing of speakers stimulates an entirely different revelation from the Holy Spirit to me.

I believe that taking notes whenever we listen to a speaker causes us to focus and to listen better. Our minds won't wander if we write down all of the thoughts that come to us as a result of what a person is saying. Almost every week I leave our church with many different notes that have proven to be extremely beneficial to me over a period of time.

I believe that God honors this kind of dedication and commitment. I am always surprised when I go to a Christian meeting to see how few people come prepared to take notes. I believe we should always have a strong attitude of expectancy that we will hear from God. We must not block the receipt of knowledge from God by limiting Him in any way as to the time, place or source of revelation He chooses to give us.

If we truly desire to receive revelation from God, we should be in His presence as often as possible. I have found that praise and worship often leads to receiving revelation knowledge from God. When we continually open our mouths and sing words of praise and thanksgiving to the Lord, we are able to come into His presence and to hear Him more clearly when He speaks to us. "Make a joyful noise to the Lord, all you lands! Serve the Lord with gladness! Come before His presence with singing!" (Psalm 100:1-2).

In addition, whenever I am looking for revelation knowledge in any specific area, I read many Christian books pertaining to that subject. I also listen to as many anointed cassette tapes as I can. I have never written a book without reading dozens of books and listening to a large number of cassette tapes pertaining to the subject I feel led to write upon.

Thomas Edison once said, "When I want to discover something, I begin by reading everything that has been done along that line in the past. I see what has been accomplished at great labor and expense in the past. I gather the data of many thousands of experiments as the starting point, and then I make several thousand more."

On another occasion this man who had over one thousand patents to his credit said, "I'm a good sponge. I absorb ideas from every source I can and put them to practical use. Then I improve on them until they become of some value. The ideas which I use are mostly the ideas of other people who don't develop them themselves."

I have saved tens of thousands of different notes that I have taken from many sources over the years. I have categorized these notes into hundreds of different alphabetical subheadings. I have more than twenty large drawers in file cabinets that are filled to overflowing with hanging folders that are crammed full of material I have put in them from every conceivable source.

I never throw anything away that I perceive to be of value. When I'm writing a book or a set of Scripture cards, I often find applicable notes that I put into a file twenty or more years ago. On several occasions I have found these notes to be the foundation for revelation knowledge that God unfolds more completely to me many years later. It only takes a few minutes each day to file this material. I have found again and again that the wonderful reservoir of material I have accumulated over the years has been invaluable to me.

I also want to share with you another concept that has been very effective for me. The times when I seem to receive the most revelation from God are immediately after I awaken from sleep, while I am exercising or immediately after I finish exercising. As I explained in detail in our book, *Increased Energy And Vitality,* I have walked a total of over fifteen thousand miles during the past thirty years. I love to walk briskly and I do this several times each week.

Vigorous exercise draws blood away from our brains and circulates it throughout our bodies. This exercise produces endorphins which are chemicals that produce a sense of well-being. I have found that the rhythmic gait of walking is very relaxing to me. I have written thousands of notes on what I heard from God while I was exercising and immediately after I finished exercising.

Finally, I would recommend that anyone who wants to receive continual revelation from the Lord should, if possible, have a specific room where that person regularly spends time with the Lord. For the first thirteen years I was a Christian I received more revelation from God in a small office in my home in New Hampshire than I did in all other places combined. I can say the same thing about an office in a bedroom in our home in Florida where I have spent thousands of precious hours alone with the Lord.

I know that our Father is pleased with His children who constantly turn to Him for revelation. I believe that God honors our persistent desire for continual revelation by giving us even more revelation. Jesus Christ explained this spiritual principle when He said, "...to everyone who has will more be given, and he will be furnished richly so that he will have an abundance..." (Matthew 25:29).

We all are different. In this chapter I have shared several thoughts about how I receive revelation knowledge from God. I hope that some of these concepts are of value to you. In the next chapter we will look into the Word of God for additional information about receiving wonderful revelation knowledge from God.

Chapter 30

Everything We Will Ever Need Has Been Put Inside of Us

When we ask Jesus Christ to be our Savior, God puts so much inside of us that we cannot even begin to comprehend all that is within us. This book is written on the subject of wisdom and knowledge so this chapter will explain what the Bible says about the wisdom and knowledge God has placed within us.

In addition to wisdom and knowledge, God also has put within each of His children all of the strength, ability, power, peace, joy, love, compassion and every other quality we will need to be completely successful from His perspective. Please study and meditate carefully on the Scripture references in this chapter so that you will learn exactly what the Word of God says about the wisdom, the knowledge and the other wonderful qualities your Father has put within you.

Parents here on earth who really love their children do their very best to provide these children with everything they need to live a good and successful life. Our heavenly Father loves us with a love that is much greater than the greatest love any human parents have ever had for any of their children. Because of His love for us, our Father has provided us with everything we will ever need throughout our lives on earth. "...His divine power has bestowed upon us all things that [are requisite and suited] to life and godliness, through the [full, personal] knowledge of Him Who called us by and to His own glory and excellence (virtue)" (II Peter 1:3).

Please underline or highlight the words "all things" in this passage of Scripture. These two words are all-inclusive. They include wisdom, knowledge, understanding, guidance and every other attribute we will need to live a godly life. We were given the ability to receive all of these attributes when Jesus Christ became our Savior.

Our Father has called each of us to excellence. He wants us to live godly lives throughout the time we spend here on earth. We are able to make withdrawals from the bountiful treasure He has placed within us as we continually yield control of our lives to Him.

We must understand that our needs are met from the inside out, not from the outside in. God didn't keep anything in heaven that we will need here on earth. At the moment we received Jesus Christ as our Savior, our loving Father deposited His entire kingdom into our hearts.

When Jesus was asked by the Pharisees when the kingdom of God would come, He replied by saying, "...The kingdom of God does not come with signs to be observed or with visible display, nor will people say, Look! Here [it is]! or, See, [it is] there! For behold, the kingdom of God is within you [in your hearts] and among you [surrounding you]" (Luke 17:20-22).

Jesus said that the kingdom of God cannot be seen with our human eyesight because the kingdom of God is within us. Please underline or highlight the word "you" in this passage of Scripture. Know that the kingdom of God is *within you.* God has placed His kingdom in our hearts and all around us.

Our Father has personally taken up residence in the hearts of every one of His children. The same Almighty God Who sits on His throne in heaven also took up residence in our hearts when we chose to receive His Son, the Messiah. "One God and Father of [us] all, Who is above all [Sovereign over all], pervading all and [living] in [us] all" (Ephesians 4:6).

We must remove any limitations about God that are predicated upon our limited human understanding. Yes, Almighty God sits on His throne in heaven where He is sovereign over everything. However, God is omnipresent. He is everywhere. God can be on His throne in heaven and at the same time live in the hearts of every one of His children on earth.

Know that your loving Father lives in your heart. Know that His wisdom, His knowledge, His guidance and His understanding are available to you all day long throughout every day of your life. Why would any of us ever look on the outside of ourselves for anything we need if we are absolutely certain that our loving Father lives in our hearts?

Our Father didn't stop there. We also must understand that the same Jesus Christ Who walked the shores of Galilee, performed great miracles, died for our sins and rose from the dead lives in the heart of every person who trusts Him as his or her Savior. Jesus Christ is omnipresent. He sits on a throne in heaven next to the throne of His Father. At the same time Jesus is able to live in the heart of every Christian.

As we grow and mature as Christians, we will be certain that Jesus Christ lives in our hearts. As the months and years go by we should have a continually increasing awareness that Jesus Christ lives in our hearts. "...Do you not yourselves realize and know [thoroughly by an ever-increasing experience] that Jesus Christ is in you...?" (II Corinthians 13:5).

If you are a Christian you can be absolutely certain that Jesus Christ lives in your heart. Every aspect of our lives should be centered around the indwelling Christ. We should be conscious throughout every day of our lives that our beloved Savior really does live inside of us.

We have seen on several occasions in this book that the Holy Spirit lives in us. God has given us the Holy Spirit as His wonderful gift to us. "Do you not know that your body is the temple (the very sanctuary) of the Holy Spirit Who lives within you, Whom you have received [as a Gift] from God?..." (I Corinthians 6:19).

We should have a continual consciousness that God the Father, God the Son and God the Holy Spirit live in our hearts. "...in Him the whole fullness of Deity (the Godhead) continues to dwell in bodily form [giving complete expression of the divine nature]. And you are in Him, made full and having come to fullness of life [in Christ you too are filled with the Godhead – Father, Son and Holy Spirit – and reach full spiritual stature]..." (Colossians 2:9-10).

Please don't read this passage of Scripture quickly and move on. I urge you to spend some time thinking about and meditating on the magnificent spiritual truth that is given to us in the amplification of Colossians 2:9-10. We are "filled with the

Godhead – Father, Son and Holy Spirit." *God the Father, God the Son and God the Holy Spirit live in the heart of every believer.*

We are given the opportunity to "reach full spiritual stature" when we turn away from the pull of the world to allow the Godhead within us to be manifested in us and through us. We can be absolutely certain that we have spiritual power on the inside of us that is infinitely greater than thermonuclear power or any other power on earth. We must not dilute this immense power through ignorance, doubt or unbelief.

Everything that Adam lost to Satan was fully restored to us by the victory Jesus Christ won when He rose from the dead. Every aspect of the glorious victory of the Lord Jesus Christ is on the inside of every believer. We simply need to learn how to trust Jesus completely to release the awesome power of His magnificent victory that already lives on the inside of us.

Do you have a continual consciousness of the magnificent spiritual treasure God has placed inside of you? We never would allow the problems of life to defeat us if we could see these problems from God's perspective. We never would give up because we would be absolutely certain that the wisdom, power and ability of God on the inside of us are much greater than any problem we will ever face.

Why should we ever be perplexed by any problem? If God lives inside of us, His wisdom also lives inside of us. Because of the price that Jesus Christ paid at Calvary, the wisdom of God goes with us wherever we go throughout every day of our lives.

We have been given the ability to tap into God's wisdom, power and ability at any hour of any day throughout our lives on earth. Too many of God's children are struggling and straining and looking feverishly for answers on the outside of themselves without beginning to comprehend that everything they will ever need has already been placed inside of them.

This chapter is filled with magnificent truths from the holy Scriptures pertaining to the wonderful spiritual treasure your loving Father has placed inside of you. Meditate continually on these facts pertaining to the treasure you have within you because of the blood that Jesus Christ shed for you at Calvary.

Dear Father, in the name of Jesus Christ, we thank You from the bottom of our hearts for Your love for us, for Your son Jesus, for the Holy Spirit and for Your Word. Dear Lord Jesus, we thank You for the incomprehensible price You paid for us at Calvary. We thank You for the wonderful promises in Your Word that tell us about the spiritual treasures You have placed inside of us. We rejoice in the fullness of the provision You have made for us so that we can carry out Your plan for our lives for Your glory.

Chapter 31

Spiritual Maturity and the Wisdom of God

Most people crave security in this uncertain world we live in. They seek security in their occupations, in their investments, in members of their families and from other external sources. We shouldn't look for security from external sources. All of the security we will need has been provided for us by Jesus Christ.

The security that so many people crave already has been placed inside of every child of God. We will take a significant step toward spiritual maturity if we will stop searching for external sources of security.

Our security should be based upon the absolute certainty that God the Father, God the Son and God the Holy Spirit live in our hearts. Our security should be based upon the fact that the kingdom of God is in our hearts. *What more security could we possibly desire?*

Everything on the outside seems so real. The things of God can seem to be vague. Just the opposite is true. Everything in the world is temporal. Everything from God is eternal. Our Father has placed inside of us all of the eternal qualities we will need to overcome all of the temporal problems we will face throughout our lives on earth.

We must not make the mistake of being too preoccupied with external things while we place too little emphasis on what is inside of us. Jesus Christ told the Pharisees to clean themselves up on the inside and to stop paying so much attention to what they were like on the outside. Jesus said, "Woe to you, scribes and Pharisees, pretenders (hypocrites)! For you clean the outside of the cup and of the plate, but within they are full of extortion (prey, spoil, plunder) and grasping self-indulgence. You blind Pharisee! First clean the inside of the cup and of the plate, so that the outside may be clean also. Woe to you, scribes and Pharisees, pretenders (hypocrites)! For you are like tombs that have been whitewashed, which look beautiful on the outside but inside are full of dead men's bones and everything impure. Just so, you also outwardly seem to people to be just and upright but inside you are full of pretense and lawlessness and iniquity" (Matthew 23:25-28).

Jesus spoke very harshly to the Pharisees. This same principle applies to us today. Some of us are too concerned with our external appearance and with the things of this world instead of living our lives from the inside out as God intends for us to live. Our Father wants our minds and our hearts to be filled to overflowing with His Word. Our Father wants us to continually surrender control of our lives to His indwelling presence so that He can live His life in us and through us.

We have seen that our hearts are the key to our lives. We have seen that our Father has instructed us to guard our hearts diligently. We should fill our hearts to overflowing with the living Word of God throughout every day of our lives. Why would we ever pass up the precious opportunity we have been given to make magnificent spiritual "deposits" into our hearts every day of our lives by meditating constantly on the holy Scriptures?

Unsaved people and immature Christians live their lives focusing primarily upon the people, places, things and events of the world they can make contact with through their senses. As we mature in the Lord, we should turn away from the way we used to think when we were immature. "When I was a child, I talked like a child, I thought like a child, I reasoned like a child; now that I have become a man, I am done with childish ways and have put them aside" (I Corinthians 13:11).

Some Christians are too comfortable. They go to church every week with the same people. They like to sit in the same seat. They usually spend a few minutes each day in prayer and Bible study. The remainder of their lives is externally oriented. They are not spiritually mature. They do not spend a significant amount of precious quiet time alone with God each day. "Brethren, do not be children [immature] in your thinking; continue to be babes in [matters of] evil, but in your minds be mature [men]" (I Corinthians 14:20).

In the world parents are concerned if their children don't grow and mature properly. Our heavenly Father is very concerned about His children who fail to grow and mature spiritually. He knows that these children will have a much more difficult time in their lives because they have not learned the things they need to learn.

Our Father wants us to turn away from immature goals. He wants us to constantly pursue His will for our lives. "Shun youthful lusts and flee from them, and aim at and pursue righteousness (all that is virtuous and good, right living, conformity to the will of God in thought, word, and deed)..." (II Timothy 2:22).

Our Father instructs us to flee from our former goals. He wants us to pursue a righteous life. Our Father wants our thoughts, words and actions to clearly indicate that we are pursuing His will for our lives.

Our Father wants us to appreciate His Word for what it is – magnificent spiritual revelation that comes to us from heaven. He wants each of His children to pay close attention to the great spiritual truths in His Word. We must not make the mistake of failing to study and meditate on the Word of God. If we do, we will miss out on the wonderful spiritual truths our Father has made available to us. "...we ought to pay much closer attention than ever to the truths that we have heard, lest in any way we drift past [them] and slip away" (Hebrews 2:1).

Our Father doesn't want us to stay in "spiritual kindergarten" throughout our lives. He wants us to progress beyond the basic teachings of Christianity. He wants us to grow continually toward the spiritual maturity that is available to each of His children. "...let us go on and get past the elementary stage in the teachings and doctrine of Christ (the Messiah), advancing steadily toward the completeness and perfection that belong to spiritual maturity..." (Hebrews 6:1).

Our Father doesn't want us to only be "Sunday Christians" who go to church every Sunday and spend just a few minutes in prayer and possibly a little time studying the Bible each day. Our Father wants us to constantly grow and mature in every area of our lives so that we will draw closer and closer to Him. "...let us grow up in every way and in all things into Him Who is the Head..." (Ephesians 4:15).

Our Father wants our minds and our hearts to be so full of His Word that Satan and his demons cannot deceive us. If our minds and our hearts are filled with the Word of God we will know how to "...keep Satan from getting the advantage over us; for we are not ignorant of his wiles and intentions" (II Corinthians 2:11).

Mature Christians know that Satan always works from the outside in and that God often works from the inside out. Satan and his demons continually attempt to use external stimuli to cause us to react in a way that is contrary to the instructions we have been given in the holy Scriptures. Satan wants us to constantly react to the circumstances in our lives. Our Father wants us to constantly react to His indwelling presence and to His Word living in our minds and in our hearts.

Many people have the wrong concept of education. They think that education means putting something on the inside from the outside. The English word "education" is derived from the Latin word "educare." The word "educare" means "to draw out." True education is based upon the concept of drawing out what has already been placed in our hearts. "Counsel in the heart of man is like water in a deep well, but a man of understanding draws it out" (Proverbs 20:5).

Our Father has provided us with wonderful spiritual counsel. We have seen that Jesus Christ referred to the Holy Spirit as our Counselor. He said, "...I will ask the Father, and He will give you another Comforter (Counselor, Helper, Intercessor, Advocate, Strengthener, and Standby) that He may remain with you forever..." (John 14:16).

If we are spiritually mature, we will learn how to draw continually from the counsel of the Holy Spirit that is available to every child of God. We should never be complacent about spiritual growth. We should understand that we cannot stand still in the area of spiritual growth and maturity.

If we constantly acquire spiritual knowledge, God promises that more spiritual knowledge will be given to us. On the other hand, if we fail to grow spiritually, the spiritual knowledge we think we have will be taken away from us. Jesus said, "Be careful therefore how you listen. For to him who has [spiritual knowledge] will more be given; and from him who does not have [spiritual knowledge], even what he thinks and guesses and supposes that he has will be taken away" (Luke 8:18).

Spiritual growth is infinite. We will never learn everything there is to learn. The more we learn, the more we will realize how much more there is to learn. The depth of God's wisdom and knowledge that is available to us is beyond the limitations of our human comprehension.

Our Father knew exactly what He was doing when He told us to renew our minds in His Word daily. He knew exactly what He was doing when He told us to meditate on the holy Scriptures throughout the day and night. Our Father doesn't want us to search for His wisdom occasionally. He wants us to hunger and thirst to continually learn everything He has made available to us.

We now are completing several chapters pertaining to receiving revelation knowledge from God. This revelation knowledge comes to us from heaven. We should place a very high priority on the opportunity we have been given to receive this precious revelation knowledge. We will not allow the things of this world to have a high priority in our lives once we know that we truly are able to receive revelation knowledge from heaven.

These revelation thoughts from God are just below the surface of our consciousness. They are easily dissipated if we are distracted by seemingly important worldly activities. Wisdom and revelation knowledge from God will be released to us if we draw close to Him for a significant period of time during every day of our lives.

Revelation knowledge cannot be taught. Revelation knowledge is "caught." In the eight chapters pertaining to revelation knowledge I have done my best to share with you what the Word of God instructs you to do to "catch" revelation knowledge in your life.

Many Christians have little or no concept of the privilege of walking in the revelation knowledge that has been made available to them. Once we begin to break through to receive revelation knowledge and see how magnificent it is, we will be highly motivated to receive still more of this wonderful knowledge from God. I pray that these chapters pertaining to revelation knowledge have helped you to have a deep and sincere desire to receive personal revelation from God so that you can learn great spiritual truths from heaven throughout the remainder of your life on earth.

We have seen the correlation between renewing our minds daily in God's Word, meditating throughout the day and night on the holy Scriptures and speaking the Word of God. The final step in this spiritual chain of events is to *do* what God's Word tells us to do. Once again, let's look at the portion of Joshua 1:8 that explains this principle. "...you shall meditate on it day and night, that you may observe and do according to all that is written in it..." (Joshua 1:8).

Our Father tells us that the desired end result of filling our minds, our hearts and our mouths with His Word is to do what He has instructed us to do. "...the word is very near you, in your mouth and in your mind and in your heart, so that you can do it" (Deuteronomy 30:14).

Isn't it interesting to see how the Word of God ties together the thoughts in our minds, the faith in our hearts, the words we speak and the things we do? We now are ready to learn what the Bible says about the relationship between obedience to God and receiving wisdom from God.

Chapter 32

Our Father Gives His Wisdom to His Obedient Children

The theme passage of Scripture of this book is James 1:5 which tells us that any child of God who lacks wisdom needs only to ask God for His wisdom and it will be given to him. We expanded this theme passage of Scripture in a subsequent chapter by adding James 1:6-8 where we are told that we should not expect to receive God's wisdom unless we ask our Father for His wisdom with single-minded, unwavering faith.

In this chapter we'll move forward in the first chapter of James. In the same chapter where we are told to ask our Father with unwavering faith for His wisdom we also are told that we must not make the mistake of listening to the Word of God without *doing* what our Father instructs us to do. "...be doers of the Word [obey the message], and not merely listeners to it, betraying yourselves [into deception by reasoning contrary to the Truth]" (James 1:22).

We give Satan and his demons an opportunity to deceive us whenever we fail to do what our Father tells us to do. Satan is able to deceive us if our reasoning and our corresponding actions do not line up with the Truth of the Word of God.

Little children here on earth will inevitably get into trouble if they fail to do what their parents tell them to do. This same principle applies to us if we fail to heed our heavenly Father's instructions. "A wise son heeds [and is the fruit of] his father's instruction and correction…" (Proverbs 13:1).

Why would we expect to receive wisdom from God if we fail to obey the specific instructions He has given us in His Book of Instructions? The Word of God explains the relationship between making wise decisions, obeying God's instructions and receiving God's blessings. "He who deals wisely and heeds [God's] word and counsel shall find good…" (Proverbs 16:20).

The Word of God repeatedly tells us that we will make wise decisions when we obey our Father's instructions. "Keep the charge of the Lord your God, walk in His ways, keep His statues, His commandments, His precepts, and His testimonies, as it is written in the Law of Moses, that you may do wisely and prosper in all that you do and wherever you turn" (I Kings 2:3).

Every Christian would like to receive the blessings of God's wisdom and to prosper in every area of life. This passage of Scripture tells us that we will make wise decisions and prosper in every area of our lives if we obey our Father's instructions. If we sincerely desire to make wise decisions and to prosper, we should study the Word of God continually to learn how our Father wants us to live our lives.

Jesus Christ explained this principle very clearly when He explained what we should do if we want to be "sensible, prudent, practical and wise." Jesus said, "...everyone who hears these words of Mine and acts upon them [obeying them] will be like a sensible (prudent, practical, wise) man who built his house upon the rock. And the rain fell and the floods came and the winds blew and beat against that house; yet it did not fall, because it had been founded on the rock" (Matthew 7:24-25).

Please underline or highlight the word "everyone" in this passage of Scripture. Know that this word includes *you.* Receive this promise as your own. Be determined to hear the Word of God continually and to obey God's instructions. Jesus said that our obedience to His instructions will cause us to be like a man who built his house upon a solid foundation of rock.

If we sincerely desire to receive wisdom or any other blessing from God, we must build our lives upon a solid, rock-like foundation of obedience to our Father's instructions. The storms of life will not cause us to fail if we do what God's Word tells us to do. We will be successful if we live our lives according to God's instructions.

Jesus went on to explain the problems we will experience if we know what God's Word says to do, but fail to obey our Father's instructions. Jesus said, "And everyone who hears these words of Mine and does not do them will be like a stupid (foolish) man who built his house upon the sand. And the rain fell and the floods came and the winds blew and beat against that house, and it fell – and great and complete was the fall of it" (Matthew 7:26-27).

Once again we see the word "everyone." This word includes *you.* We shouldn't expect to receive wisdom or anything else from our Father if we hear His instructions and *do not obey them.* Jesus said that Christians who make this mistake are like foolish people who build a house upon a foundation of sand. Christians who fail to obey God's instructions will inevitably experience a "great and complete fall" when they are faced with severe storms in their lives.

Our Father repeatedly tells us that we will be wise if we do what He says to do and that we will be stupid and foolish if we learn what He wants us to do and then fail to obey His instructions. Jesus said, "...wisdom is vindicated (shown to be true and divine) by all her children [by their life, character, and deeds]" (Luke 7:35).

We show whether we are receiving divine wisdom by our character and by the way we live. If we know what our Father tells us to do, we can only expect to receive His wisdom and other blessings if we obey His instructions. Jesus said, "If you know these things, blessed and happy and to be envied are you if you practice them [if you act accordingly and really do them]" (John 13:17).

Our Father repeatedly promises to bless us when we are obedient. If He is pleased with the way we live, He promises to give us wisdom, knowledge and joy. "...to the person who pleases Him God gives wisdom and knowledge and joy..." (Ecclesiastes 2:26).

The relationship between receiving God's wisdom and obeying God's instructions is very clear. We show if we truly love our Father to the degree that we learn and obey His instructions. "...the [true] love of God is this; that we do His commands [keep His ordinances and are mindful of His precepts and teaching]. And these orders of His are not irksome (burdensome, oppressive, or grievous)" (I John 5:3).

We show our love for our heavenly Father by doing what He tells us to do. This passage of Scripture goes on to say that God's instructions "are not irksome, burdensome, oppressive or grievous." Satan tries to make us think that we won't enjoy life if we do what God instructs us to do. Satan is a liar (see John 8:44). Our lives will be full, meaningful and enjoyable when we live the way our Father tells us to live.

Our Father wants His children to obey the following specific instructions that King Solomon gave to his son. King Solomon said, "My son, forget not my law or teaching, but let your heart keep my commandments; for length of days and years of a life [worth living] and tranquility [inward and outward and continuing through old age till death], these shall they add to you" (Proverbs 3:1-2).

We are told that we will enjoy "length of days and years of a life worth living" if we obey God's instructions. Our lives will be long, worthwhile and fulfilling if we live the way our Father instructs us to live.

This passage of Scripture also promises that God's children who obey His instructions will receive "inward and outward tranquility continuing through old age until death." *How could we ask for any greater blessing?* We all would like to experience absolute tranquility throughout the remainder of our lives right up until the day we die. Our Father promises to give us this wonderful blessing *if* we will learn and obey His instructions.

Our Father knows what is best for us. His wisdom is far superior to our limited human wisdom. We should be absolutely determined to study and meditate continually on the holy Scriptures to learn how our Father wants us to live. We then should do whatever He tells us to do. "...Whatever He says to you, do it" (John 2:5).

Our Father has made His wisdom available to each of His children. The Bible is filled with many specific instructions telling us exactly how our Father wants us to live. In addition to giving us a comprehensive Book of Instructions, our Father also has given us the Holy Spirit to be our guide.

Our Father will not reach down from heaven to make us do what He wants us to do. He has given each of us the freedom to choose how we will live our lives. We each choose whether we will serve God or whether we will ignore God's instructions because we choose to pursue our own selfish desires. "...choose for yourselves this day whom you will serve..." (Joshua 24:15).

This chapter is filled with specific facts from the Word of God showing us clearly the relationship between receiving God's wisdom and other blessings from God and obeying the instructions our Father has given us in His Book of Instructions. I pray that each person reading these Scripture references will be absolutely determined to learn God's instructions and to faithfully obey these instructions.

Chapter 33

Learn How to Pray Effectively for the Wisdom of God

The Bible instructs us to pray to God continually throughout every day of our lives. I believe that praying for God's wisdom should be one of our most frequent prayer requests. Do you have a daily prayer list? If you do, I recommend that you consider writing a reminder to pray for the wisdom of God at or near the top of this prayer list.

I have increased my prayers for God's wisdom since I started to write this book. I believe that God has answered these prayers. I pray that our loving Father will bless you, dear reader, as a result of your continual prayers for His wisdom.

I believe we should always pray for God's wisdom before we make any major decision. Jesus Christ is our example in every area of our lives. When the time came for Jesus to select His apostles, He spent an entire night praying to God. "...He went up into a mountain to pray, and spent the whole night in prayer to God. And when it was day, He summoned His disciples and selected from them twelve, whom He named apostles (special messengers)..." (Luke 6:12-13).

I can't understand why any Christian would choose a spouse, buy a home or an automobile or make any other major decision without first praying repeatedly for God's wisdom. We should never make any major decision until we have peace deep down inside of ourselves that our Father approves of this decision. I have prayed many times for God's wisdom before making a major decision. God has answered each of these prayers. Thank you, dear Father.

Our Father has promised to give us His wisdom, but we have seen that James 1:5 instructs us to *ask Him for His wisdom.* We won't receive God's wisdom automatically. Some Christians fail to receive wisdom from God simply because they do not ask their Father to give them His wisdom. "...You do not have, because you do not ask" (James 4:2).

James 1:5 is the theme Scripture for this book. We should anchor our prayers upon this specific promise whenever we ask God for wisdom. I believe we should speak this promise to God as we pray. We should freely admit that our human wisdom is inadequate. We should ask our Father to give us His wisdom. We should have absolute faith that our Father will give us His wisdom just as He has promised.

We have seen that subsequent passages of Scripture in the first chapter of James tell us that we should ask God for His wisdom with unwavering faith. Whenever we pray for God's wisdom, we should pray with absolute faith that God will answer our prayer. Jesus said, "...whatever you ask for in prayer, having faith and [really] believing, you will receive" (Matthew 21:22).

The word "whatever" in this passage of Scripture includes wisdom from God. We will see God's wisdom manifested in our lives when we combine James 1:5-7 with Matthew 21:22 and continually anchor our prayers of faith upon these passages of Scripture.

Our prayers are most effective when we have a close personal relationship with the Lord and when our hearts are filled with the purposes and promises of God. Jesus Christ said, "If you live in Me [abide vitally united to Me] and My words remain in you and continue to live in your hearts, ask whatever you will, and it shall be done for you" (John 15:7).

The words "ask what you will" include God's wisdom. Jesus tells us that we will receive an answer to this prayer. However, the word "if" at the beginning of this passage of Scripture is very important. We will receive an answer from God *if* we meet two specific conditions.

If we sincerely believe we will receive answers to our prayers for God's wisdom or any other prayer request, we will receive an answer from God if we "live in Jesus Christ and abide vitally united to Him." A close relationship with Jesus Christ is vitally important to receiving answers to our prayers.

Second, we are told that the Word of God should live continually in our hearts. I sincerely believe that constant meditation on the holy Scriptures is the spiritual "key" that unlocks the blessings of the kingdom of God. If our hearts are filled to overflowing with God's Word and if we have a close personal relationship with Jesus Christ, we have every reason to believe that our Father will give us His wisdom when we ask Him for it.

Do you ever wonder if God hears your prayers? The Word of God assures us that our Father hears our prayers whenever we pray according to His will. "...this is the confidence (the assurance, the privilege of boldness) which we have in Him: [we are sure] that if we ask anything (make any request) according to His will (in agreement with His own plan), He listens to and hears us" (I John 5:14).

A prayer for God's wisdom obviously is a prayer that is according to His will because James 1:5 instructs us to pray for God's wisdom. The Word of God and the will of God are the same. We can be absolutely assured that our Father hears us when we pray asking for His wisdom.

Because we are certain that our Father hears our prayers, we also should have absolute faith that He will answer our prayers. "And if (since) we [positively] know that He listens to us in whatever we ask, we also know [with settled and absolute knowledge] that we have [granted us as our present possessions] the requests made of Him" (I John 5:15).

This passage of Scripture tells us that our Father will "grant us as our present possessions the requests made of Him." Do the words "present possessions" mean that God will always give us His wisdom instantly whenever we pray for His wisdom? I believe that God answers our prayers of faith for His wisdom instantly in the spiritual realm. However, we often have to wait faithfully and patiently for the answer to our prayers to be manifested in the natural realm.

Isn't it wonderful to be *absolutely certain* that our Father *hears us* when we pray according to His will and to *know* that He *will* answer these prayers? I believe we should be conscious of I John 5:14-15 whenever we pray. We can always have absolute confidence that our Father hears our prayers and that He will answer our prayers whenever we pray with persevering faith for something that is in His will.

Our Father tells us that, instead of being worried and anxious about the circumstances in our lives, we should always come to Him in prayer. "Do not fret or have any anxiety about anything, but in every circumstance and in everything, by prayer and petition (definite requests), with thanksgiving, continue to make your wants known to God. And God's peace [shall be yours, that tranquil state of a soul assured of its salvation through Christ, and so fearing nothing from God and being content with its earthly lot of whatever sort that is, that peace] which transcends all understanding shall garrison and mount guard over your hearts and minds in Christ Jesus" (Philippians 4:6-7).

Why would we ever worry when we have been given the privilege of praying? *Why* would we ever worry if we are absolutely certain that our Father will answer our prayers? Instead of worrying about anything, we are told that in "every circumstance and in everything" we should pray.

Our Father wants us to come to Him in prayer whenever we have a need. He instructs us to pray "with thanksgiving." Why wouldn't we thank our Father when we pray if we truly believe He will answer our prayers? We shouldn't withhold our thanks until we actually receive the manifestation of His answer to our prayers. We should show our faith in God by thanking Him *when we pray.*

If we obey these specific instructions from God, we are told that we will receive God's peace. We will be calm, quiet and confident deep down inside of ourselves because of our certainty that our Father has answered our prayer request. The peace of God that we will receive when we pray in this way is *so magnificent that it surpasses all limitations of our human understanding.* The peace of God is so great that it actually will *guard* our minds and our hearts. Thank you, dear Father, for this wonderful promise.

We can be absolutely certain that our Father will answer our prayers for His wisdom or any other prayer request that is according to His will if we obey these specific instructions when we pray. We should pray continually for God's wisdom. "...be constant in prayer" (Romans 12:12). Our Father wants us to persevere with unwavering faith whenever we ask for His wisdom or anything else. "Be unceasing in prayer [praying perseveringly]..." (I Thessalonians 5:17).

We should never underestimate the importance of praying fervently with unwavering faith that our Father will answer our prayers. "...The earnest (heartfelt, continued) prayer of a righteous man makes tremendous power available [dynamic in its working]" (James 5:16).

Christians are righteous because Jesus Christ has paid the price for our sins that enables each of us to be righteous before God. Because of the sacrifice of Jesus Christ we have been given the privilege of approaching the throne of God with our prayers. When we pray continually with unwavering faith in God, *the tremendous, dynamic power of Almighty God is made available to us.*

Praying for God's wisdom should become such a habit that we should never go through a day without asking God for His wisdom on several different occasions. Our Father does not limit the availability of His wisdom. We have seen that He has promised to pour out His wisdom upon us abundantly. We should take God at His word. We should pray often for His wisdom with absolute faith that He will answer our prayers.

Can you imagine what would happen if all members of a particular church prayed fervently throughout every day believing that they would receive wisdom from God? I pray that several churches, as a result of reading this book, will undertake this project. If all members of a church pray continually with faith for the wisdom of God, I believe this church will be used in a mighty way by God for His glory. Please write to me if your church undertakes this project and I will join you in your prayers.

The Bible also tells us that our Father will answer our prayers when two or more of His beloved children come to Him with faith in a prayer of agreement. Jesus said, "...I tell you, if two of you on earth agree (harmonize together, make a symphony together) about whatever [anything and everything] they may ask, it will come to pass and be done for them by My Father in heaven" (Matthew 18:19).

If two or more children of God agree in faith that God will answer a specific prayer request, God promises to answer these prayers. We should pray often with other believers for "anything and everything." These all-inclusive words obviously include praying for wisdom from God. We can be certain that our Father will answer these prayers.

This chapter is filled with many spiritual truths from the Word of God in regard to praying for God's wisdom or any other prayer request. I urge you to meditate continually on these Scripture references so that your prayer life will be more effective. We now will look into God's Word to see what it says about the relationship between a close relationship with God and receiving wisdom from God.

Chapter 34

We Can Only Receive God's Wisdom if We Know Him Intimately

Our Father created us to enjoy a close and intimate relationship with Him. I don't believe we can consistently receive God's wisdom until we learn how to enter into and remain in His presence. If we truly desire a close relationship with God, we should initiate the action to come close to Him. We can be assured that our Father *will* come close to us *if* we come close to Him. "Come close to God and He will come close to you..." (James 4:8).

We have seen that *The Amplified Bible* defines the wisdom of God as "comprehensive insight into the plans and purposes of God." If we desire comprehensive insight into the plans and promises of any person, shouldn't we have a close relationship with that person? We shouldn't expect to receive comprehensive insight into our Father's plans and purposes unless we have established a close relationship with Him. "The

Lord looked down from heaven upon the children of men to see if there were any who understood, dealt wisely, and sought after God, inquiring for and of Him and requiring Him [of vital necessity]" (Psalm 14:2).

This passage of Scripture tells us that the Lord looks down from heaven searching for people "who understand Him, deal wisely, seek Him and inquire for and of Him." A close relationship with the Lord is not a "nice to have" – we are told that this close relationship is a *vital necessity*. Since this book is written primarily about the subject of receiving wisdom from God, I want to point out that this passage of Scripture emphasizes the relationship between "dealing wisely" and seeking God as a vital necessity.

We have seen that Solomon received an abundance of God's wisdom. I believe that Solomon's desire to receive God's wisdom came from the advice he received from his father, King David, about the importance of a close personal relationship with God. David said, "And you, Solomon my son, know the God of your father [have personal knowledge of Him, be acquainted with, and understand Him; appreciate, heed, and cherish Him]" … (I Chronicles 28:9).

King David emphasized the importance of a personal relationship with God. He told his son that he needed to know God personally so that he could understand Him. We will receive "insight and understanding" from God when we know Him intimately. "…the knowledge of the Holy One is insight and understanding" (Proverbs 9:10).

Our Father wants our relationship with Him to be much closer than our relationship with any human being on earth. Jesus said, "He who loves [and takes more pleasure in] father or mother more than [in] Me is not worthy of Me; and he who loves [and takes more pleasure in] son or daughter more than [in] Me is not worthy of Me..." (Matthew 10:37).

Jesus said that we aren't worthy of Him if we love our parents, our children (or anyone else) more than we love Him. Our love for Jesus Christ should be our absolute #1 priority. Nothing else should even come close. We always will be filled with love for the members of our family and for other people if we have a close relationship with Jesus Christ.

If we truly want to serve our Lord Jesus Christ, we should always put Him first ahead of anyone and anything else. Jesus said, "If anyone comes to Me and does not hate his [own] father and mother [in the sense of indifference to or relative disregard for them in comparison with his attitude toward God] and [likewise] his wife and children and brothers and sisters - [yes] and even his own life also - he cannot be My disciple" (Luke 14:26).

The word that is translated "hate" in this passage of Scripture doesn't mean the same as the word "hate" means today. This word means that we should never place a greater emphasis on a close relationship with anyone here on earth than we do on our relationship with the Lord. The amplification in this passage of Scripture says that we should have a "sense of indifference to or relative disregard for" members of our family "in comparison with our attitude toward God." We cannot be disciples for the Lord or consistently receive His wisdom and other blessings unless we always put Him in first place in our lives.

Our close relationship with the Lord should be the center of our existence. We will receive manifestation of God's strength and the ability to do great things for Him if we know Him intimately. "...the people who know their God shall prove themselves strong and shall stand firm and do exploits [for God]" (Daniel 11:32).

The Word of God tells us exactly what we should do if we want to know God intimately. "...this is how we may discern [daily, by experience] that we are coming to know Him [to perceive, recognize, understand, and become better acquainted with Him]: if we keep (bear in mind, observe, practice) His teachings (precepts, commandments)" (I John 2:3).

How can we discern on a daily basis if we truly are drawing closer to the Lord? What should we do if we have a sincere desire "to perceive, recognize, understand and become better acquainted with Him?" We are told that we will enjoy this close relationship if we obey the instructions He gives us in His Word.

Jesus Christ said that we will show how much we really love Him by filling our minds and our hearts with His instructions and by doing what He tells us to do. "The person who has My commands and keeps them is the one who [really] loves Me; and whoever [really] loves Me will be loved by My Father, and I [too] will love him and will show (reveal, manifest) Myself to him. [I will let Myself be clearly seen by him and make Myself real to him]" (John 14:21).

We will become increasingly conscious of our Father's love for us if we show our love for Jesus Christ by faithfully obeying His instructions. Jesus promises to reveal Himself to us and to make Himself real to us when we show our love for Him by doing what He has instructed us to do.

Would you like to see the Lord and enjoy a close personal relationship with Him? We are told exactly what to do if we want to enjoy this blessing. The Bible instructs us to "...pursue that consecration and holiness without which no one will [ever] see the Lord" (Hebrews 12:14).

Our lives should be consecrated and holy if we truly desire a close relationship with the Lord. A holy and a consecrated life is a life that is completely dedicated to the Lord. "...let us know (recognize, be acquainted with, and understand) Him; let us be zealous to know the Lord [to appreciate, give heed to, and cherish Him]..." (Hosea 6:3).

We are given explicit instructions that tell us exactly what to do if we want to enjoy a close relationship with the Lord and if we want to understand Him. The Lord doesn't reveal Himself to casual seekers. We should have a zealous desire to know the Lord intimately. A person who has a zealous desire to know the Lord will be absolutely focused upon attaining this wonderful goal.

We should have a deep appreciation for the opportunity we have been given to enjoy a close personal relationship with the Lord. We did not earn and we do not deserve this privilege. We must not waste this precious opportunity. We should seek the Lord wholeheartedly. We should have a deep and sincere desire to continually be in His presence. "Seek the Lord and His strength; yearn for and seek His face and to be in His presence continually!" (I Chronicles 16:11).

We shouldn't expect to receive a continual outpouring of wisdom or any other blessings from the Lord if we haven't shown a sincere and continuing desire to know Him intimately. If you would like to study and meditate on several additional Scripture references that will help you to draw closer to the Lord, you might be interested in our Scripture Meditation Cards, *A Closer Relationship With The Lord.*

I believe you will learn a great deal about enjoying a closer relationship with the Lord if you meditate continually on these Scripture references and if you listen to our eighty-five minute cassette tape that contains a great deal of information that cannot fit into the limited space of the Scripture cards. If you obey God's specific instructions for a close relationship with Him, you will see your relationship with Him deepening.

In this book we are talking specifically about receiving wisdom from God. We saw in James 1:6-8 that our Father will only give us His wisdom when we ask for His wisdom with deep and unwavering faith in Him. A definite relationship exists between our faith in God and how well we know Him.

How can we really trust God if we don't have a close relationship with Him? Which people here on earth do you trust most? Deep trust in another person invariably is based upon a close relationship with that person.

If we know the Lord intimately and if we trust Him completely, we will be very grateful for everything He has done for us. Our gratitude should be so deep and heartfelt that we will praise the Lord continually. "I will bless the Lord at all times; His praise shall continually be in my mouth" (Psalm 34:1).

We cannot know anyone on earth intimately unless we spend a great deal of time alone with that person. We can only know about them if we don't spend a lot of time alone with people. This same principle applies to our relationship with the Lord.

Unfortunately, some Christians don't really put the Lord first. They only have a surface relationship with Him. They attend church each week and they spend a little time each day in prayer, but they aren't deeply committed to the Lord throughout every day of their lives. Jesus Christ explained that the Pharisees had this type of relationship with Him. He said, "...These people [constantly] honor Me with their lips, but their hearts hold off and are far distant from Me" (Mark 7:6).

Christians who only have a distant relationship with the Lord don't yearn with all of their hearts to draw close to Him.

They don't understand that their souls will be filled with joy if they learn how to remain in the presence of the Lord. "...You will enrapture me [diffusing my soul with joy] with and in Your presence" (Acts 2:28).

Nothing on earth can compare with the tremendous blessings we will experience from a close, intimate, personal relationship with the Lord. We will enjoy this wonderful personal relationship throughout eternity when we are in heaven. Jesus Christ has provided each of us with the opportunity to experience a wonderful preview of this relationship during our lives on earth.

We must not fail to take advantage of the precious opportunity we have been given to enjoy the sweet and refreshing presence of the Lord. A close relationship with the Lord should be the first priority in our lives. *Why* would we ever allow anything or anyone to come ahead of this magnificent opportunity we have been given?

As we begin to experience the wonder of being in the presence of the Lord, we will desire to come into His presence again and again and again. We will learn how to abide in His presence with joy. We will turn away from preoccupation with the things of the world to continually draw closer to our wonderful Lord. Worldly activities that used to be very important to us will become insignificant. Nothing in this world will be more important to us than to draw closer to the Lord on a continual and ongoing basis.

In this chapter we have learned about the wonderful blessings that are available to us when we learn how to enjoy a close and intimate relationship with the Lord. In the next chapter we'll look into God's Word to see exactly what it says about being quiet before the Lord so that we can enjoy His wonderful presence to the utmost.

Chapter 35

Enjoy Times of Refreshing from the Presence of the Lord

When we are tempted to struggle with difficult problems that we face, we will find that we experience a wonderful refreshing when we turn away from these worldly concerns to enter into the glorious presence of the Lord. "...that times of refreshing (of recovering from the effects of heat, of reviving with fresh air) may come from the presence of the Lord..." (Acts 3:19).

Anything else we can do with our time is completely insignificant when this alternative is compared with the precious opportunity we each have been given to spend quality time alone with the Lord on a daily basis. *What appointment on your daily appointment schedule can possibly be more important than the privilege you have been given to have a daily appointment with Almighty God?*

Why would any of us ever allow business appointments, social appointments or recreational events to come ahead of the privilege of spending time alone with the Lord? How can appointments with men and women who were created by God take precedence over the unique opportunity we have been given to enjoy the presence of God Who created every person on earth? Doesn't it make sense that children of God who spend quality time alone each day with their Father will receive more of His wisdom and His other blessings than other believers who spend little or no quality time alone with their Father?

Jesus Christ paid a tremendous price for each of us. Because He died on the cross for us and then rose from the dead, our personal relationship with Him should take first place in every aspect of our lives. "...seeing He is the Beginning, the Firstborn from among the dead, so that He alone in everything and in every respect might occupy the chief place [stand first and be preeminent]" (Colossians 1:18).

Our hearts should be so filled with gratitude for everything Jesus Christ has done for us that we will always be conscious of His indwelling presence. Every aspect of our lives should revolve around Him. We should never allow anything or anyone to take precedence in any way over "...Christ, Who is our life..." (Colossians 3:4).

We now are ready to look at a Scripture reference we have seen before in a slightly different context. In the Sermon on the Mount Jesus instructed us to seek God's kingdom and God's righteousness ahead of everything else. Jesus assured us that God will meet our needs when we truly keep Him first in every aspect of our lives. Jesus said, "...seek (aim at and strive after) first of all His kingdom and His righteousness (His way of doing and being right), and then all these things taken together will be given you besides" (Matthew 6:33).

If we understand that a close relationship with the Lord is a "vital necessity," we will not allow anything to come ahead of our relationship with Him. Because this relationship is our top priority, we will put the Lord in first place and we will keep Him in first place. "...If you seek Him [inquiring for and of Him and requiring Him as your first and vital necessity] you will find Him..." (I Chronicles 28:9).

Once we experience the wonder of God's presence, we will crave to come into His presence continually. God is wonderfully unique. No person on earth can even remotely compare to God. We are absolutely blessed to have been given the opportunity to draw close to God. "...I am God, and there is no one else; I am God, and there is none like Me" (Isaiah 46:9).

Once we begin to understand the magnitude of the opportunity we have been given to draw close to God, we will be consumed by this privilege. We will not allow anything to come ahead of our determination to draw close to God throughout every day of our lives. We'll be like the psalmist who said, "...I have no delight or desire on earth besides You" (Psalm 73:25).

Our desire to draw closer to the Lord should increase continually. Our desire to pursue selfish goals should decrease. John the Baptist said, "He must increase, but I must decrease. [He must grow more prominent; I must grow less so]" (John 3:30).

Our Best Friend lives in our hearts. Because our Best Friend is always with us, we will never lack for an opportunity to enjoy wonderful companionship with Him. Our Best Friend is waiting to fellowship with us twenty-four hours a day throughout every day of our lives.

If you are a human parent, don't you cherish the quiet and intimate moments you spend with your children? Our heavenly Father is no different. The fact that Almighty God wants to spend quality time alone with each of us is overwhelming.

We all have many faults and shortcomings. Although it may seem incongruous that the God of the universe wants to spend time with each of us with all of our imperfections, James 4:8 indicates that He does want to spend precious time fellowshipping with us. Our Father loves each of us unconditionally regardless of our faults and imperfections.

Our Father does not make the decision as to whether or not He will have a daily visit with His children. He will never force Himself on us. We have seen in James 4:8 that we each decide whether we will initiate the contact to spend precious time each day with our loving Father.

Many people experience a natural pull toward lakes, mountains, oceans and other beautiful places created by God. When they seek recreation, they want to get as close as possible to these beautiful places. Going to lakes, mountains and oceans is nice, but we must understand that we have been given the privilege of spending precious quiet time alone each day with the One Who created these lakes, mountains and oceans. Why would we ever settle for exclaiming over the beauty of a sunset when we have the opportunity to draw closer each day to the One Who creates every sunset?

Unsaved people have to look to external sources for happiness. They don't have God living inside of them. I'm not saying that we shouldn't enjoy the beautiful places God has made. I am saying that we should never allow any external attractions to come ahead of the privilege of drawing close to God on a daily basis. We don't have to wait for weekends or vacations to experience the wonder of being in God's presence.

Mature Christians continually turn away from the discordant sounds of the world to enjoy precious quiet time alone with the Lord. The atmosphere is quiet, calm and peaceful deep down inside of ourselves where the Lord makes His home.

We should take full advantage of the privilege of visiting with the Lord each day in the beautiful calm, quiet and peaceful atmosphere where He lives. We can learn to live in His presence all day long.

Jesus Christ fully understood the importance of spending time alone with His Father. When large numbers of people came to Him for teaching and healing, Jesus didn't put this opportunity first. Instead, He actually turned away from these needy people to spend time alone praying to His Father. "...great crowds kept coming together to hear [Him] and to be healed by Him of their infirmities. But He Himself withdrew [in retirement] to the wilderness (desert) and prayed" (Luke 5:15-16).

Can you imagine how these people must have felt when they came to Jesus Christ expecting to have Him teach them and to be healed of their sicknesses only to see Him turn away and leave them? Jesus had His priorities right. I believe Jesus desired this time alone with God so that He could minister more effectively to these people. This same principle applies to us today. If we truly desire to be effective doing what our Father has called us to do, we first must spend a considerable amount of time with the goal of living in His presence.

We have just seen that Jesus focused on time alone with God before He ministered to people. Jesus also wanted to be alone with God after He had ministered to large crowds of people. On one occasion, after Jesus had fed five thousand men and their wives and children from five loaves of bread and two fish, he dismissed these people. He then went up into the hills to be alone, praying to His Father. "...after He had dismissed the multitudes, He went up into the hills by Himself to pray. When it was evening, He was still there alone" (Matthew 14:23).

Jesus began His earthly ministry by spending forty days alone in prayer and fasting. This time alone with God provided the foundation for the miracles that occurred during His earthly ministry. We should make the decision to follow His example throughout every day of our lives.

Many of us have been inspired by the ministries of Dr. Billy Graham and other devoted and mature Christian leaders. If we could follow these Christian leaders around and observe what they do in their everyday lives, I believe we would find that they each spend a considerable amount of time alone with the Lord on a daily basis. These busy leaders are never too busy to spend time with God.

What exactly should we do during our quiet time alone with the Lord? We draw close to God when we pray to Him. We draw close to God when we study and meditate on His Word. We draw close to God when we listen to Him speaking to us. We draw close to God when we are very quiet as we enjoy the wonder and intimacy of His presence.

One of the best ways to hear God speaking to us is to pray constantly. Prayer isn't a one-sided conversation. When we pray correctly, we talk to God and we listen to God. The more we pray, the better we will be able to hear our Father speaking to us.

We have seen that we come into God's presence when we praise Him and worship Him. We should praise God and thank Him constantly. Throughout every day of our lives our mouths should open again and again to express our deep heartfelt gratitude by saying things like, "Thank you so much, dear Lord. I love You, dear Lord. I praise You, precious Lord. I worship You. I glorify You. I magnify you. I exalt You. I lift You up. Hallelujah!" "From the rising of the sun to the going down of it and from east to west, the name of the Lord is to be praised!" (Psalm 113:3).

I believe that continual praise, worship and thanksgiving also bring large numbers of angels into action on our behalf. I also believe that a continual attitude of praise and worship dispels Satan and his demons from any opportunity to attempt to influence us.

In this chapter we have laid an additional foundation for spending precious quiet time alone with the Lord on a daily basis. In the next chapter we will look into the holy Scriptures in more detail for specific information telling us how to draw closer to the Lord throughout every day of our lives.

Chapter 36

Our Most Important Daily Appointment

Some of us are so busily engaged in various activities we think are important that we fail to set aside precious quiet time each day to be alone with the Lord. "The apostles [sent out as missionaries] came back and gathered together to Jesus, and told Him all that they had done and taught. And He said to them, [As for you] come away by yourselves to a deserted place, and rest a while – for many were [continually] coming and going, and they had not even leisure enough to eat" (Mark 6:30-31).

In this passage of Scripture we read about the apostles coming back from their activities as missionaries to tell Jesus about everything they had done. Did Jesus urge them to go out again immediately and do even more? No, He didn't. Jesus told them to go to a quiet place to rest for awhile. Jesus said that many people are so busy with their activities that they don't even take enough time to eat.

The last portion of this passage of Scripture could apply to many people today in this era of fast food restaurants. Some people are so busy that they often rush in and out of these restaurants to gulp down their food. Some people are so busy that their minds never rest. When they should be sleeping at night, their minds are always racing as they focus continually on many things that are important to them. "...his mind takes no rest even at night. This is also vanity (emptiness, falsity, and futility)!" (Ecclesiastes 2:23).

We are told that this kind of a lifestyle is vain, empty and futile. Our Father doesn't want us to make the mistake of living our lives at a breakneck pace even if our activities are worthy. He planned for us to rest one day a week and to live our lives in balance on the other days.

I believe we should examine our activities at the end of each day to ask ourselves, "What did I do today that has eternal significance?" We will be able to see our activities from God's perspective if we apply this daily standard of measurement to our lives. We can learn from the following occurrence how our Lord Jesus wants us to spend our time.

One day Jesus went into a small village to visit two sisters named Martha and Mary. Please be very honest as you evaluate your life by reading the following words from Jesus Christ. Are you a "Mary" or are you a "Martha?"

"...Jesus entered a certain village, and a woman named Martha received and welcomed Him into her house. And she had a sister named Mary, who seated herself at the Lord's feet and was listening to His teaching. But Martha [overly occupied and too busy] was distracted with much serving; and she came up to Him and said, Lord, is it nothing to You that my sister has left me to serve alone? Tell her then to help me [to lend a hand and to do her part along with me]! But the Lord replied to her by saying, Martha, Martha, you are anxious and troubled about many things; there is need of only one or but a few things. Mary has chosen the good portion [that which is to her advantage], which shall not be taken away from her" (Luke 10:38-42).

Unfortunately, some of us live like Martha when Jesus clearly explains that He wants us to live like Mary. Martha was too busy doing things she thought were important. As a result, she was distracted from a wonderful opportunity to fellowship with Jesus. Martha thought that her activities were important because such an honored guest had come to their home. She was concerned that Mary sat at the feet of Jesus listening to His teaching instead of helping her.

Martha urged Jesus to tell Mary to help her with her busy activities. Martha thought that preparing and serving food for Jesus was more important than listening to Him. Jesus replied to Martha just as He would reply to many of us today. He told Martha that she was "anxious and troubled about many things" when she should have "chosen the good portion."

Instead of being so busy, Martha should have followed Mary's example to sit at the feet of Jesus to learn great eternal truths. We should learn from what Jesus teaches us here. In order to have time to fellowship with God, we should organize our lives so that we do our daily tasks quickly and efficiently.

Are you setting aside precious time each day to draw close to the Lord to learn great eternal truths that you will take to heaven with you when you die? We must understand that fellowshipping with God, receiving God's wisdom and being taught continually by God are much more important than any worldly activities.

Unfortunately, many well-intentioned Christians have absolutely no concept of what it is like to spend quiet time alone with the Lord each day. They are so busy going places and doing things that they miss out completely on learning the great truths the Lord wants to reveal to them.

We must understand that we will never *find* time to be alone with the Lord. We should *make* this time available by giving this precious daily time with the Lord the top priority it deserves. We should never try to work our time with the Lord into a busy schedule. Instead, we should schedule every other aspect of our lives around our daily time with the Lord.

Jesus Christ successfully completed the busiest and most important schedule that ever existed, but He consistently set aside time to be alone with His Father. We should follow His example. We should never place other seemingly important activities ahead of our time with the Lord.

We might be criticized by other people because we isolate ourselves each day to spend wonderful time alone with the Lord. We should never base our daily priorities on an attempt to please people. If we want to please someone, we should please the Lord by turning away from worldly activities to spend quality time alone with Him each day.

We should cherish the wonderful opportunity we have been given to spend intimate time with God each day. We can be certain that our Father will provide enough time each day for us to spend time alone with Him and still accomplish everything else that is truly important. We should trust God with our time just as we trust Him with every other aspect of our lives. I believe you will find that your time seems to multiply and that you are able to accomplish more in your life as a result of consistently spending time with the Lord.

I believe that giving time to the Lord each day is very similar to tithing our income to the Lord. I see no difference in the spiritual realm between time and money. When we tithe on the income we receive, we give the Lord the first ten percent of our income (see Malachi 3:8-12). If we understand the importance of giving the Lord the first ten percent of our income, I believe we also should plan to give Him at least ten percent of our waking hours. We cannot make a better investment.

If a person sleeps an average of seven hours a night, this person is awake for seventeen hours each day. Ten percent of that time is 1.7 hours per day. I believe we should round this 1.7 hours off to spend at least two hours of daily quiet time with the Lord. Christians who faithfully tithe on their income know that the Lord makes the ninety percent of their income after their tithe go farther than one hundred percent of their income without a tithe. This same principle applies to our time.

I made the decision to "tithe" my time to the Lord soon after I became a Christian. In those early days I kept careful records of this time just as I kept records in my checkbook of the amount of money I invested in tithes and offerings. I still have the records I kept at that time. I spent forty-two hours with the Lord in my first month as a Christian, eighty-nine hours the second month, seventy-two hours the third month, eighty hours the fourth month, eighty-nine hours the fifth month and ninety-three hours the sixth month.

The seeds that I planted with my time many years ago and the seeds of the time I have planted with the Lord since then have produced a tremendous harvest in my life. I stopped keeping these strict hourly records once I firmly established the habit of tithing my time to the Lord, but I have continued this principle. We should spend our time wisely each day if we truly want to receive wisdom from God. "...teach us to number our days, that we may get us a heart of wisdom" (Psalm 90:12).

For many years I have completed a checklist each day where I briefly inspect what I expect in many areas of my life. Some of the items on my daily checklist are personal areas pertaining to my relationship with family members, diet and exercise. Other areas on my daily checklist are spiritual areas I want to check on.

Every day of my life I rank myself on my daily Bible study, Scripture meditation, prayer, worship and listening to the Lord. My system may seem legalistic to you, but I can assure you that this daily checklist makes it absolutely impossible for me to rationalize. When I spend a few minutes at the end of each day completing this checklist, I know exactly what I have done and what I haven't done. If I'm off the track, I know it. I can make the necessary adjustments immediately instead of allowing bad habits to obtain a foothold in my life.

Some Christians initially find that spending a considerable amount of time alone with the Lord each day is difficult. A significant adjustment is required because this much quiet time is so foreign to their previous lifestyle. Please be patient if you are faced with this dilemma. Know that you are doing what the Lord wants you to do. Trust the Lord to work everything out over a period of time.

As we grow and mature as Christians, we eventually will delight in our quiet time alone with the Lord each day. I can assure you that you will experience this absolute delight if you persevere and if you trust the Lord to reveal Himself to you. Once you begin to hear the voice of the Lord clearly this quiet time will immediately become the most important time in your life. You will never again even think of missing this wonderful time alone with the Lord each day.

I don't think we need to spend all of our quiet time alone with the Lord in an enclosed area. I often credit a portion of my exercise time as time with the Lord. I have enjoyed a great deal of precious time with the Lord when I take long walks by myself in the beautiful scenery He has created. As I walk, I pray, I worship the Lord and I listen to Him speak to me.

Any Christian who has not experienced the joy and contentment of time alone with the Lord has missed out on life's greatest blessing. The fulfillment we experience when we actually hear the Lord speaking to us and guiding us is almost impossible to describe. The marvelous flow of enlightenment from being in God's presence is beautiful beyond description.

Some people are lonely whenever they spend a lot of time alone. Loneliness has its roots in separation from God. Loneliness began in the Garden of Eden. Adam and Eve experienced loneliness for the first time when they turned away from God. Jesus Christ was never lonely. He knew that His Father was always with Him. Jesus said, "...He Who sent Me is ever with Me; My Father has not left Me alone..." (John 8:29).

Unbelievers are always alone because God doesn't live in their hearts. They have to look outside of themselves in an attempt to find companionship. This book is filled with facts from the holy Scriptures explaining that God the Father, God the Son and God the Holy Spirit are with us throughout every minute of every hour of every day of our lives.

Some people are terrified to be alone. They can't stand silence. If they are quiet too long, they immediately turn on a radio or a television set, listen to music, call someone on the telephone or go some place to be with other people. Some people cannot spend even one hour without some form of external stimulation. *Loneliness is the pain of being alone. Solitude is the glory of being alone.* As we grow and mature as Christians, we will relish our quiet time alone with the Lord.

We live in a temporal and dying world that is filled with noise. Our generation is the noisiest generation in history. We must not allow ourselves to be constantly distracted by the clamor of the world. We must learn how to turn away from noise, activities, people, places, things and events to be quiet before the Lord each day. The great things in life are not noisy. The great things in life are quiet, calm and still. The great things in life don't come to us from the outside in. The great things in life come to us from the inside out.

Worldly counselors often advise lonely people to engage in many activities with other people. Some of these people find that they are lonely in the midst of a crowd of people who are engaged in worldly activities. Other people escape loneliness temporarily when they are engaged in social activity, but they find they are right back where they started when they come back from the crowds to be alone again. The very best cure for loneliness is a close relationship with the Lord. Christians who are lonely must learn how to spend quality time alone with the Lord each day.

When we spend a considerable amount of time with people we love here on earth, we inevitably draw closer to these people. This same principle applies to our time with the Lord. As we spend more time with the Lord we will know Him better. As we continually draw closer to the Lord we will experience more and more of His wonderful love for us.

Christians who learn how to enjoy their time with the Lord will find that they are able to take a "mini vacation" every day of their lives. They are able to find refreshment from their busy activities in their precious time alone with the Lord. We should get to the point where we eagerly anticipate this spiritual "island" in the midst of the busy and hectic lifestyle that many of us are engaged in.

Our daily time with the Lord should become a deeply ingrained habit. *Good habits are just as hard to break as bad habits.* If you persevere in establishing this habit, you soon will find that your daily time with the Lord passes so rapidly that you cannot believe it. Time flies by when we are with the timeless One. The things of this world become dim in comparison to the enlightenment we receive during our time with the Lord every day.

There is no better place to be than to be alone with the Lord. Everything we yearn for deep down inside of ourselves can and will be experienced to the fullest when we consistently spend quality time with the Lord. Nothing on earth can remotely compare to the magnificent time of revelation and refreshing that is available to every child of God who makes the quality decision to spend precious time alone with the Lord every day.

Chapter 37

Spend Quality Time with the Lord Early in the Morning

We discussed tithing our time to the Lord in the last chapter. I believe a significant portion of the time we give to the Lord should come in the early morning hours. The psalmist David often prayed to the Lord early in the morning. He then waited for the Lord to speak to his heart. David said, "In the morning You hear my voice, O Lord; in the morning I prepare [a prayer, a sacrifice] for You and watch and wait [for You to speak to my heart]" (Psalm 5:3).

Our Father cares very deeply about each of us. We are important to Him. He wants to visit with us each morning. "What is man that You should magnify him and think him important? And that You should set Your mind upon Him? And that You should visit him every morning?..." (Job 7:17-18).

As we come to God each morning He will show us what He wants us to do during the upcoming day. The psalmist

David prayed to God in the morning saying, "Cause me to hear Your loving-kindness in the morning, for on You do I lean and in You do I trust. Cause me to know the way wherein I should walk, for I lift up my inner self to You" (Psalm 143:8).

When we tithe from our income, we are instructed to give God the "firstfruits" of our income. We shouldn't pay all of our bills and then give God whatever money remains. Instead, we should give God the first ten percent of our income just as the people in Bible times gave Him the firstfruits from their harvest.

Proverbs 3:9-10 tells us to give God the firstfruits of our income. We are told that these financial seeds will be blessed abundantly by God. In Genesis 4:2-5 we see that God blessed Abel because he gave the firstfruits of his sheep, but He failed to bless Abel's brother, Cain, because Cain gave God the "left-overs" of his harvest.

I believe this same spiritual principle applies to us giving God the firstfruits of our time each day. Sometimes we become sleepy after a few minutes of Bible study at night and we don't learn as much as we could. I believe we should pray each night before we go to sleep and I believe that we should meditate on the Word of God at night, but I believe that our principal Bible study time should be early in the morning.

We are fresh and rested when we give God the firstfruits of each day. Our minds are clear. Everything is quiet. Telephones haven't started to ring. The activities of the upcoming day haven't begun. There are no obstacles that can distract us from drawing close to our precious Lord during this quiet time at the beginning of each day.

In the last chapter I explained why I believe we should "tithe" at least two hours each day to the Lord. I like to spend at least one hour of this time with the Lord early in the morning. I then spend at least one more hour with the Lord (and usually much more) throughout the day and night as I pray continually, meditate constantly on the holy Scriptures, praise the Lord and worship Him and listen to Him speaking to me.

I believe the early morning hours are a wonderful time to be taught by the Lord. We should come to the Lord each morning with a humble, teachable and expectant attitude. We should follow the example of the prophet Isaiah who, prophesying about Jesus Christ, said, "...He wakens Me morning by morning, He wakens My ear to hear as a disciple [as one who is taught]" (Isaiah 50:4).

Isaiah prophesied that God would awaken Jesus each morning to teach Him. This same principle applies to us today. Our Father wants each of us to build a solid foundation for every day of our lives. Will we rise early and spend precious time with God each morning or will we go to bed late, arise late and rush off to our busy activities without establishing a solid spiritual foundation for the upcoming day?

We definitely are giving the Lord the best hours of the day if we give Him the first part of each day when we are well rested and fresh. The Bible compares the morning hours with grass that "flourishes and springs up." It compares the evening hours with grass that has been "mown down and withered." "...In the morning they are like grass which grows up – in the morning it flourishes and springs up; in the evening it is mown down and withers" (Psalm 90:5-6).

Jesus Christ was an early riser. He spent precious quiet time with His Father long before dawn. Jesus often went to a place where He could be completely alone as He prayed to His Father. "...in the morning, long before daylight, He got up and went out to a deserted place, and there He prayed" (Mark 1:35).

The Bible tells us that many people rose before dawn to be taught by Jesus. On one occasion we are told that a large crowd of people gathered at dawn waiting for Jesus to come into the temple to teach them. "...Jesus went to the Mount of Olives. Early in the morning (at dawn), He came back into the temple [court], and the people came to Him in crowds..." (John 8:1-2).

The Bible tells us that other men of God were early risers. "...Abraham rose early in the morning..." (Genesis 22:3). The psalmist David said, "...I will awake right early [I will awaken the dawn]!" (Psalm 57:8).

David often spent wonderful quality time with the Lord before dawn. We have just seen that Jesus awakened "long before daylight." I believe it is very beneficial to spend precious time with the Lord before the sun rises.

In our morning time with the Lord we should pray for wisdom and guidance during the upcoming day. We should study the Word of God in the morning. We should praise the Lord and worship Him in the morning. We have been instructed to praise the Lord from the time the sun comes up until the sun goes down (see Psalm 113:3). We should be very quiet before the Lord each morning so that we can hear what He wants to tell us.

In previous chapters I have mentioned that we renew our minds by studying the holy Scriptures. I believe we should renew our minds by studying the Word of God every morning. I believe we should begin the process of meditating on the holy Scriptures that will continue throughout the remainder of the day and the night. The psalmist said, "...I am awake before the cry of the watchman, that I may meditate on Your word" (Psalm 119:148).

When this passage of Scripture was written, night watchmen often cried out loudly to awaken sleeping people. Their cry was similar to the ringing of the alarm clocks we set today. If you haven't been spending a significant amount of time with the Lord early in the morning, I assure you that your life will be transformed if you set your alarm clock to go off one hour earlier. If you establish this habit consistently over a period of time you will have similar habits to Jesus Christ, Abraham and the psalmist who spent wonderful quality time with God in the early morning hours.

Some people believe that changing an established daily routine to get up an hour earlier in the morning to spend time with the Lord is difficult. In most areas of the United States our government tells us to change our clocks one hour each day in the spring and again in the fall based upon government regulations pertaining to Daylight Savings Time. If the government can tell us when to get up earlier, we should be able to tell ourselves when to get up earlier to spend precious time with the Lord.

One of the best ways to get up earlier in the morning is to go to bed earlier at night. Christians shouldn't be "night people." Our Father created us to be "morning people." The Bible repeatedly refers to Satan as darkness and to God as light. Christians are referred to in the Bible as sons of light and sons of the day." We don't belong to the darkness of the late night hours. "...you are all sons of light and sons of the day; we do not belong either to the night or to darkness" (I Thessalonians 5:5).

Some unbelievers stay up very late at night to party, to drink alcoholic beverages and to engage in illicit immoral activities. Our Father wants us to do just the opposite. "The night is far gone and the day is almost here. Let us then drop (fling away) the works and deeds of darkness and put on the [full] armor of light. Let us live and conduct ourselves honorably and becomingly as in the [open light of] day, not in reveling (carousing) and drunkenness, not in immorality and debauchery (sensuality and licentiousness)…" (Romans 13:12-13).

I believe the saying "Early to bed and early to rise makes a man healthy, wealthy and wise" is absolutely true. I have found that I can get by with less sleep and that I am healthier and much more energetic when I repeatedly feed myself the spiritual food of God's Word early in the morning.

We have seen that the Word of God energizes. I believe that any sleep we might lose by arising early to study and meditate on the holy Scriptures is more than offset by the energizing effect we receive from continually studying and meditating on the living Word of God.

God never sleeps (see Psalm 121:4). Have you ever had the experience of waking up early in the morning to find that a precious thought is at the forefront of your consciousness before you are completely awake? I have enjoyed this wonderful experience on hundreds of different occasions over the years. I can't tell you how many times I have written many wonderful notes from the Lord in the early morning hours.

Sometimes these notes essentially amount to taking dictation from the Lord. I have found the early morning hours to be extremely productive. After you experience this phenomenon I believe you will be highly motivated to consistently spend more quality time alone with the Lord during the early morning hours.

When we pray for wisdom and guidance from God we often will receive the answer to this prayer early in the morning. We can expect to receive wonderful revelation from the Lord if we have prepared during the preceding day with prayers of faith and by obeying our Father's instructions to meditate on the holy Scriptures throughout the day and night.

I believe our minds are similar to incubators. A hen incubates her eggs when she sits on them to hatch them. The heat of the hen's body creates a favorable environment for her eggs to hatch. Many farmers now heat eggs artificially to hatch them. Premature babies often are kept in incubators to protect them from dying when they are small and frail.

This same principle of incubation can be used with the seeds we plant to receive revelation knowledge from the Lord. We plant these seeds each day by prayers of faith and by Bible study and meditation. I believe that the Lord causes these spiritual seeds to incubate in our minds and in our hearts while we sleep. Proper preparation often results in receiving answers to our prayers when we receive wonderful revelation from the Lord early in the morning.

This chapter is filled with biblical references pertaining to the quality of the early morning hours. I pray that many people who read this book will be highly motivated to spend more time with the Lord at the beginning of each day. I believe you will receive wonderful blessings from the Lord if you make this quality decision and stick to it.

Chapter 38

Pride and Self-Confidence Block Us from God's Blessings

Most of the chapters in this book are positive, encouraging and uplifting. This chapter is not positive, encouraging and uplifting because it explains the penalties we will pay if we are proud and self-confident instead of being humble and trusting the Lord to do what we know we cannot do ourselves. This chapter consists primarily of warnings from God telling us that, if we are proud, we can fail to receive the wisdom and the other blessings He wants to give us.

Our Father doesn't want us to have so much confidence in our human wisdom and our human abilities that we fail to understand how desperately we need Him. God has no respect for people who are proud of their human wisdom and understanding. "...He regards and respects not any who are wise in heart [in their own understanding and conceit]" (Job 37:24).

We must understand that our human wisdom is very limited. People who trust completely in their human wisdom cannot live an effective life. They will fail to accomplish anything that has any eternal significance. "…who [limited to human wisdom] knows what is good for man in his life, all the days of his vain life which he spends as a shadow [going through the motions but accomplishing nothing]?…" (Ecclesiastes 6:12).

We cannot be proud if we sincerely desire to receive wisdom from God. God hates pride. He opposes people who are proud. "…God sets Himself against the proud (the insolent, the overbearing, the disdainful, the presumptuous, the boastful) – [and He actually opposes, frustrates, and defeats them]…" (I Peter 5:5).

Who would ever want to be opposed by Almighty God? God says that He will set Himself against people who are proud. If we are proud, we can be certain that God will cause us to be very frustrated. He will ultimately defeat every proud person.

Pride is so powerful that it changed God's angels into devils. The Archangel Lucifer who was very close to God fell from heaven because of his pride. "How have you fallen from heaven, O light-bringer and daystar, son of the morning! How you have been cut down to the ground, you who weakened and laid low the nations [O blasphemous, satanic king of Babylon!] And you said in your heart, I will ascend to heaven; I will exalt my throne above the stars of God; I will sit upon the mount of assembly in the uttermost north. I will ascend above the heights of the clouds; I will make myself like the Most High" (Isaiah 14:12-14).

Pride caused Lucifer to attempt to exalt himself above God. Please notice that the words "I will" are used five times in this passage of Scripture. God created us to seek His will, not our will. If we continually pursue our selfish desires and trust in our human abilities, our pride will ultimately cause us to fall just as Lucifer's pride and ambition caused him to fall from heaven.

Pride caused Lucifer to become Satan. Satan wants us to make the same mistake he made. He wants us to be so proud and conceited that we will fall into condemnation as he did. We should be very careful that we don't "...[develop a beclouded and stupid state of mind] as the result of pride [be blinded by conceit, and] fall into the condemnation that the devil [once] did" (I Timothy 3:6).

Proud people have a tendency to overestimate their own wisdom and their human abilities. Proud people often underestimate the wisdom and ability of other people. Our Father doesn't want us to have "...a proud look [the spirit that makes one overestimate himself and underestimate others]..." (Proverbs 6:17).

We must heed the warning the apostle Paul gave to the Romans if we want to receive wisdom or any other blessings from God. Paul said, "...by the grace (unmerited favor of God) given to me I warn everyone among you not to estimate and think of himself more highly than he ought [not to have an exaggerated opinion of his own importance]..." (Romans 12:3).

We make a big mistake if we think too highly of ourselves. God created some people with a significant amount of human ability. We should never boast about the human wisdom and talents our Creator has given to us. "...Let not the wise and skillful person glory and boast in his wisdom and skill..." (Jeremiah 9:23).

Our Father wants us to be humble at all times. He wants us to be willing to do anything He asks us to do. We should never overestimate our human abilities. We should never be conceited because of our human wisdom. "...give yourselves to humble tasks. Never overestimate yourself or be wise in your own conceits" (Romans 12:16).

Many unbelievers take training courses and read books in an attempt to increase their self-confidence. The self-confidence that the world prizes so highly is exactly the opposite of what our Father wants to see in us. There is no place in the Bible where we are told to be self-confident. Our Father wants our confidence to be in Him, not in ourselves. Self-confidence ultimately will destroy us. "...why should you [get puffed up and] destroy yourself [with presumptuous self-sufficiency]?" (Ecclesiastes 7:16).

God gave the apostle Paul many talents and abilities. Even though he was very gifted, Paul knew that he should not be confident in himself. Paul said that we should "...put no confidence or dependence [on what we are] in the flesh and on outward privileges and physical advantages and external appearances - though for myself I have [at least grounds] to rely on the flesh. If any other man considers that he has or seems to have reason to rely on the flesh and his physical and outward advantages, I have still more!" (Philippians 3:3-4).

Paul refused to place his trust in his human abilities. We should follow his example. We make a big mistake if we place our trust in our human wisdom and our human abilities. "Woe to those who are wise in their own eyes and prudent and shrewd in their own sight!" (Isaiah 5:21).

People who trust in their human wisdom are conceited. *The Amplified Bible* always identifies self-confident people by calling them fools. "Do you see a man wise in his own eyes and conceit? There is more help for a [self-confident] fool than for him" (Proverbs 26:12).

Gifted people who are proud of their God-given human abilities are not inclined to pay the price of consistently studying and meditating on the Word of God. They are so caught up with themselves that they have no desire to understand God's ways. They think they have all of the answers they will need. "A [self-confident] fool has no delight in understanding but only in revealing his personal opinions and himself" (Proverbs 18:2).

Many self-confident people don't want to listen. Their ears are closed to the things of God. They actually despise the wisdom of God. "Speak not in the ears of a [self-confident] fool, for he will despise the [godly] Wisdom of your words" (Proverbs 23:9).

Most self-confident people are completely unaware of the severe problems they ultimately will face as a result of their pride and self-confidence. Their careless self-confidence ultimately will bring about their destruction. "...the careless ease of [self-confident] fools shall destroy them" (Proverbs 1:32).

Mature Christians place a high priority on receiving wisdom from God. Self-confident people focus primarily on the things of the world. "A man of understanding sets skillful and godly Wisdom before his face, but the eyes of a [self-confident] fool are on the ends of the earth" (Proverbs 17:24).

We can clearly see that our Father does not want His beloved children to be proud and self-confident. He also warns us against associating with people who are self-confident. "...he who associates with [self-confident] fools is [a fool himself and] shall smart for it" (Proverbs 13:20).

We make a big mistake if our confidence is in ourselves. If we sincerely desire to receive wisdom from God, we must understand our human inadequacies. "He who leans on, trusts in, and is confident of his own mind and heart is a [self-confident] fool, but he who walks in skillful and godly Wisdom shall be delivered" (Proverbs 28:26).

I pray that the numerous warnings against pride and self-confidence in this chapter will have a significant impact upon you. I believe that one of the biggest liabilities any person can have is to receive a lot of God-given natural talent and ability if this person does not have the maturity and humility to appreciate these gifts from God. Now that we have seen facts from the holy Scriptures concerning pride and self-confidence, we are ready to look into the Word of God to see what it says about the relationship between humility and receiving wisdom from God.

Chapter 39

Our Father Gives His Wisdom to His Humble Children

Knowledge can be a double-edged sword. Knowledge is desirable, but the Bible teaches us that some people become overly proud as a result of what they have learned. "...knowledge causes people to be puffed up (to bear themselves loftily and be proud)..." (I Corinthians 8:1).

Pride has caused many leaders to fall. After all that we have read about King Solomon and the magnificent wisdom he received from God we must understand that Solomon ultimately became proud in spite of the wisdom God gave to Him. Solomon's pride caused him to disobey God. "...King Solomon [defiantly] loved many foreign women – the daughter of Pharaoh, women of the Moabites, Ammonites, Edomites, Sidonians, and Hittites. They were of the very nations of whom the Lord said to the Israelites, You shall not mingle with them, neither shall they mingle with you, for surely they will turn away your hearts after their gods. Yet Solomon clung to these in love. He had 700 wives, princesses, and 300 concubines, and his wives turned away his heart from God" (I Kings 11:1-3).

God told the Israelites about many women He didn't want them to associate with. God knew that these women could cause the Israelites to turn away from Him. In spite of the wisdom that God gave him, Solomon disobeyed these specific instructions from God because of his defiant pride. These women did exactly what God said they would do. They turned Solomon's heart away from God.

We must remain humble when God blesses us with His wisdom. We should fear God at all times if we want to continue to receive His wisdom. We should always walk in humble obedience to the instructions in God's Word. We should continually yield our lives to the guidance of the Holy Spirit.

We should always thank our Father and give Him the glory whenever He blesses us with His wisdom. We should never give in to the temptation to take God's glory for ourselves. Our Father does not give His glory to others. "I am the Lord; that is My name! And My glory I will not give to another…" (Isaiah 42:8).

People have thanked me profusely on many occasions when I have given them what seemed to be anointed advice. Whenever I receive this response, I always try to say, "Don't thank me. Thank God. The advice I gave you came through me, not from me."

We should direct all praise to the Lord instead of praising ourselves or allowing others to praise us. "…let him who boasts and glories boast and glory in the Lord. For [it is] not [the man] who praises and commends himself who is approved and accepted, but [it is the person] whom the Lord accredits and commends" (II Corinthians 10:17-18).

If anyone ever could have exalted Himself for what He did, Jesus Christ was that person. Jesus was always meek and humble. He said, "...I am gentle (meek) and humble (lowly) in heart..." (Matthew 11:29).

Being used by God can be difficult because pride can creep in. On several occasions I have enjoyed success in a particular endeavor because of the anointing of God and, realizing that I had exhibited pride because of what God had done through me, I have repented and asked God to forgive me.

If we exalt ourselves, we always will be humbled. We shouldn't expect to receive God's wisdom and other blessings from our Father unless we consistently humble ourselves before Him and before one another. Jesus said, "Whoever exalts himself [with haughtiness and empty pride] shall be humbled (brought low), and whoever humbles himself [whoever has a modest opinion of himself and behaves accordingly] shall be raised to honor" (Matthew 23:12).

Jesus was not interested in receiving recognition from human beings. The only recognition He wanted was recognition from God for successfully doing what His Father called Him to do during His earthly ministry. Jesus said, "I receive not glory from men [I crave no human honor, I look for no mortal fame]" (John 5:41).

Jesus Christ is our example in every area of our lives. Our Father wants us to be humble just as His beloved Son always was humble. "Let this same attitude and purpose and [humble] mind be in you which was in Christ Jesus: [Let Him be your example in humility]..." (Philippians 2:5).

All truly great servants of God are humble. "…Moses was very meek (gentle, kind, and humble)…" (Numbers 12:3). In the last chapter we saw that God gave the apostle Paul many talents and abilities. Paul was very humble in spite of his gifts and talents. He knew that his accomplishments for the Lord were done through him, not by him. Paul said, "…I know that nothing good dwells within me, that is, in my flesh…" (Romans 7:18).

Abraham Lincoln is an excellent example of a great leader who was truly humble. President Lincoln once said, "I must confess that I am driven to my knees by the overwhelming conviction that I have nowhere else to go. My wisdom and that of all about me is insufficient to meet the demands of the day."

All leaders should understand how inadequate they are in themselves. We all need God's wisdom. Our Father only gives His wisdom to His children who are humble. "When swelling and pride come, then emptiness and shame come also, but with the humble (those who are lowly, who have been pruned or chiseled by trial, and renounce self) are skillful and godly Wisdom and soundness" (Proverbs 11:2).

Our Father instructs every person who receives His wisdom to remain humble. People who truly are wise are always humble. "Who is there among you who is wise and intelligent? Then let him by his noble living show forth his [good] works with the [unobtrusive] humility [which is the proper attribute] of true wisdom" (James 3:13).

Do you want God to guide you? Do you want God to teach you? We must understand that our Father only gives these blessings to His children who truly are humble and teachable. "He leads the humble in what is right, and the humble He teaches His way" (Psalm 25:9).

We do not deserve to receive blessings from God. We are able to receive our Father's blessings because of His grace and because of His love for us. Our Father gives favor to His children who are humble. "...He gives His undeserved favor to the low [in rank], the humble, and the afflicted" (Proverbs 3:34).

Our awareness of our human inadequacy should be so strong that we rely totally, completely and absolutely upon God. We are God's children. Little children know how inadequate they are. They don't attempt to solve difficult problems that they cannot solve. They don't worry about these problems. They turn to their parents with absolute trust. Our Father wants us to come to Him with simple childlike trust.

Jesus Christ chose to set aside His deity when He came to earth as the Son of Man. Jesus depended upon God to do everything in Him and through Him. We saw in a previous chapter that Jesus knew He could not do what God wanted Him to do with His human abilities. Jesus said,"...I assure you, most solemnly I tell you, the Son is able to do nothing of Himself (of His own accord)..." (John 5:19).

If the greatest Man Who ever lived on this earth knew that He could not solve difficult problems by Himself, *why* would any of us ever think we can solve difficult problems with our human wisdom, knowledge and understanding? We must understand how helpless we are without the assistance of Jesus Christ. Jesus said, "...apart from Me [cut off from vital union with Me] you can do nothing" (John 15:5).

Please underline or highlight the word "you" in this passage of Scripture. Know that Jesus Christ is talking to *you.* We must understand the vital importance of staying close to Jesus Christ at all times. We cannot accomplish any goals with eternal significance unless we continually turn to Jesus Christ to do in us and through us what we cannot possibly do ourselves.

When we face difficult challenges we should know that we can do all things through the strength of Jesus Christ. "I have strength for all things in Christ Who empowers me [I am ready for anything and equal to anything through Him Who infuses inner strength into me; I am self-sufficient in Christ's sufficiency]" (Philippians 4:13).

This magnificent promise from the Word of God has sustained me on many occasions when I was faced with difficult problems. I enjoy meditating on the *Amplified Bible* version of Philippians 4:13. We should know that the strength, wisdom and ability of Jesus Christ are available to us whenever we are faced with any difficult problem. We are "ready for anything and equal to anything" because Jesus Christ lives in our hearts. Jesus is more than sufficient. He will provide everything we need if we dare to place all of our trust in Him.

We do not have the ability to solve many difficult problems, but we can rejoice because our Father promises to provide everything we need. "Not that we are fit (qualified and sufficient in ability) of ourselves to form personal judgments or to claim or count anything as coming from us, but our power and ability and sufficiency are from God" (II Corinthians 3:5).

Humility isn't something that is manifested consciously. Humility is a quality that is manifested from deep down inside of ourselves. Humble Christians know that God is everything and they are nothing without Him. Humble Christians know that they need the wisdom, strength and ability of God throughout every day of their lives. They know that they are completely dependent upon God.

When we are in the Lord's presence, we will see how insignificant we really are. The Lord promises to exalt us and lift us up and give meaning to our lives if we humble ourselves before Him. "Humble yourselves [feeling very insignificant] in the presence of the Lord, and He will exalt you [He will lift you up and make your lives significant]" (James 4:10).

In the last two chapters we have clearly seen that pride blocks us from receiving the wisdom of God. We have seen that we must be humble if we want to receive wisdom from God. In the next chapter we'll look into the Word of God to see how we should submit ourselves to God to find His will for our lives and to carry out the assignment He has given to each of us.

Chapter 40

Experience Fulfillment by Accomplishing God's Will for Your Life

All Christians should understand the importance of seeking God's will for their lives. The Bible tells us that every day of our lives was planned before God created us. "Your eyes saw my unformed substance, and in Your book all the days [of my life] were written before ever they took shape, when as yet there was none of them" (Psalm 139:16).

God has a specific and exact plan for every person He created. After we ask Jesus Christ to be our Savior, our Father wants us to devote our lives to seeking, finding and carrying out His plan for our lives. "...we are God's [own] handiwork (His workmanship), recreated in Christ Jesus, [born anew] that we may do those good works which God predestined (planned beforehand) for us [taking paths which He prepared ahead of time], that we should walk in them [living the good life which He prearranged and made ready for us to live]" (Ephesians 2:10).

Our Father wants each of us to follow "paths which He prepared ahead of time." He wants us to live "the good life" He has arranged for us. We should not devote our lives to the pursuit of selfish goals. "...so that he can no longer spend the rest of his natural life living by [his] human appetites and desires, but [he lives] for what God wills" (I Peter 4:2).

In this book we have looked at the earthly ministry of Jesus Christ several times to see the example Jesus has set for us in many different areas. We now are ready to use Jesus as our example once again. Jesus did not seek His own will. His sole desire was to do His Father's will. Jesus said, "...I do not seek or consult My own will [I have no desire to do what is pleasing to Myself, My own aim, My own purpose] but only the will and pleasure of the Father Who sent Me" (John 5:30).

I believe that the Word of God points each of us toward God's plan for our lives. We will delight in carrying out God's will for our lives if we fill our hearts with the Word of God through constant meditation on the holy Scriptures. We will be like the psalmist who said, "I delight to do Your will, O my God; yes, Your law is within my heart" (Psalm 40:8).

The Word of God explains the will of God for the lives of all of His children. As we continually draw closer to God our Father will give us the energy, power and desire to please Him by successfully carrying out the specific plan He has for each of our lives. "...it is God Who is all the while effectually at work in you [energizing and creating in you the power and desire], both to will and to work for His good pleasure and satisfaction and delight" (Philippians 2:13).

In this chapter we are briefly examining Scripture references pertaining to the will of God. If you would like additional detailed instructions from the holy Scriptures on seeking, finding and carrying out God's will for your life, you might want to purchase our Scripture Meditation Cards and the accompanying cassette tape, *Find God's Will For Your Life.* I urge you not to purchase the Scripture cards without the cassette tape if you are interested in obtaining this information. If you truly want to find God's will for your life, you will find invaluable instructions on this eighty-five minute cassette tape that contains additional instruction that could not possibly be included in the abbreviated Scripture cards.

If we pursue selfish personal goals, we shouldn't expect to receive God's help in achieving these goals. If we sincerely seek God's will for our lives, we can expect to encounter many obstacles that cannot possibly be overcome with our limited human wisdom, strength and ability. God lives in our hearts. Nothing will be able to stop us if we turn to Him with absolute and unwavering faith as we seek to carry out His will for our lives. "...if this doctrine or purpose or undertaking or movement is of human origin, it will fail (be overthrown and come to nothing); but if it is of God, you will not be able to stop or overthrow or destroy them..." (Acts 5:38-39).

God is omnipotent – He has unlimited power and authority. Nothing can stop God except when we block Him through doubt and unbelief (see Mark 6:1-6). "...Job said to the Lord, I know that You can do all things, and that no thought or purpose of Yours can be restrained or thwarted" (Job 42:1-2).

Christians who do not understand the importance of seeking, finding and carrying out their Father's will for their lives will ultimately find that their lives lack fulfillment. We cannot experience true fulfillment, meaning and satisfaction without seeking, finding and carrying out God's plan for our lives. The achievement of selfish goals provides only temporary and fleeting satisfaction.

Our Father wants us to know Him intimately and to long to carry out the assignment He has for us. He will satisfy us and give us the deep fulfillment we yearn for if we seek Him continually and if we sincerely desire to carry out His will for our lives. "...He satisfies the longing soul and fills the hungry soul with good" (Psalm 107:9).

Many people know that there must be something that will give them the fulfillment, meaning and satisfaction they yearn for, but they don't know where to find these wonderful blessings. We will love our lives when we receive wisdom from our Father that shows us how He wants us to live. Our lives will be prosperous and successful before God. "He who gains Wisdom loves his own life; he who keeps understanding shall prosper and find good" (Proverbs 19:8).

Our Father wants us to grow and mature to the point where we understand that we cannot experience fulfillment from worldly possessions. We all have seen people who lusted after earthly possessions only to find that they received no lasting satisfaction after they obtained these possessions. People who lust after the things of the world will never be satisfied. "...[the lust of] the eyes of man is never satisfied" (Proverbs 27:20).

Our lustful desires can only offer temporary satisfaction because the world we live in is temporary. The will of God is eternal. If we seek, find and carry out God's plan for our lives, we will experience a great deal of fulfillment here on earth because our accomplishments will have eternal significance. "...the world passes away and disappears, and with it the forbidden cravings (the passionate desires, the lust) of it; but he who does the will of God and carries out His purposes in his life abides (remains) forever" (I John 2:17).

In this chapter we have learned that the pursuit of selfish goals cannot provide satisfaction, meaning and fulfillment. In the next chapter we will look into the Word of God to see what it says about the relationship between selflessness and our ability to receive and utilize the wisdom of God.

Chapter 41

Selfless Christians Receive the Wisdom of God

Selfishness blocks us from receiving the wisdom of God. Selflessness enables us to receive wisdom from God. Selfish people inherit their tendency toward selfishness from the sins of Adam and Eve. Mature Christians are selfless – they turn away from selfish goals. Their primary goal in life is to serve God.

God created Adam before He created Eve. God told Adam that he could eat freely from every tree in the Garden of Eden except "the tree of the knowledge of good and evil and blessing and calamity." God told Adam that he would die if he ate fruit from this tree. "...the Lord God took the man and put him in the Garden of Eden to tend and guard and keep it. And the Lord God commanded the man, saying, You may freely eat of every tree of the garden; but of the tree of the knowledge of good and evil and blessing and calamity you shall not eat, for in the day that you eat of it you shall surely die" (Genesis 2:15-17).

God then said that it was not good for Adam to be alone. He created Eve to be Adam's wife. Soon after God created Eve she was tempted by Satan to eat from the tree God had forbidden Adam to eat from. One of the reasons that Eve succumbed to Satan's temptation was because she thought it would *make her wise* if she ate fruit from this tree. Like many people in the world today, Eve was looking for wisdom in the wrong place.

Eve disobeyed God's instructions because of her desire for wisdom and because she thought the fruit would taste good. Eve ate fruit from that tree. She also gave some of the forbidden fruit to Adam. He also ate this fruit. "...when the woman saw that the tree was good (suitable, pleasant) for food and that it was delightful to look at, and a tree to be desired in order to make one wise, she took of its fruit and ate; and she gave some also to her husband, and he ate" (Genesis 3:6).

Adam and Eve sinned by disobeying specific instructions from Almighty God. They experienced spiritual death because of their disobedience. They separated themselves from the wisdom of God and from every other blessing from God.

Adam and Eve were conscious for the first time of their separation from God when they heard God coming soon after they sinned. They did something they never would have done before they sinned. They attempted to hide from God. "...they heard the sound of the Lord God walking in the garden in the cool of the day, and Adam and his wife hid themselves from the presence of the Lord God among the trees of the garden" (Genesis 3:8).

Adam and Eve were separated from God because of their sin. All human beings except Jesus Christ who have lived since that time have inherited a sin nature because of the sin of Adam and Eve. Every person on earth has a sin nature. The most giving, loving person you know has a sin nature. We all were born with a capacity to sin and to pursue selfish goals. Jesus was not a direct descendant of Adam and Eve. He did not inherit their sinful nature because He was born of a virgin.

God sent His beloved Son to earth to give us the opportunity to be redeemed from our sins. When we ask Jesus Christ to become our Savior, we are made righteous before God by the shed blood of Jesus Christ. Jesus took our sin nature upon Himself. When Jesus becomes our Savior, we are given the opportunity to choose to turn away from selfish goals to pursue the life of service we were created for.

God has given each of us freedom of choice. We all would be robots if God didn't give us the freedom to choose. The freedom of choice God has given to us causes all of us to make some choices that are not for the glory of God. "All things are legitimate [permissible - and we are free to do anything we please], but not all things are helpful (expedient, profitable, and wholesome). All things are legitimate, but not all things are constructive [to character] and edifying [to spiritual life]. Let no one then seek his own good and advantage and profit, but [rather] each one of the other [let him seek the welfare of his neighbor]" (I Corinthians 10:23-24).

Our Father wants us to continually make choices that are "constructive to character and edifying to spiritual life." We each are faced daily with our own sin nature. Instead of pursing selfish goals throughout every day of our lives, we must make the choice moment by moment whether we will live in the Spirit or live in the flesh. Our Father wants us to die to selfish desires. He wants us to live to serve Him and to help others.

We can only overcome our selfish, lustful desires if we yield control of our lives to the Holy Spirit. Many Christians are constantly in a war between their carnal, selfish nature and their desire to yield control of their lives to the Holy Spirit. This battle has been won for us, but we must choose throughout each day of our lives to walk in the victory that has been given to us by Jesus Christ. Only Jesus can enable us to live selfless lives instead of constantly pursuing worldly goals.

When I was a young man, I liked the song, "I'll Do It My Way." I used to sing that song with gusto because I was devoted to the pursuit of my selfish goals. If I heard that song today I would immediately say, "No, no. I'll do it Your way, Lord."

True freedom doesn't come from an "I'll do it my way" attitude. God's ways are very different from the ways of the world. We find true freedom in the last place most people would expect to find it. *The pursuit of selfish goals imprisons us. Selflessness sets us free.*

Selfishness separates us from the love of God, the wisdom of God and the power of God. We can be set free from the bondage of selfishness by the resurrection power of our Lord Jesus Christ. From the time we ask Jesus to be our Savior, our lives ideally should be a steady progression of spiritual growth from being self-centered to being Christ-centered.

God created us to serve Him. We must turn away from preoccupation with selfish goals so that we can find what our Father has called us to do to with our lives. The wisdom of God is available to all of God's children who are totally dedicated to serving Him.

Immature people cannot understand this principle. They believe that life would be wonderful if they could have their own way in everything. True freedom only comes from putting Jesus Christ first, other people second and ourselves last. I like to explain this principle by using the following three words expressed vertically:

Jesus
Others
Yourself

The first letter of each of these words spells the word "joy." We can only experience the joy of the Lord to the degree that we are mature enough to keep Jesus Christ and God's plan for our lives in first place, to put the interests of other people in second place and to put our own selfish desires in last place where they belong.

Throughout every day of our lives we continually decide whether the Holy Spirit will control our lives or whether we will pursue selfish goals. The apostle Paul said, "...I say, walk and live [habitually] in the [Holy] Spirit [responsive to and controlled and guided by the Spirit]; then you will certainly not gratify the cravings and desires of the flesh (of human nature without God). For the desires of the flesh are opposed to the [Holy] Spirit, and the [desires of the] Spirit are opposed to the flesh (godless human nature); for these are antagonistic to each other [continually withstanding and in conflict with each other], so that you are not free but are prevented from doing what you desire to do" (Galatians 5:16-17).

Paul explained that we only can overcome the lustful craving of our flesh by continually yielding control of our lives to the Holy Spirit. He explained that the desires of the flesh and the desires of the Holy Spirit are completely opposite. We will release more and more control of our lives to the Holy Spirit as we grow and mature as Christians. We will understand that God created us in such a way that we receive much more satisfaction from giving and serving then we receive from getting and taking.

God didn't put us on earth to please ourselves. He didn't create us to pursue our own interests. We should always follow the example of Jesus Christ Who never pursued selfish goals. "...Christ did not please Himself [gave no thought to His own interests]..." (Romans 15:3).

God created us in such a way that we will only experience fulfillment of the deepest desires of our hearts by yielding control of our lives to Him. "[Live] as children of obedience [to God]; do not conform yourselves to the evil desires [that governed you] in your former ignorance [when you did not know the requirements of the Gospel]" (I Peter 1:14).

We will experience a constant attitude of gratitude as we grow and mature as Christians. We will think constantly of everything the Lord has done for us that we did not earn and do not deserve. We will have a deep desire to do anything we can to repay the Lord for all He has done for us. "What shall I render to the Lord for all His benefits toward me? [How can I repay Him for all His bountiful dealings?]" (Psalm 116:12).

We couldn't repay the Lord for all He has done for us if we spent every minute of every hour of every day of the remainder of our lives striving to repay Him. The only way we can even begin to repay the Lord is by cheerfully surrendering control of our lives to Him. "...He died for all, so that all those who live might live no longer to and for themselves, but to and for Him Who died and was raised again for their sake" (II Corinthians 5:15).

Jesus Christ can only become the Lord of our lives if we die to ourselves. Jesus produced a tremendous ultimate harvest of an immense number of souls when He willingly died on a cross at Calvary. We can only produce a great harvest for Him if we willingly die to our selfish desires. Jesus said, "I assure you, most solemnly I tell you, Unless a grain of wheat falls into the earth and dies, it remains [just one grain; it never becomes more but lives] by itself alone. But if it dies, it produces many others and yields a rich harvest" (John 12:24).

Jesus Christ lives in our hearts. He can and will control our lives to the degree that we willingly yield control to Him because we trust completely in Him to live His life in us and through us. We should follow the example of the apostle Paul who said, "I have been crucified with Christ [in Him I have shared His crucifixion]; it is no longer I who live, but Christ (the Messiah) lives in me; and the life I now live in the body I live by faith in (by adherence to and reliance on and complete trust in) the Son of God, Who loved me and gave Himself up for me" (Galatians 2:20).

We must turn completely away from our selfish desires if we sincerely want to follow Jesus Christ. We should draw closer and closer to Jesus as we gladly yield control of our lives to Him. Jesus said, "...If anyone intends to come after Me, let him deny himself [forget, ignore, disown, and lose sight of himself and his own interests] and take up his cross, and [joining Me as a disciple and siding with My party] follow with Me [continually, cleaving steadfastly to Me]" (Mark 8:34).

Jesus wants us to turn away from temporal, selfish goals to focus on the pursuit of goals that have eternal significance. Our lives will produce results that have eternal significance if we continually surrender control of our lives to the Lord. Jesus said, "...whoever wants to save his [higher, spiritual, eternal] life, will lose it [the lower, natural, temporal life which is lived only on earth]; and whoever gives up his life [which is lived only on earth] for My sake and the Gospel's will save it [his higher, spiritual life in the eternal kingdom of God]" (Mark 8:35).

We each make a continual decision whether we want to live "the lower life" or "the higher life." We will be much more inclined to yield control of our lives to the Holy Spirit if we obey our Father's instructions to fill our minds and our hearts each day with His Word. We will receive wisdom from God if we allow the Holy Spirit to control our lives. We will experience wonderful peace, joy, meaning and fulfillment in our lives as we die to our selfish desires to devote our lives to carrying out the assignment God has given to us.

We should never give glory to anyone or anything ahead of the glory we give to Jesus Christ. We should crucify our carnal, worldly and selfish desires just as Jesus was crucified for us. We should have the attitude of the apostle Paul who said, "...far be it from me to glory [in anything or anyone] except in the cross of our Lord Jesus Christ (the Messiah) through Whom the world has been crucified to me, and I to the world!" (Galatians 6:14).

We open ourselves to the influence of Satan whenever we pursue lustful, selfish desires. We should offer our lives to God instead of making this mistake. "Do not continue offering or yielding your bodily members [and faculties] to sin as instruments (tools) of wickedness. But offer and yield yourselves to God..." (Romans 6:13).

I hope this chapter has encouraged you to willingly surrender control of your life to the Lord. In the next chapter we'll look into the Word of God for specific instruction that tells us exactly *how* to yield control of our lives to the Lord.

Chapter 42

God Is the Potter and We Are the Clay

Our constant desire throughout every day of our lives should be for the Lord to continually live His life in us and through us. I believe we should pray often, saying something like the following, "Dear Father, in the name of your beloved Son, Jesus Christ, I ask You to live Your life in me and through me. Use me in any way You want to use me. I live to serve You, dear Lord. I surrender my life to You."

If we sincerely desire to serve God, we need to grow and mature until we are able to put our selfish desires on the cross each day as we yield control of our lives to the Holy Spirit. As we grow and mature we should become like the apostle Paul who said, "...I die daily [I face death every day and die to self]" (I Corinthians 15:31).

Some Christians turn to God only when they are faced with severe problems. Our Father wants us to draw close to

Him throughout every day of our lives during good times and during bad times. He wants us to yield control of our lives to Him throughout each day. He wants us to trust Him completely to do in us and through us what we cannot possibly do ourselves.

We must be broken before we can be used to the fullest by the Lord. In the natural realm things that are broken and repaired usually do not have as much value as they had before they were broken. In the spiritual realm we must be broken before we can be made whole.

Brokenness can come in one of two ways. Sometimes the wrong choices we make bring trials and tribulations into our lives that ultimately will cause us to come to a place of brokenness before God. We will become broken before God if we obey our Father's instructions to fill our minds and our hearts with His Word each day and if we deeply and sincerely desire to yield control of our lives to Him.

Our lives should be controlled by the Word of God and by the Spirit of God dwelling in our hearts. Ideally, our brokenness should come voluntarily from the inside out instead of coming involuntarily from the outside in as a result of being broken as a reaction to the circumstances we face.

We should be so grateful to Jesus Christ and trust Him so deeply that we will gladly yield control of our lives to Him. We actually should regard ourselves as prisoners of Jesus Christ just as the apostle Paul did. He said, "...I, Paul, [am] the prisoner of Jesus the Christ..." (Ephesians 3:1).

The Bible compares yielding our lives to God to a potter and his clay. Our Father is the Potter. Our lives should be like clay. We should gladly allow our Father to mold us and to shape us. "…O Lord, You are our Father; we are the clay, and You our Potter, and we all are the work of Your hand" (Isaiah 64:8).

We shouldn't be in control of our lives. God should be in control of our lives. Our lives will only be meaningful before God if we accept ourselves as He created us and if we allow Him to shape us and to mold us. "Woe to him who strives with his Maker! - a worthless piece of broken pottery among other pieces equally worthless [and yet presuming to strive with his Maker]! Shall the clay say to him who fashions it, What do you think you are making? or, Your work has no handles?" (Isaiah 45:9).

We should never question God. We should never criticize God. We should never ask God why He made us the way He did. God is the Potter. He has the right to create and mold His clay any way He desires. "…who are you, a mere man, to criticize and contradict and answer back to God? Will what is formed say to him that formed it, Why have you made me thus? Has the potter no right over the clay, to make out of the same mass (lump) one vessel for beauty and distinction and honorable use, and another for menial or ignoble and dishonorable use?" (Romans 9:20-21).

No two people are alike. When God created us, He made each person different. God has specific assignments for each person He created. We should trust Him completely. We should focus on yielding to Him if we want Him to use us more.

Our Father knows exactly how to mold us and shape us. He is omniscient. He knows every little detail about every one of His children. Because our Father knows each of us so intimately, we should never hesitate to yield control of our lives to Him. Dying to self is the most productive thing we can do with our lives.

We only will be able to experience manifestation of God's presence in us and through us to the degree that we die to ourselves. The absolute surrender that seems so reprehensible to many unsaved people and immature Christians actually enables us to receive our Father's wisdom and all of the other blessings He wants to give to each of His beloved children.

I believe we should follow the example of Hudson Taylor who was a great missionary in the first part of the Twentieth Century. This great man of God once said, "I used to ask God to help me. Then I asked if I might help Him. I ended by asking Him to do His work through me."

These three sentences explain very simply the evolution of growth and maturity that should take place in our lives. We continually ask God to help us when we first become Christians. Some people never get past this stage. Their constant prayers are, "I want…I want…I want."

Our gratitude toward God should increase as we grow and mature. We will have a deep desire to serve God in any way we can as we begin to comprehend the magnitude of what our heavenly Father and His beloved Son, Jesus Christ, have done for us. We will have a deep desire to serve God in any way we can. This desire is commendable, but we should take this desire one step further. The best way we can serve God is to continually ask Him to do His work through us.

Our Father wants each of us to work with Him and for Him. He is the Chief Executive Officer. Each of His children is similar to a junior executive who should work closely with Him at all times. "…we are fellow workmen (joint promoters, laborers together) with and for God…" (I Corinthians 3:9).

We are God's hands and feet here on earth. We are God's eyes and ears. We are God's mouth. Our Father has created our spirits, our souls and our bodies to be used by Him for His glory.

James 1:5-9, the foundation passage of Scripture for this book, tells us that our Father will give us His wisdom if we ask Him with unwavering faith. Our primary goal should be to use the wisdom our Father gives us to serve Him. Our Father desires to pour out His wisdom abundantly in us, on us, and through us so that we can spread the gospel and minister effectively to other people.

The wisdom of the world is primarily self-seeking. The wisdom of God has been made available to us so that we can serve God effectively. We are not here on earth for other people to serve us. We should follow the example of Jesus Christ by dedicating ourselves to serve Him. Jesus said, "...whoever wishes to be great among you must be your servant, and whoever desires to be first among you must be your slave – just as the Son of Man came not to be waited on but to serve, and to give His life as a ransom for many [the price paid to set them free]" (Matthew 20:26-28).

We should turn away from all prideful thoughts and all desire for recognition from other human beings if we truly want to receive God's wisdom so that we can serve Him effectively. The only recognition we should desire for our service to God should be to hear Him say to us after we have served Him, "Well done, good and faithful servant."

We should desire to receive this commendation from God when we serve Him here on earth. We should desire above all else to hear Him say these words to us when we first see Him face to face in heaven.

Jesus Christ left the glory of heaven to come to earth to serve God. We should follow His example of service. Jesus said, "If anyone serves Me, he must continue to follow Me [to cleave steadfastly to Me, conform wholly to My example in living and, if need be, in dying] and wherever I am, there will My servant be also. If anyone serves Me, the Father will honor him" (John 12:26).

We can only serve Jesus Christ to the degree we are willing to follow Him. We should "cleave" to Jesus without wavering. Our Father will honor us if we serve Jesus Christ. He will use us in a great way if we have a zealous desire to serve Him. "Never lag in zeal and in earnest endeavor; be aglow and burning with the Spirit, serving the Lord" (Romans 12:11).

We should "burn with the Spirit" as we yield control of our lives to the Holy Spirit because of our sincere desire to serve the Lord. Everything we say and everything we do should be said and done in the name of Jesus Christ. We should place total dependence on Him as we praise God continually. "...whatever you do [no matter what it is] in word or deed, do everything in the name of the Lord Jesus and in [dependence upon] His Person, giving praise to God the Father through Him" (Colossians 3:17).

We now have completed everything I originally wanted to write about in this book. However, as I looked at the research I did in preparing to write this book, I saw that one significant way to receive wisdom from God has not been covered. In the final chapter of this book we will look into the Word of God to see how our Father often gives us manifestation of His wisdom through other people.

Chapter 43

We Should Seek Counsel from Mature Christians

We have seen that our Father often uses repetition to emphasize specific principles He wants us to clearly understand. In this chapter we will see that the Word of God repeatedly tells us to seek wise counsel from others to help us to make important decisions. "... the person of understanding will acquire skill and attain to sound counsel [so that he may be able to steer his course rightly]..." (Proverbs 1:5).

Our Father instructs us to attend church regularly (see Hebrews 10:25). We should prayerfully and carefully seek the church our Father wants us to attend. When we need counsel from others we can seek counsel from the leaders of our church - the pastor, assistant pastors, elders, deacons, teachers and other leaders within the church. These leaders have been placed in their positions of leadership because of their maturity as Christians.

As we grow and mature as Christians we should develop close relationships with other Christians who are mature in the Lord. Whenever I face a difficult problem, I often turn to five or six mature Christians who are very close to me. I respect the mature judgment of these people. On many occasions my mature Christian friends have pointed me toward a solution to a problem that I never could have found on my own.

When we need to make a difficult decision we should have the desire to receive counsel from several people. The Bible says that we often will fail if we do not receive wise guidance. We are told that we will be safe if we consistently turn to many people for counsel. "Where no wise guidance is, the people fall, but in the multitude of counselors there is safety" (Proverbs 11:14).

We usually will be frustrated if we attempt to make decisions without receiving wise counsel from mature Christians. Sometimes we need counsel from several different people before we are able to make the best possible decision. "Where there is no counsel, purposes are frustrated, but with many counselors they are accomplished" (Proverbs 15:22).

Whenever I am faced with a difficult problem I take careful notes from each of the discussions I have with the people I turn to for counsel. I talk with each person as long as necessary to learn everything I can from the wisdom God has given to that person. I then neatly rewrite my notes from that conversation. I then prayerfully ask another mature Christian for counsel. I repeat the same process. I continue to seek counsel until I believe in my heart that I have received all of the counsel I need.

After I have talked to these counselors I often follow a system that I learned many years ago when I read wise advice from Benjamin Franklin. He said, "When confronted with two courses of action, I jot down on a piece of paper all the arguments in favor of each one. Then, on the opposite side of the page, I write the arguments against each one. By weighing the arguments pro and con and canceling them out one against the other, I take the counsel indicated by what remains."

I often review the notes I have rewritten from meetings with several counselors. Sometimes I break down this composite advice into categories. I then list these categories in what I believe is the proper order of importance. I list the pros and cons in each subheading on different sides of a line that I draw down the center of several pieces of paper.

As I go through this process I inevitably find that a pattern begins to emerge from the advice I received from these people. The cumulative effect of the notes I have taken from several people often has led me toward a solution I never could have found on my own. I am always grateful for the counsel I receive from these people. "The way of a fool is right in his own eyes, but he who listens to counsel is wise" (Proverbs 12:15).

We should rejoice over the wise advice we receive from our counselors. These people really care about what we are going through. Their counsel comes from deep down in their hearts. "Oil and perfume rejoice the heart; so does the sweetness of a friend's counsel that comes from the heart" (Proverbs 27:9).

When we turn to mature Christians for counsel we often will find that the Holy Spirit speaks to us through these people. The Holy Spirit will speak through another person to give us wise advice that this person could not give directly with his or her limited human intelligence and understanding. When people come to me for counsel I often say, "We have a problem if we look for an answer from my human wisdom. Let's pray and ask the Lord to give us His wisdom."

No matter how mature we think we are or how many years we have been a Christian, we never will arrive at the point where we shouldn't seek counsel from others. Sometimes people who have risen to positions of leadership think they have all of the answers they need. They fail to receive the wonderful counsel that is available to them from others. "Better is a poor and wise youth than an old and foolish king who no longer knows how to receive counsel (friendly reproof and warning)..." (Ecclesiastes 4:13).

On many occasions the same people who have given me such wonderful counsel have turned to me for counsel when they have needed advice. I am always very grateful when I am used by the Lord to help any of the people who have been used by the Lord to help me. We are here to serve the Lord and to help one another.

In this chapter I have talked about receiving counsel from mature Christians. We should be very careful about seeking counsel from people who are not Christians. These ungodly people might have a lot of worldly wisdom, but they are not connected to the Word of God and the Spirit of God. "Blessed (happy, fortunate, prosperous, and enviable) is the man who walks and lives not in the counsel of the ungodly [following their advice, their plans and purposes]..." (Psalm 1:1).

Many people who seem to be very intelligent and knowledgeable are only intelligent and knowledgeable in the ways of the world. They have no knowledge of God's ways. Have you ever heard someone talk about "the blind leading the blind?" Did you know that these words came from Jesus Christ Who spoke to the Pharisees saying, "...if a blind man leads a blind man, both will fall into a ditch" (Matthew 15:14)?

We often will "fall into a ditch" if we act upon the counsel we receive from ungodly people. We should seek counsel from people who are able to receive wisdom from God instead of seeking counsel from people who are blind to God's ways. "He who walks [as a companion] with wise men is wise..." (Proverbs 13:20).

Ideally, we should only turn for advice to mature Christians who have spent many years obeying God's instructions to continually fill their minds and their hearts with His Word. We should seek counsel from believers who are close enough to God to hear His voice. We must understand that the best counsel we can receive comes *through* other people, not from other people.

In addition to seeking counsel from mature Christians, we also are instructed to receive constructive criticism and correction from the Lord and from other believers. Our Father often will give us constructive criticism because He loves us so much. We should always be completely open to changing our ways to do whatever He tells us to do. "Those whom I [dearly and tenderly] love, I tell their faults and convict and convince and reprove and chasten [I discipline and instruct them]. So be enthusiastic and in earnest and burning with zeal and repent [changing your mind and attitude]" (Revelation 3:19).

We have seen that we should consistently seek counsel from mature Christians. If we truly want to make wise decisions, we also should be willing to receive constructive criticism from these people because we know that they have our best interests at heart. "Hear counsel, receive instruction, and accept correction, that you may be wise in the time to come" (Proverbs 19:20).

We have seen that the Word of God repeatedly tells us that we will receive blessings from God when we are humble. If we truly are humble and teachable, our minds and our hearts will be fertile soil to receive advice from others, to be taught by others and to receive constructive criticism from others.

We should never be so proud that we look at constructive criticism with disdain. We should understand that mature Christians who correct us actually are being kind to us when they give us the constructive criticism we need to receive. "Let the righteous man smite and correct me - it is a kindness..." (Psalm 141:5).

The words "righteous man" in this passage of Scripture refer to people who are righteous before God as a result of accepting and believing in the sacrifice the Lord Jesus Christ made for them. We should allow these people to "smite us." The word "smite" in this context means "to strike out against."

Sometimes we need to hear words that we don't want to hear. If we are humble and teachable, we won't react negatively when we receive constructive criticism. "... he who hates reproof is like a brute beast, stupid and indiscriminating" (Proverbs 12:1).

Some of the best advice I have ever received has come from loving friends who dared to risk my displeasure by giving me the constructive criticism I badly needed to receive. We make a big mistake if we ignore this constructive criticism. "The ear that listens to the reproof [that leads to or gives] life will remain among the wise. He who refuses and ignores instruction and correction despises himself, but he who heeds reproof gets understanding" (Proverbs 15:31-32).

No one likes to be criticized. However, we often cannot receive the understanding we must have unless we are willing to receive constructive criticism. When we receive this criticism we should always ask ourselves, "What is this person's intent? Is this criticism constructive? If so, what could the

Lord be trying to teach me through this person's constructive criticism?"

Proud people turn away from people when they don't want to hear their criticism. If we trust the person who is criticizing us, we often will find that we are looking directly into the eyes of the Lord if we will listen humbly to the constructive criticism we are receiving. We will understand that the Lord is gently and constructively trying to teach us through loving human beings who risk our displeasure by daring to correct us.

This chapter is filled with many specific instructions from the Word of God pertaining to the advice and constructive criticism our Father wants to give us through other believers. I pray that you always will be open to the counsel and constructive criticism the Lord wants you to receive from Him and from other Christians who know you and love you.

Conclusion

Our Father has done His part. He has made His wisdom available to us to use for His glory throughout our lives. This book is solidly anchored upon 501 Scripture references that tell us how to receive manifestation of God's wisdom.

If you are very serious about receiving wisdom from God, I urge you to read this book more than once. Continued study and meditation are required to understand the contents of this book because it contains so much Scripture.

The first reading of this book will give you a scriptural foundation to build upon. Several people over the years have written to us to say that they have read one of our books so many times that the pages fell out. They have written to order a new copy of that particular book.

Use a highlighter or underline scriptural references that are significant to you when you review this book. Make notes pertaining to the scriptural instructions in the margins of each page, in a separate notebook or on file cards. You also can enter this scriptural information into a computer.

Study the information in this book to get the Scripture references up off the printed pages of the book into your mind. Meditate continually on key passages of Scripture so that they will drop from your mind down into your heart. Continue to meditate until the Word of God flows out of your mouth and you have programmed yourself to obey God's instructions and to step out in faith on God's promises.

The Scripture references in this book are filled with the wisdom of God and the power of God. Saturate yourself in these promises and instructions from God's throne in heaven. Receive with unwavering faith the magnificent wisdom your Father has promised to give to you.

Our Father doesn't want us to just pay mental assent to His Word. He wants us to obey His instructions. He wants us to step out in faith on His promises. He wants us to make this total commitment to Him so that we will receive all of the wisdom, guidance, knowledge and understanding He has made available to us.

You now have an opportunity to help many other people learn about God's wisdom. Please pray and ask the Lord to show you friends and loved ones who could benefit from the contents of this book. From the beginning of our ministry we have made a quantity discount available to every reader so that you can share our publications with others at minimal cost. See the order forms in the back of the book for specific information that will help you to help others with the scriptural instructions that are explained in this book.

Also, please pray about giving a copy of this book to any government leaders who are in your personal sphere of influence. Government leaders at all levels of government are constantly faced with complex problems. *How* can these government leaders attempt to do their jobs in these uncertain times with the limitations of their human wisdom? *All government leaders need the wisdom of God.*

Can you imagine the effect this book would have if the President of the United States, every United States Senator, every United States Congressman or Congresswoman, the governor of every state and all local government officials had a copy of this book and studied and meditated on the Scripture references on a daily basis? Please do everything you can to get this book into the hands of every possible government official in our country and other English speaking countries. My book, *Trust God for Your Finances,* has been translated into nine foreign languages. We are trusting God for this book on His wisdom to reach every known language.

If you know government officials who have asked Jesus Christ to be their Savior, they will be able to understand the scriptural principles that are explained in this book. Government officials who have not asked Jesus Christ to be their Savior can learn about eternal salvation from this book. They then can join the other people who have come into the kingdom of God as a result of accepting the salvation message that is contained in the appendix of each of our books. Please pray for the salvation of any unsaved people who receive a copy of this book from you.

Also, please pray about giving copies of this book to other people in positions of leadership, particularly the pastor of your church. I believe wholeheartedly that any church where the pastor, the assistant pastors, all elders and deacons and all members of the church staff will study and meditate on the Scripture references in this book will find that their church will operate much more powerfully and efficiently.

If you like what you have read in this book, please look to see if any of our other publications might help you. Please review the following checklist of benefits carefully. See if any of the following specific benefits that are explained in our publications are of interest to you.

Overcome worry and fear

Book: *Conquering Fear*

Scripture cards and cassette tape: *Freedom from Worry and Fear*

Increase your faith in God

Scripture cards and cassette tape: *Continually Increasing Faith in God*

Find God's will for your life

Book: *God's Will for Your Life*

Scripture cards and cassette tapes: *Find God's Will for Your Life*

Receive healing from sickness

Scripture cards and cassette tape: *Receive Healing from the Lord.*

Improved health

Book: *Increased Energy and Vitality.*

Financial success by following God's instructions

Book: *Trust God for Your Finances*

Scripture cards and cassette tape: *Financial Instructions from God*

Assurance of God's indwelling presence

Scripture cards and cassette tape: *God is Always With You.*

Experiencing peace with God and the peace of God

Book: *Deep Inner Peace*

Scripture cards and cassette tape: *Enjoy God's Wonderful Peace*

Your Father's love for you

Scripture cards and cassette tape: *Our Father's Wonderful Love*

Draw closer to the Lord

Scripture cards and cassette tape: *A Closer Relationship with the Lord*

Increased patience and perseverance

Book: *Never, Never Give Up*

Your eternal home in heaven

Book: *What Will Heaven Be Like?*

Overcoming adversity in your life

Book: *Soaring above the Problems of Life*

Scripture cards and cassette tape: *Receive God's Blessing in Adversity*

Effective Bible study

Book: *How to Study the Bible*

Sharing eternal salvation with others

Book: *100 Years from Today*

Calm confidence in a crisis

Book: *Quiet Confidence in the Lord*

Each of these topics is covered in scriptural detail in our books, Scripture Meditation Cards and cassette tapes. In addition, I have recorded 35 individual cassette tapes to provide additional teaching on these and other subjects. I have worked for over a quarter of a century to pull all of this scriptural material together by topic so that you can study and meditate on God's Word in each of these areas. I pray that many of our publications and cassette tapes will be a blessing to you and, through you, to many other people.

Finally, I pray that this book on the wisdom of God has blessed you abundantly. I pray that you will take full advantage of the opportunity your Father has given you to receive His wonderful wisdom. God bless you.

Appendix

This book contains a comprehensive set of biblical instructions that explain how to receive wisdom, knowledge, guidance and understanding from the Lord. These instructions are given to God's children - those human beings who have entered into His kingdom. I ask each person reading this book, "Have *you* entered into the kingdom of God?"

We don't enter into the kingdom of God by church attendance, baptism, confirmation, teaching Sunday school or living a good life. We can only enter into the kingdom of God if we are "born again." Jesus said, "...I assure you, most solemnly I tell you, that unless a person is born again (anew, from above), he cannot ever see (know, be acquainted with, and experience) the kingdom of God" (John 3:3).

Some people are so caught up with their own religious denomination and their personal beliefs that they completely miss God's instructions on how to enter His kingdom. We must be born spiritually. This process starts by admitting that we are sinners. We then must repent of these sins. "...unless you repent (change your mind for the better and heartily amend your ways, with abhorrence of your past sins), you will all likewise perish and be lost eternally" (Luke 13:5).

Many people miss out on eternal life in heaven because they are trusting in the goodness of their own lives to get them to heaven. This is a tragic mistake. With the exception of Jesus Christ, every person who has ever lived is a sinner. "...None is righteous, just and truthful and upright and conscientious, no, not one" (Romans 3:10). We all are sinners. "...all have sinned and are falling short of the honor and glory which God bestows and receives" (Romans 3:23).

God doesn't have degrees of sin. If we have committed one sin, we are just as guilty as someone who has committed many sins. "For whosoever keeps the Law [as a] whole but stumbles and offends in one [single instance] has become guilty of [breaking] all of it" (James 2:10).

In addition to acknowledging our sins and repenting of them, we must take one additional step. "...if you acknowledge and confess with your lips that Jesus is Lord and in your heart believe (adhere to, trust in, and rely on the truth) that God raised Him from the dead, you will be saved. For with the heart a person believes (adheres to, trusts in, and relies on Christ) and so is justified (declared righteous, acceptable to God), and with the mouth he confesses (declares openly and speaks out freely his faith) and confirms [his] salvation" (Romans 10:9-10).

We must do more than just pay mental assent to the crucifixion of Jesus Christ to receive eternal salvation. We must know that we are sinners. We must believe deep down in our hearts that Jesus Christ paid the full price for all of our sins and that He took our place on the cross at Calvary. We must know that Jesus died for us and that He has risen from the dead. We must believe totally, completely and absolutely that we will live eternally in heaven only because of the price that Jesus Christ paid for us.

If we really believe these spiritual truths in our hearts, we will speak them with our mouths. We may feel timid about doing this at first, but speaking of Jesus builds our faith tremendously and builds faith in others. We should tell other people that we have been born again, that we are Christians and that we trust completely in Jesus Christ for our eternal salvation. We are not saved until we believe these scriptural truths in our hearts and freely confess them to others with our mouths.

All of us were born naturally on the day our mothers gave birth to us. We must have a second birth in order to be born spiritually. "You have been regenerated (born again), not from a mortal origin (seed, sperm), but from one that is immortal by the ever living and lasting Word of God" (I Peter 1:23).

God doesn't reveal Himself to us through our intellects. He reveals Himself through our hearts. We may be adults in the natural realm, but we need to start all over again as children in the spiritual realm. We must have childlike faith. "...unless you repent (change, turn about) and become like little children [trusting, lowly, loving, forgiving], you can never enter the kingdom of heaven [at all]" (Matthew 18:3).

The following prayer will result in your spiritual birth if you truly believe these words in your heart and if you boldly confess them to others with your mouth. "Dear Father God, I come to you in the name of Jesus Christ. I admit that I am a sinner. I know there is no way I can enter into Your kingdom based upon the sinful life I have led. I am genuinely sorry for my sins. I believe in my heart that Jesus Christ is Your Son and that He died on the cross to pay for my sins. I believe that You raised Him from the dead and that He is alive today, sitting at

Your right hand. I trust completely in Him as my only way of receiving eternal salvation. Thank You, dear Lord Jesus. Thank You, dear Father. Amen."

You have been "born again" if you pray this prayer from your heart and if you confess these heartfelt beliefs with your mouth. You have been given a fresh new start "...if any person is [ingrafted] in Christ (the Messiah) he is a new creation (a new creature altogether); the old [previous moral and spiritual condition] has passed away. Behold, the fresh and new has come!" (I Corinthians 5:17).

Welcome to the family of God!

Study Guide

What Did You Learn from This Book?

Many individuals, Bible study groups, Sunday school classes and home fellowship groups have carefully reviewed the Scripture references in our books and Scripture Meditation Cards to learn from the Word of God. The following questions have been designed as a study guide for these individuals and groups to receive maximum retention from the 501 Scripture references contained in this book.

Over the years we have received numerous testimonies from members of Bible study groups, Sunday school classes and home fellowship groups in regard to the scriptural truths they have learned by discussing Scripture references from our books or our Scripture Meditation Cards. The following testimonies that we received as I was writing this book are an example of many similar testimonies we have received.

A man from Iowa said, "Approximately ten married couples from our church meet each week. For the past several months our weekly meetings have been centered around your Scripture cards, *Continually Increasing Faith in the Lord.* We read each card. Then we discuss it. Sometimes we have so much discussion that we can only cover two or three Scripture cards in one meeting. Everyone in our group is very enthused about these Scripture cards. We soon will be ordering another set of Scripture cards for continued discussion."

A man from New Hampshire said, "The mens' group from our church meets each Tuesday night. We have been studying your Scripture cards, *Find God's Will for Your Life,* for several weeks. At the beginning of each meeting we pick a specific number of cards. Then, we listen to your cassette tape explaining the Scripture references on these cards. We then discuss each of these Scripture references. Many of the men have become much more sensitive to what God wants them to do with their lives as a result of this project."

Both of these comments are about our Scripture Meditation Cards because we stopped writing books for almost five years to write and publish ten sets of Scripture Meditation Cards. The following comprehensive Study Guide will enable any individuals, Bible study groups, Sunday school classes or home fellowship groups to carefully study what the Word of God has to say about receiving wisdom, knowledge, guidance and understanding from God. We are unable to find questions that will enable us to include all of the 501 Scripture references in this Study Guide, but you will find that most of the Scripture references have been covered in our question and answer format.

This book can only help you if you are persuaded by the Word of God and by the Holy Spirit to obey the specific instructions from the holy Scriptures that are contained in this book. We believe the following questions will provide you with a thorough overview of the contents of this book.

	Page Ref.
1. What definition is used in *The Amplified Bible* to explain the meaning of the wisdom of God? (Colossians 1:28)	15
2. How can you be certain that your Father will give His wisdom to you? (James 1:5)	16
3. What does our Father say about the amount of wisdom He is willing to give to us? (James 1:5 and Ephesians 1:7-9)	16-17
4. This book contains several passages of Scripture that explain the incomprehensible depth of the wisdom of God. What examples do you remember that will help you to understand the tremendous magnitude of God's wisdom? (Romans 11:33, Psalm 104:24-25, Psalm 147:4-5, Daniel 2:20-22, Psalm 139:1-4, Hebrews 4:13, Exodus 15:11)	17-20
5. What does the Bible tell us about the relationship between wisdom from God, the quality of our lives and our life expectancy? (Proverbs 9:11, Isaiah 46:4, Proverbs 13:14 and Proverbs 3:15-18)	21-22
6. What comparison does the Bible make between the immense power of the wisdom of God and traditional sources of power in the world? (Ecclesiastes 9:16, Ecclesiastes 9:18, Proverbs 24:5, Ecclesiastes 7:19, Proverbs 21:22 and Ecclesiastes 10:10)	22-23

7. The wisdom of God is not available to people who have not asked Jesus Christ to be their Savior. How does Satan attempt to stop unbelievers from understanding their need for eternal salvation through Jesus Christ? (John 12:40, Ephesians 2:2, II Corinthians 4:4, Romans 8:7, John 8:47, Ephesians 4:17-18 and I Corinthians 1:21) 27-30

8. How can we be certain that God Himself will give each of us the desire to receive eternal salvation as a result of asking Jesus Christ to be our Savior? (John 6:44 and I Timothy 2:3-4) 31-32

9. What exactly does the Bible say must occur before a person can receive eternal salvation through Jesus Christ? (John 3:3, Luke 13:5, Romans 10:9 and I John 1:8) 32-33

10. What does the Bible say about being able to understand the Word of God after we are saved when we could not understand the Bible before we were saved? (Colossians 1:13, II Corinthians 3:16, II Corinthians 4:3, II Corinthians 5:17, Romans 6:4 and Romans 7:22) 33-34

11. The Bible tells us that the wisdom of God is hidden from many people. How can you be absolutely certain that the wisdom of God is not hidden from you? (Matthew 13:11, Proverbs 2:7, I Corinthians 2:7, Colossians 2:2-3, I Corinthians 1:24, John 1:1 and Revelation 19:13) 37-38

12. What does the word "tradition" mean from a scriptural perspective? Can traditional thinking

21. What is the relationship between fearing the Lord, studying the Word of God and receiving wisdom from God? (Deuteronomy 17:19, Psalm 119:38, Psalm 19:8-10, Psalm 119:127 and Proverbs 13:13) 48-50

22. What is the scriptural relationship between the Spirit of the Lord, the fear of the Lord and receiving wisdom and understanding from the Lord? (Isaiah 11:2-3) 50-51

23. What condition must exist if we truly want the Lord to be our teacher? (Psalm 25:12 and Psalm 25:14) 51-52

24. What relationship exists between the fear of the Lord and our relationship with Satan? (Proverbs 8:13 and Proverbs 19:23) 52

25. What should we do if we want our Father to keep His eye upon us at all times? (Psalm 33:18) 52

26. What does it mean when the Bible tell us that wisdom from God is "the principal thing?" How does this Old Testament principle relate to other instructions in the Bible that tell us to put God first? (Proverbs 4:7, Deuteronomy 6:5-6, Matthew 22:37-38 and Matthew 6:33) 55-56

27. What are we instructed to do to get wisdom from God so that this wisdom will guard us, exalt us and bring us honor and promotion? (Proverbs 4:5-6 and Proverbs 4:8-9) 57-58

28. Why did God pour out such an abundance of His wisdom upon King Solomon?(I Kings 3:5, I Kings 3:9-13 and I Kings 4:29-31) 58-59

48. What benefits did the psalmist receive from the Word of God when he was suffering from affliction? (Psalm 119:25 and Psalm 119:50) 100

49. What does it mean when the Word of God is compared to "great spoil?" How can we tell what our real treasures are? (Psalm 119:162 and Matthew 6:21) 100-101

50. Why should we continually be in awe of the Word of God? Why are we wise if we obey the instructions in the holy Scriptures? (Psalm119:161 and Proverbs 8:33) 101-103

51. Why does our Father instruct us to continually renew our minds in His Word? (Proverbs 23:19,II Timothy 2:25 and Psalm 119:70-72) 105-108

52. Our lives will be transformed if we obey our Father's instructions to renew our minds in His Word. What does the word "transform" mean? How does this potential for transformation apply to your life? (Romans 12:2, Matthew 17:2 and Romans 6:6) 108-109

53. How often does our Father want us to renew our minds in His Word? What blessings does He promise to give to His children who obey these instructions? (Ephesians 4:22-23, Colossians 3:9-10 and II Corinthians 4:16).......... 109-111

54. What does it mean when we are instructed to "brace up our minds?" (I Peter 1:13, Psalm 119:28 and Acts 17:11) 111-112

55. What caused Judas Iscariot, who once was a beloved disciple of Jesus Christ, to make the

61. Why should we always pray before we begin our daily Bible study? What should we pray for? (Psalm 119:18-19) 129

62. Why is it so important to hold tightly to the instructions we are given in the Word of God? (Proverbs 4:13) 130-131

63. When we study the Bible continually God's instructions and promises come up off the printed pages of the Bible into our minds. Why is it important for us to learn how to get the wisdom of the Word of God from our minds down into our hearts? (Psalm 51:6, Romans 10:10, Hebrews 11:1, Colossians 3:16, Proverbs 23:7, Proverbs 3:21-22 and Psalm 37:31) 133-135

64. Plants or trees that are pruned are cut so that unnecessary portions are removed. Many people have to be "pruned" by learning through adversity. How were the disciples of Jesus Christ "cleansed and pruned already?" Why should we follow their example? (John 15:3) 135-136

65. The Bible repeatedly instructs us to store up the Word of God in our minds and our hearts. What blessings will we receive if we obey these instructions? (Deuteronomy 11:18, Job 22:22-23, Proverbs 7:1, Proverbs 10:14 and II John 2) 130-137

66. Why do some people have heavy hearts? What are we instructed to do if we want to have a glad heart? How will we react to the circumstances in our lives if we have a glad heart? (Proverbs 12:25, Proverbs 15:15 and Psalm 19:8) 138

67. What did Jesus Christ mean when He said we should abide in His Word? What blessings did Jesus tell us we will receive if we abide in His Word? (John 8:31-32) 138-139

68. The Word of God promises that we will make our way prosperous, that we will deal wisely and that we will have good success. What three things does God tell us to do if we want to receive these wonderful benefits? (Joshua 1:8) 141-144

69. We will prosper and come to maturity if we delight in the Word of God and if we continually meditate on God's Word throughout the day and night. We are told that we will be like a tree planted next to a stream of water if we obey these instructions. What does this statement mean? How does it apply to your life today? (Psalm 1:2-3) 144-146

70. What do many people focus upon when they are faced with adversity instead of meditating continually on God's promises? (Isaiah 33:18) 146-149

71. What is the difference between memorizing the Word of God and meditating on the Word of God? What exactly do we do when we meditate on God's Word? 151-157

72. Why is it so important for our ears to hear our mouths speaking the Word of God when we meditate on the holy Scriptures? (Jeremiah 23:28 and Romans 10:17) 159-165

73. We never stand still in the area of spiritual growth. We are either moving forward or moving back-

do to prepare ourselves for God's wisdom to flow out of our mouths? What blessings will we receive if we speak the Word of God continually? (II Timothy 2:16, Psalm 49:3, Proverbs 20:15 and Ecclesiastes 10:12-14) 189-190

86. What should mature Christians do if they are tempted to speak in anger? What results will inevitably occur? (Proverbs 29:11 and Proverbs 15:1) 190-191

87. In James 1:5 God promises to give liberally of His wisdom to everyone who asks Him. This promise is a conditional promise. What are the conditions to this promise? (James 1:5-8) 193-194

88. How do some people essentially call God a liar even though they have no intention of calling Him a liar? (I John 5:10) 196

89. Why did the Israelites in the desert fail to benefit from the wonderful promise they received from God? (Hebrews 4:2) 196-197

90. Our Father wants us to have total, absolute and unwavering faith in all of His promises. How did Abraham show unwavering faith in God in the face of a seemingly impossible situation? How should we apply this attitude in our lives today? How can we use this principle to rebuke Satan and his demons? (Romans 4:19-21, Proverbs 4:25-27 and Ephesians 4:27) 197-198

91. We become justified before God when Jesus Christ becomes our Savior. What instruction did our Father give in four different places in the

124. Many unsaved people and immature Christians are externally oriented. The Lord is internally oriented. How does He look at us? What is the "real us?" (I Samuel 16:7 and I Peter 3:4) 245-246

125. Our Father wants to give us wonderful revelation knowledge that cannot be received by our senses. What does He instruct us to do so that we will be able to receive this revelation knowledge from Him? (I Corinthians 2:9-11 and Ephesians 1:17-18) 246-248

126. The world's definition of fame and being great from God's perspective are quite different. What has Jesus Christ instructed us to do if we desire to be great from His perspective? (Mark 10: 43-45) 249-250

127. Why should we always be prepared to write down any revelation the Lord gives us as soon as we receive it? 250-253

128. What instructions have we been given to obey if we sincerely desire to come into the presence of the Lord? (Psalm 100:1-2) 253-255

129. What should we do if we deeply and sincerely desire to receive more revelation knowledge from God? (Matthew 25:29) 255

130. Our Father has provided everything we will need during our lives on earth. What are we instructed to do to receive His provision? (II Peter 1:3)...............258

131. We cannot see the kingdom of God with our human eyesight. Where is the kingdom of God located? (Luke 17:20-22) 258-259

132. What do the words "the Godhead" mean? How can your constant awareness of the Godhead revolutionize the quality of your life? (Ephesians 4:6, II Corinthians 13:5, I Corinthians 6:19 and Colossians 2:9-10) 259-262

133. The world seeks security from external sources. God's security comes from the inside out. Jesus Christ called the Pharisees hypocrites because they looked good on the outside, but they were not clean on the inside. How do these words apply to us today? (Matthew 23:25-28) 263-265

134. Our Father wants each of us to grow and mature spiritually. What goal does He want us to pursue as we turn away from our previous immature behavior? (I Corinthians 13:11, I Corinthians 14:20, II Timothy 2:22, Hebrews 2:1, Hebrews 6:1 and Ephesians 4:15) 265-266

135. How can we keep Satan from getting an advantage over us? (II Corinthians 2:11) 267

136. How does the Lord's concept of education differ from the way that many people in the world look at education? (Proverbs 20:5) 267

137. What does the amplification of the word "Comforter" in *The Amplified Bible* explain that the Holy Spirit will do for us if we trust Him completely? (John 14:16) 267-268

138. Does the spiritual knowledge we have obtained remain intact if we fail to continue to grow and mature spiritually? (Luke 8:18) 268-269

155. We have been given the opportunity to receive manifestation of the tremendous, dynamic power of Almighty God in answer to our prayers. How are we instructed to pray in order to receive this manifestation of God's power? (James 5:16) 282-283

156. Why should we pray, whenever possible, in a prayer of agreement with one or more Christians? (Matthew 18:19) 283

157. Our Father wants to have a close relationship with each of His beloved children. What is required to initiate this close relationship? (James 4:8) 285

158. What does our Father look for when He looks down from heaven to find His children who are operating in His wisdom? (Psalm 14:2) 286

159. What are we instructed to do if we sincerely want to receive insight and understanding from God? (I Chronicles 28:9 and Proverbs 9:10) 286

160. How did Jesus Christ compare the relationship with the members of our families here on earth to our relationship with Him? (Matthew 10:37) .. 286-287

161. Jesus explained that we should "hate" our fathers, our mothers, our wives (or husbands), our children, our brothers, our sisters and ourselves if we truly desire to serve as His disciples. What does this difficult-to-understand statement actually mean? (Luke 14:26) 287

162. What is required from us if we want to "prove ourselves strong and stand firm and do exploits for God?" (Daniel 11:32) 287

A few words about Lamplight Ministries

Lamplight Ministries, Inc. originally began in 1983 as Lamplight Publications. After ten years as a publishing firm with a goal of selling Christian books, Lamplight Ministries was founded in 1993. Jack and Judy Hartman founded Lamplight Ministries with a mission of continuing to sell their publications and also to give large numbers of these publications free of charge to needy people all over the world.

Lamplight Ministries was created to allow people who have been blessed by our publications to share in financing the translation, printing and distribution of our books into other languages and also to distribute our publications free of charge to jails and prisons. Over the years many partners of Lamplight Ministries have shared Jack and Judy's vision. As the years have gone by Lamplight Ministries' giving has increased with each passing year. Tens of thousands of people in jails and prisons and in Third World countries have received our publications free of charge.

Our books and Scripture Meditation Cards have been translated into eleven foreign languages – Armenian, Danish, Greek, Hebrew, German, Korean, Norwegian, Portuguese, Russian, Spanish and the Tamil dialect in India. The translations in these languages are not available from Lamplight Ministries in the United States. These translations can only be obtained in the countries where they have been printed.

The pastors of many churches in Third World countries have written to say that they consistently preach sermons in their churches based upon the scriptural contents of our publications. We believe that, on any given Sunday, people in several churches in many different countries hear sermons that are based upon the scriptural contents of our publications. Praise the Lord!

Jack Hartman was the sole author of twelve Christian books. After co-authoring one book with Judy, Jack and Judy co-authored ten sets of Scripture Meditation Cards. Judy's contributions to *God's Wisdom Is Available To You* was so significant that she is the co-author of this book. Jack and Judy currently are working on several other books that they believe the Lord is leading them to write as co-authors.

We invite you to request our newsletter to stay in touch with us, to learn of our latest publications and to read comments from people all over the world. Please write, fax, call or email us. You are very special to us. We love you and thank God for you. Our heart is to take the gospel to the world and for our books to be available in every known language. Hallelujah!

Lamplight Ministries, Inc.,
PO Box 1307, Dunedin, Florida, 34697. USA
Phone: 1-800-540-1597 • Fax: 1-727-784-2980 • website: lamplight.net • email: gospel@tampabay.rr.com

We offer you a substantial quantity discount

From the beginning of our ministry we have been led of the Lord to offer the same quantity discount to individuals that we offer to Christian bookstores. Each individual has a sphere of influence with a specific group of people. We believe that you know many people who need to learn the scriptural contents of our publications.

The Word of God encourages us to give freely to others. We encourage you to give selected copies of these publications to people you know who need help in the specific areas that are covered by our publications. See our order form for specific information on the quantity discounts of 40% to 50% that we make available to you so that you can share our books and cassette tapes with others.

A request to our readers

If this book has helped you, we would like to receive your comments so that we can share them with others. Your comments can encourage other people to study our publications to learn from the scriptural contents of these publications.

When we receive a letter containing comments on any of our books, cassette tapes or Scripture Meditation Cards, we prayerfully take out excerpts from these letters. These selected excerpts are included in our newsletters and occasionally in our advertising and promotional materials.

If any of our publications have been a blessing to you, please share your comments with us so that we can share them with others. Tell us in your own words what a specific publication has meant to you and why you would recommend it to others. Please give as much specific information as possible.

We will need your written permission to use all or any part of your comments. We will never print your name or street address. We simply use the initials of your first and last name and the state or country you live in (E.G., Illinois).

Thank you for taking a few minutes of your time to encourage other people to learn from the scripture references in our publications.

Books by Jack and Judy Hartman

Conquering Fear – Many people in the world today are afraid because they see that various forms of worldly security are disappearing. Our Father does not want us to be afraid. He has told us 366 times in His Word that we should not be afraid. This book is filled with scriptural references that explain the source of fear and how to overcome fear.

Deep Inner Peace is based upon more than 200 Scripture references that explain how to overcome worry and fear, how to develop quiet confidence in the Lord and how to receive manifestation of God's peace at all times regardless of the circumstances we face. We have received hundreds of letters from people who were on the verge of suicide, who received help with drug and alcohol problems and who received comfort when they were faced with serious illness or severe tragedy.

God's Will For Our Lives teaches from the holy Scriptures why we are here on earth, what our Father wants us to do with our lives and how to experience the meaning and fulfillment we can only experience when we are carrying out God's will. God had a specific plan for each of our lives before we were born. He has given each of us abilities and talents to carry out the assignment He has given to us.

God's Wisdom Is Available To You explains from more than 500 Scripture references how to receive the wisdom our Father has promised to give to us. God looks at the wisdom of the world as "foolishness" (see I Corinthians 3:19). You will learn how to receive the revelation knowledge, guidance and wisdom from God that bypasses sense knowledge.

How to Study the Bible. Many Christians attempt to study the Bible and give up because they are unable to find a fruitful method of Bible study. This book explains in detail the method that Jack Hartman uses to study the Bible. This practical, step-by-step technique will give you a definite, specific and precise system for studying the Word of God. Any person who sincerely wants to study the Bible effectively can be helped by this book and our two cassette tapes on this subject.

Increased Energy and Vitality. Jack and Judy Hartman are senior citizens who are determined to be in the best possible physical condition to serve the Lord during the remainder of their lives. They have spent many hours of study and practical trial and error to learn how to increase their energy and vitality. This book is based upon more than 200 Scripture references that will help you to increase your energy and vitality so that you can serve the Lord more effectively.

Never, Never Give Up devotes the first five chapters to a scriptural explanation of patience and the remaining thirteen chapters to scriptural instruction pertaining to the subject of perseverance. This book is based upon almost 300 Scripture references that will help you to learn exactly what our loving Father instructs us to do to increase our patience and perseverance.

Nuggets of Faith – Jack Hartman has written over 100,000 spiritual meditations. This book contains some of his early meditations on the subject of increasing our faith in God. It contains 78 "nuggets" (average length of three paragraphs) to help you to increase your faith in God.

100 Years from Today tells exactly where each of us will be one hundred years from now if Jesus Christ is our Savior and where we will be if Jesus Christ is not our Savior. This simple and easy-to-understand book has helped many unbelievers to receive Jesus Christ as their Savior. This book leads the reader through the decision to eternal salvation. The book closes by asking the reader to make a decision for Jesus Christ and to make this decision now.

Quiet Confidence in the Lord is solidly anchored upon more than 400 Scripture references that explain how to remain calm and quiet in a crisis situation. You will learn from the Word of God how to control your emotions when you are faced with severe problems and how to increase your confidence in the Lord by spending precious quiet time alone with Him each day.

Soaring Above the Problems of Life has helped many people who were going through severe trials. This practical "hands on" book is filled with facts from the Word of God. Our Father has given each of us specific and exact instructions telling us how He wants us to deal with adversity. This book is written in a clear and easy-to-understand style that will help you to learn to deal with the adversity that we all must face in our lives.

Trust God for Your Finances is currently in its nineteenth printing with more than 150,000 copies in print. This book which has been translated into nine foreign languages contains over 200 Scripture references that explain in a simple, straightforward and easy-to-understand style what the Word of God says about our Father's instructions and promises pertaining to our finances.

What Will Heaven Be Like? explains from more than 200 Scripture references what the Bible tells us about what heaven will be like. Many people have written to tell us how much this book comforted them after they lost a loved one. We have received many other letters from terminally ill Christians who were comforted by scriptural facts about where they would be going in the near future.

Scripture Meditation Cards and Cassette Tapes by Jack and Judy Hartman

Each set of Scripture Meditation Cards consists of 52 2-1/2 inch by 3-1/2 inch cards that can easily be carried in a pocket or a purse. Each set of Scripture cards includes approximately 75 Scripture references and is accompanied by an 85-minute cassette tape that explains every passage of Scripture in detail.

Freedom From Worry and Fear

The holy Scriptures tell us repeatedly that our Father does not want us to be worried or afraid. There is no question that God doesn't want us to be worried or afraid, but what exactly should we do if we have a sincere desire to overcome worry and fear? You will learn to overcome worry and fear from specific factual instructions from the Word of God. You will learn how to have a peaceful mind that is free from fear. You'll learn to live one day at a time forgetting the past and not worrying about the future. You'll learn how to trust God completely instead of allowing worry and fear to get into your mind and into your heart.

Enjoy God's Wonderful Peace

Peace with God is available to us because of the sacrifice that Jesus Christ made for us at Calvary. In addition to peace with God, Jesus also has given us the opportunity to enjoy the peace of God. You will learn how to enter into God's rest to receive God's perfect peace that will enable you to remain calm and quiet deep down inside of yourself regardless of the circumstances you face. You will learn exactly what to do to experience God's peace that is so great that it surpasses human understanding. The Holy Spirit is always calm and peaceful. We can experience His wonderful peace if we learn how to yield control of our lives to Him.

Find God's Will for Your Life

The Bible tells us that God had a specific plan for every day of our lives before we were born. Our Father will not reveal His will for our lives to us if we seek His will passively. He wants us to hunger and thirst with a deep desire to live our lives according to His will. God's plan for our lives is far over and above anything we can comprehend with our limited human comprehension. We cannot experience deep meaning, fulfillment and satisfaction in our lives without seeking, finding and carrying out God's will for our lives.

Receive God's Blessings in Adversity

The Lord is with us when we are in trouble. He wants to help us and He will help us according to our faith in Him. He wants us to focus continually on Him instead of dwelling upon the problems we face. We must not give up hope. Our Father will never let us down. He has made provision to give us His strength in exchange for our weakness. Our Father wants us to learn, grow and mature by facing the problems in our lives according to the instructions He has given us in His Word. We must persevere in faith to walk in the magnificent victory that Jesus Christ won for us.

Financial Instructions from God

Our loving Father wants His children to be financially successful just as loving parents here on earth want their children to be successful. God's ways are much higher and very different from the ways of the world. Our Father doesn't want us to follow the world's system for financial prosperity. He wants us to learn and obey His instructions pertaining to our finances. You will learn how to renew your mind in the Word of God so that you will be able to see your finances in a completely different light than you see them from a worldly perspective. You will be given step-by-step instructions to follow to receive financial prosperity from God.

Receive Healing from the Lord

Many people are confused by the different teachings about whether God heals today. Are you sick? Would you like to see for yourself exactly what the Bible says about divine healing? Study the Word of God on this important subject. Draw your own conclusion based upon facts from the holy Scriptures. You will learn that Jesus Christ has provided for your healing just as surely as He has provided for your eternal salvation. You will learn exactly what the Word of God instructs you to do to increase your faith that God will heal you.

A Closer Relationship with the Lord

Because of the price that Jesus Christ paid at Calvary all Christians have been given the awe-inspiring opportunity to come into the presence of Almighty God. These Scripture cards clearly explain the secret of enjoying a sweet and satisfying relationship with the Lord. Many Christians know about the Lord, but He wants us to know Him personally. We should have a deep desire to enjoy a close personal relationship with our precious Lord. He has promised to come close to us if we sincerely desire a close relationship with Him.

Our Father's Wonderful Love

God showed His love for us by sending His beloved Son to earth to die for our sins. Jesus Christ showed His love for us by taking the sins of the entire world upon Himself on the cross at Calvary. The same love and compassion that was demonstrated during the earthly ministry of Jesus

Christ is available to us today. Because of the sacrifice of Jesus Christ all Christians are the beloved sons and daughters of Almighty God. God is our loving Father. Our Father doesn't want us to seek security from external sources. He wants us to be completely secure in His love for us. You will learn from the Word of God exactly how faith works by love and how to overcome fear through love.

God is Always with You

God is not far away. He lives in our hearts. We must not neglect the gift that is in us. We are filled with the Godhead – Father, Son and Holy Spirit. Why would we ever be afraid of anything or anyone if we are absolutely certain that God is always with us? God's power and might are much greater than we can comprehend. He watches over us at all times. He wants to help us. He wants us to walk in close fellowship with Him. His wisdom and knowledge are available to us. He wants to guide us throughout every day of our lives.

Continually Increasing Faith in God

We all are given the same amount of faith to enable us to become children of God. Our Father wants the faith that He gave us to grow continually. We live in the last days before Jesus Christ returns. We must learn how to develop deeply rooted faith in God. You will learn how to walk in the authority and power you have been given over Satan and his demons. You can walk in victory over the circumstances in your life. You will learn exactly what the holy Scriptures tell us to do to receive manifestation of God's mighty strength and power. You will learn the vital importance of the words you speak. You will learn that there is only one way to control the words you speak when you are under severe pressure in a crisis situation.

Why you cannot combine orders for quantity discounts for Scripture Meditation Cards with other products

We desire to make the purchase of our products as *simple* as possible. However, we are unable to combine orders for our Scripture Meditation Cards with orders for our other products.

The reason for this decision is that the cost of printing and packaging Scripture Meditation Cards is much higher in proportion to the purchase price than the price of printing books. If we wanted to offer the same percentage quantity discount that we offer with our books, the cost for one set of Scripture Meditation Cards would have to be $7. This price was unacceptable to us.

We decided to offer each individual set of Scripture Meditation Cards for a reasonable price of $5 including postage. In order to keep this price for individual sets of Scripture Meditation Cards this low we had to develop an entirely different price structure for quantity discounts. Please see the enclosed order form for information on these discounts.

Cassette Tapes by Jack Hartman

01H How to Study the Bible (Part 1) – 21 scriptural reasons why it's important to study the Bible

02H How to Study the Bible (Part 2) – A detailed explanation of a proven, effective system for studying the Bible

03H Enter Into God's Rest – Don't struggle with loads that are too heavy for you. Learn what God's Word teaches about relaxing under pressure.

04H Freedom From Worry – A comprehensive scriptural explanation of how to become free from worry

05H God's Strength, Our Weakness – God's strength is available if we can admit our human weakness and trust instead in His unlimited strength.

06H How to Transform Our Lives – A scriptural study of how we can change our lives through a spiritual renewal of our minds.

07H The Greatest Power in the Universe (Part 1) – The greatest power in the universe is love. This tape explains our Father's love for us.

08H The Greatest Power in the Universe (Part 2) – A scriptural explanation of our love for God and for each other, and how to overcome fear through love.

09H How Well Do You Know Jesus Christ? – An Easter Sunday message that will show you Jesus as you never knew Him before.

10H God's Perfect Peace – In a world of unrest, many people search for inner peace. Learn from God's Word how to obtain His perfect peace.

11H Freedom Through Surrender – Many people try to find freedom by "doing their own thing." God's Word says that freedom comes from surrendering our lives to Jesus Christ.

12H Overcoming Anger – When is anger is permissible and when is it a sin? Learn from the Bible how to overcome the sinful effects of anger.

13H Taking Possession of Our Souls – God's Word teaches that patience is the key to the possession of our souls. Learn from the Word of God how to increase your patience and endurance.

14H Staying Young in the Lord – Some people try to cover up the aging process with makeup, hair coloring and hairpieces. Learn from the Bible how you can offset the aging process.

15H Two Different Worlds – Specific instructions from the Word of God to help you enter into and stay in the presence of God.

16H Trust God For Your Finances – This tape is a summary of the highlights of Jack's best-selling book, *Trust God For Your Finances.*

17H The Joy of the Lord – Learn how to experience the joy of the Lord regardless of the external circumstances in your life.

18H Let Go and Let God – Our Father wants us to give our problems to Him and leave them with Him because we have complete faith in Him..

19H Guidance, Power, Comfort and Wisdom – Learn the specific work of the Holy Spirit Who will guide us, empower us, comfort us and give us wisdom.

20H Go With God – This tape is based on 35 Scripture references that explain why and how to witness to the unsaved.

21H One Day at a Time – Our Father doesn't want us to dwell on the past nor worry about the future. Learn how to follow biblical instructions to live your life one day at a time.

22H Never, Never Give Up – Endurance and perseverance are often added to our faith as we wait on the Lord, releasing our will to His.

23H The Christ-Centered Life – Some Christians are still on the throne of their lives pursuing personal goals. Learn how to center every aspect of your life around the Lord Jesus Christ.

24H Fear Must Disappear – The spirit of fear cannot stand up against perfect love. Learn what perfect love is and how to attain it.

25H Internal Security – Some Christians look for security from external sources. In this tape, Jack shares his belief that difficult times are ahead of us and the only security in these times will be from the Spirit of God and the Word of God living in our hearts.

26H Continually Increasing Faith – Romans 12:3 tells us that all Christians start out with a specific amount of faith. In these last days before Jesus returns, we will all need a stronger faith than just the minimum. This tape offers many specific suggestions on what to do to continually strengthen our faith.

27H Why Does God Allow Adversity? – Several Scripture references are used in this tape to explain the development of strong faith through adversity.

28H Faith Works by Love – Galatians 5:6 tells us that faith works by love. Christians wondering why their faith doesn't seem to be working may find an answer in this message. A life centered around the love of the Lord for us and our love for others is absolutely necessary to strong faith.

29H There Are No Hopeless Situations – Satan wants us to feel hopeless. He wants us to give up hope and quit. This tape explains the difference between hope and faith. It tells how we set our goals through hope and bring them into manifestation through strong, unwavering faith.

30H Walk By Faith, Not By Sight – When we're faced with seemingly unsolvable problems, it's easy to focus our attention on the problems instead of upon the Word of God and the Spirit of God. In this tape, Jack gives many personal examples of difficult situations in his life and how the Lord honored his faith and the faith of others who prayed for him.

31H Stay Close to the Lord – Our faith is only as strong as its source. A close relationship with the Lord is essential to strong faith. In this tape, Jack explores God's Word to give a thorough explanation of how to develop a closer relationship with the Lord.

32H Quiet Faith – When we're faced with very difficult problems, the hardest thing to do is to be still. The Holy Spirit, however, wants us to remain quiet and calm because of our faith in Him. This message carefully examines the Word of God for an explanation of how we can do this.

33H When Human Logic is Insufficient – Human logic and reason often miss God. This message explains why some Christians block the Lord because they're unable to bypass their intellects and place their trust completely in Him.

34H The Good Fight of Faith – In this message, Jack compares the "good fight of faith" with the "bad" fight of faith. He explains who we fight against, where the battle is fought, and how it is won.

ORDER FORM FOR BOOKS AND CASSETTE TAPES

Book Title	Quantity	Total
God's Wisdom is Available to You ($12.00)	_______	_______
Increased Energy and Vitality ($10.00)	_______	_______
Quiet Confidence in the Lord ($9.00)	_______	_______
Never, Never Give Up ($8.00)	_______	_______
Trust God For Your Finances ($8.00)	_______	_______
Deep Inner Peace ($8.00)	_______	_______
What Will Heaven Be Like? ($8.00)	_______	_______
Conquering Fear ($8.00)	_______	_______
Soaring Above the Problems of Life ($8.00)	_______	_______
God's Will For Our Lives ($8.00)	_______	_______
How to Study the Bible ($5.00)	_______	_______
Nuggets of Faith ($5.00)	_______	_______
100 Years From Today ($5.00)	_______	_______

Cassette Tapes (please indicate quantity being ordered) • *$5 each*

_____01H _____02H _____03H _____04H _____05H _____06H
_____07H _____08H _____09H _____10H _____11H _____12H
_____13H _____14H _____15H _____16H _____17H _____18H
_____19H _____20H _____21H _____22H _____23H _____24H
_____25H _____26H _____27H _____28H _____29H _____30H
_____31H _____32H _____33H _____34H

Price of books and tapes _______
Minus 40% discount for 5-9 items _______
Minus 50% discount for 10 or more items _______
Net price of order _______
Add 15% ***before discount*** for shipping and handling _______
(Maximum of $50 for any size order)
Florida residents only, add 7% sales tax _______
Tax deductible contribution to Lamplight Ministries, Inc. _______
Enclosed check or money order (do not send cash) _______
(Please make check payable to Lamplight Ministries, Inc. and mail to: PO Box 1307, Dunedin, FL 34697)

MC____ Visa____ AmEx____ Disc.____ Card # _______________
Exp Date __________ Signature _______________
Name _______________
Address _______________
City _______________
State or Province __________ Zip or Postal Code __________
(Foreign orders must be submitted in U.S. dollars.)

ORDER FORM FOR BOOKS AND CASSETTE TAPES

Book Title	Quantity	Total
God's Wisdom is Available to You ($12.00)	______	______
Increased Energy and Vitality ($10.00)	______	______
Quiet Confidence in the Lord ($9.00)	______	______
Never, Never Give Up ($8.00)	______	______
Trust God For Your Finances ($8.00)	______	______
Deep Inner Peace ($8.00)	______	______
What Will Heaven Be Like? ($8.00)	______	______
Conquering Fear ($8.00)	______	______
Soaring Above the Problems of Life ($8.00)	______	______
God's Will For Our Lives ($8.00)	______	______
How to Study the Bible ($5.00)	______	______
Nuggets of Faith ($5.00)	______	______
100 Years From Today ($5.00)	______	______

Cassette Tapes (please indicate quantity being ordered) • *$5 each*

______01H	______02H	______03H	______04H	______05H	______06H
______07H	______08H	______09H	______10H	______11H	______12H
______13H	______14H	______15H	______16H	______17H	______18H
______19H	______20H	______21H	______22H	______23H	______24H
______25H	______26H	______27H	______28H	______29H	______30H
______31H	______32H	______33H	______34H		

Price of books and tapes ______
Minus 40% discount for 5-9 items ______
Minus 50% discount for 10 or more items ______
Net price of order ______
Add 15% ***before discount*** for shipping and handling ______
(Maximum of $50 for any size order)
Florida residents only, add 7% sales tax ______
Tax deductible contribution to Lamplight Ministries, Inc. ______
Enclosed check or money order (do not send cash) ______

(Please make check payable to Lamplight Ministries, Inc. and mail to: PO Box 1307, Dunedin, FL 34697)

MC____ Visa____ AmEx____ Disc.____ Card # ______________________
Exp Date __________ Signature ______________________
Name ______________________
Address ______________________
City ______________________
State or Province __________ Zip or Postal Code __________
(Foreign orders must be submitted in U.S. dollars.)

ORDER FORM FOR SCRIPTURE MEDITATION CARDS AND CASSETTE TAPES

Due to completely different price structure for the production of Scripture Meditation Cards and 85-minute cassette tapes, we offer a different quantity discount which cannot be combined with our other quantity discounts. The following prices *include shipping and handling*. $5 per card deck or cassette tape; $4 for 5-9 card decks or cassette tapes; $3 for 10 or more card decks or cassette tapes.

SCRIPTURE MEDITATION CARDS	QUANTITY	PRICE
Find God's Will for Your Life	______	______
Financial Instructions from God	______	______
Freedom from Worry and Fear	______	______
A Closer Relationship with the Lord	______	______
Our Father's Wonderful Love	______	______
Receive Healing from the Lord	______	______
Receive God's Blessing in Adversity	______	______
Enjoy God's Wonderful Peace	______	______
God is Always with You	______	______
Continually Increasing Faith in God	______	______
CASSETTE TAPES		
Find God's Will for Your Life	______	______
Financial Instructions from God	______	______
Freedom from Worry and Fear	______	______
A Closer Relationship with the Lord	______	______
Our Father's Wonderful Love	______	______
Receive Healing from the Lord	______	______
Receive God's Blessing in Adversity	______	______
Enjoy God's Wonderful Peace	______	______
God is Always with You	______	______
Continually Increasing Faith in God	______	______

TOTAL PRICE ______

Florida residents only, add 7% sales tax ______

Tax deductible contribution to Lamplight Ministries, Inc. ______

Enclosed check or money order (do not send cash) ______

Please make check payable to Lamplight Ministries, Inc. and mail to:
PO Box 1307, Dunedin, FL 34697

MC____ Visa____ AmEx____ Disc.____ Card # ______________________

Exp Date __________ Signature ______________________

Name ______________________

Address ______________________

City ______________________

State or Province __________ Zip or Postal Code __________

(Foreign orders must be submitted in U.S. dollars.)

The Vision of Lamplight Ministries

Lamplight Ministries, Inc. is founded upon Psalm 119:105 which says, "Your word is a lamp to my feet and a light to my path." We are so grateful to our loving Father for His precious Word that clearly shows us the path He wants us to follow throughout every day of our lives.

From the beginning of our ministry God has used us to reach people in many different countries. Our vision is to share the instructions and promises in the Word of God with multitudes of people in many different countries throughout the world.

We are believing God for the finances to provide the translation of our publications into many different foreign languages. We desire to give our publications free of charge to needy people all over the world who cannot afford to purchase them.

We are believing God for many partners in our ministry who will share our vision of distributing our publications which are solidly anchored upon the Word of God. It is our desire to provide these publications in every foreign language that we possibly can.

We yearn to share the Word of God with large numbers of people in Third World countries. We yearn to share the Word of God with large numbers of people in prisons and jails. These people desperately need to learn and obey God's instructions and to learn and believe in God's promises.

Please pray and ask the Lord if He would have you help us to help needy people all over the world. Thank you and God bless you.